E

PELICAN BOOKS

A560

THE GROWTH OF PLANTS

G. E. Fogg was born at Langar, Nottinghamshire, in 1919 and educated at Dulwich College, Queen Mary College, London, and St John's College, Cambridge. During the Second World War he took part in a survey of the seaweed resources of Britain and worked as an industrial plant physiologist on weed control. In 1955 he joined the Department of Botany, University College, London, where he remained until appointed to his present position of Professor of Botany at Westfield College, London, in 1960. The physiology of the simpler plants and their importance in the sea and fresh-water are his main research interests and provide the subjects of his two books, *The Metabolism of Algae* (1953) and *Algal Cultures and Phytoplankton Ecology* (1965). On various pretexts he has managed to travel widely in Scandinavia, the U.S.A., Africa, India, and the Far East and has recently worked with the British Antarctic Survey in the South Orkneys. He has served as Botanical Secretary of the Society for Experimental Biology and as Programme Secretary of the Xth International Botanical Congress. In 1965 he was elected a Fellow of the Royal Society. Professor Fogg, who is married and has a son and a daughter, includes gardening among his recreations but freely admits that the results do no credit to plant physiology.

G. E. FOGG

THE GROWTH OF PLANTS

WITH
TWENTY-FOUR PLATES AND
FIFTY-THREE TEXT
FIGURES

PENGUIN BOOKS

Penguin Books Ltd, Harmondsworth, Middlesex, England
Penguin Books Inc., 3300 Clipper Mill Road, Baltimore, Md 21211, U.S.A.
Penguin Books Australia Ltd, Ringwood, Victoria, Australia

—

First published 1963
Reprinted 1964, 1966, 1967

—

Copyright © G. E. Fogg, 1963

—

Made and printed in Great Britain
by Richard Clay (The Chaucer Press) Ltd, Bungay, Suffolk
Set in Monotype Baskerville

To

PROFESSOR W. H. PEARSALL, F.R.S.,

who has often advocated that books on plant physiology

should be published in disposable form,

in gratitude for his friendship and counsel

CONTENTS

Contents

PREFACE

AT a time when science is valued and supported as never before, the study of plants is something of a Cinderella. Indeed, to many otherwise well-informed persons botany is not a science at all but the art of recognizing flowers. The reasons for this lack of appreciation of the importance and content of present-day botany are various, but it cannot be said that the subject matter is without economic value or intellectual interest. Ultimately, human survival depends, and is likely always to depend, on plant growth. In the past it has sufficed to rely on natural vegetation and on crops grown by traditional methods, evolved slowly through the ages by trial and error, but with the sharp increase in the world's human population during this century this is no longer adequate, and it is certain that in the near future every resource of botanical science will have to be drawn upon to avoid disaster. The life and growth of plants are the resultants of the interactions of a multitude of processes and are among the most complicated things that the scientist has attempted to investigate. Experimental methods as precise as any of those used by physical scientists are needed in the study of the details of a plant's activities, and the understanding of the interrelations which are the essence of its life calls for thinking of a high order and of a kind which is characteristically biological.

It is hoped that this book may convey something of the interest and practical possibilities which lie in the study of plant growth. The aim has been to give a general account of present-day plant physiology for the reader with little or no background knowledge beyond a smattering of chemistry. It is hoped that in attempting to achieve lucidity there has been no undue sacrifice of accuracy, so that perhaps the book may also serve as an elementary text.

*

The suggestion that this book should be written came from Professor Michael Abercrombie, F.R.S., and I am extremely grateful to him for his encouragement and gentle persistence in seeing that the task was carried through. My thanks must also be expressed to Mr P. J. Syrett for his critical reading of the typescript and for

numerous helpful suggestions for its improvement. I am also grateful to Mr R. Brinsden and to various colleagues, to whom ack-
nowledgement is made elsewhere, for their help in illustrating the
book.

G. E. FOGG

Chorleywood, Buckinghamshire
July 1961

ACKNOWLEDGEMENTS

The following acknowledgements are made for the use of photographs: Plates 3–5, by R. Brinsden, by courtesy of Dr D. J. B. White; Plate 6, by R. Brinsden, by courtesy of Dr L. Fowden; Plate 7, by M. S. C. Birbeck, Chester Beatty Research Institute, by courtesy of Prof. W. O. James; Plates 8 and 9, by courtesy of Dr R. Scott Russell; Plate 10, by courtesy of Prof. H. K. Porter and the Council of the Royal Society; Plates 11 and 12, by courtesy of Prof. R. L. Wain and the Council of the Royal Society; Plate 13, by courtesy of Prof. R. L. Wain and the Editor, *Annals of Applied Biology*; Plates 14–16, by courtesy of Dr P. W. Brian and I.C.I. Ltd; Plates 17, 20, and 21, by courtesy of R. Brinsden; Plates 18 and 19, by courtesy of Prof. F. Skoog; Plates 22 and 23, by courtesy of Dr W. W. Schwabe; Plate 24, by courtesy of Prof. A. S. Crafts.

Acknowledgements are also made to the following for permission to quote from published works: Oxford University Press, for the quotations from the works of Christopher Fry; Longmans, Green and Co., for the translation from van Helmont in E. J. Russell's *Soil Conditions and Plant Growth*; Jonathan Cape Ltd, for the quotation from Han Suyin's *A Many-Splendoured Thing*; Interscience Publishers Inc., for the quotation from E. I. Rabinowitch's *Photosynthesis and Related Processes*.

INTRODUCTION

> *The arithmetic*
> *Of cause and effect I've never understood.*
> *How many beans make five is an immense*
> *Question, depending on how many*
> *Preliminary beans preceded them.*
>
> CHRISTOPHER FRY
> (*The Dark is Light Enough*)

CHAPTER I

Plant Growth and its Complexities

PLANTS grow and multiply, but, unlike animals, they do this without obviously seeking out and devouring food and without having any apparent active mating behaviour. Aristotle defined plants in words to this effect over 2,000 years ago, and it is still an acceptable statement of their general characteristics. Growth without visible intake of food materials is usually the most striking activity of a plant and, consciously or unconsciously, we look for evidence of this when trying to decide whether a particular object is a plant or not. While it is usually imperceptible over short periods of time, growth is otherwise obvious and examples are familiar. There is no need to dwell on this or on the various implications that plant growth may have for us – of food or profit, when a crop thrives; of effort, when the lawn needs mowing yet again; or of mystery, when one contemplates the transformation of a seemingly dead seed into a flourishing plant.

Understanding the processes by which plants keep alive and grow is the aim of the science of plant physiology. As we shall see, a great variety of processes, all of them concerned in one way or another in growth, go on in plants, but no one of them can be singled out as the all-important one for growth and used as a means of defining it. In fact, although most people will feel fairly sure of what they understand by the word, 'growth' has little precise meaning in the strictly scientific sense. The immediate difficulty is that there is no one obvious starting-point for this book. However, since it is usually taken as meaning increase in size, we may begin by considering growth from this point of view.

In plant physiology, as in any other science, measurement

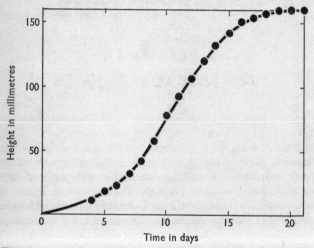

Fig. 1. Growth in height of a lupin seedling. (Data of Pfeffer.)

and numerical precision are of first importance, and much can be learnt about the way in which plants increase in size from simple measurements of height made at suitable intervals of time. Some results obtained in this way with a seedling lupin (*Lupinus albus*) * show growth in height beginning rather slowly, increasing to a maximum, then slowing down again so that the graph obtained by plotting height against

---

* The common names of plants will generally be used, but for the sake of scientific accuracy the Latin name will be given when a species is first mentioned.

time is like an oblique S in shape (Fig. 1). Another way of looking at it is to plot the daily increment in height against time; this gives a curve falling off more or less symmetrically on either side of a peak (Fig. 2), again showing the growth rate as speeding up then slowing down. The pattern of growth represented by these two curves is characteristic of plants in general, although rates and final amounts vary enormously. Growth is sometimes imperceptible, even over a period of years, but annual plants such as maize (*Zea mays*) and sunflower (*Helianthus annuus*) may attain heights of ten feet or more in the growing season, and extraordinarily high

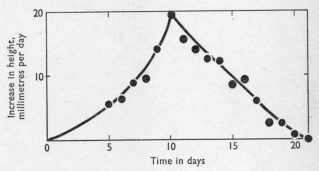

Fig. 2. Growth in height of a lupin seedling. The data of Fig. 1 replotted as daily increments.

rates of increment are shown by bamboos (e.g. *Dendrocalamus giganteus*); travellers' tales of hats hung on bamboos at night being out of reach by the following morning have some basis in fact, for an increase in height of 41 centimetres per day has been recorded for these plants.

The situation is more complicated in perennial than in annual plants, since the growth pattern is repeated each season. A graph constructed from measurements of a tree taken at intervals, say of a week, would show steps, each corresponding to a growing season, although the whole curve in general outline would conform to the same pattern as for annual plants. A graph made from measurements taken only once per year at corresponding times would not show these steps. Since it is tiresome to make measurements of a single tree over its complete life-span, and since trees may carry an accurate record of their age in the growth-rings in their trunks, data are most conveniently obtained by measuring the heights of trees of different ages. Data of this sort for the beech (*Fagus sylvatica*) are given in Fig. 3. The points when plotted may be scattered rather widely on

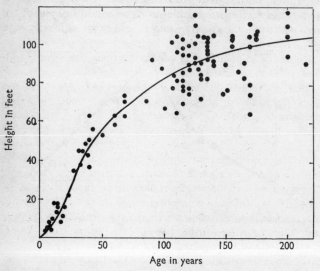

Fig. 3. The relation of height to age in beech trees growing on chalk and limestone soils. (Data of Brown, 1953.)

either side of the ideal graph, especially those for the older trees, and illustrate the variability of material with which the plant physiologist has to contend. This variability arises both from differences in nature, individual beech trees having their own inherited peculiarities, and nurture, conditions such as quality of soil, amount of sunshine, exposure to wind, and so on being different for each tree. Nevertheless, the points lie about a curve which is essentially of the same

S-shaped form as that in Fig. 1, although the initial increase in slope is scarcely perceptible when the graph is plotted on a small scale so that the exaggerated upper part of the S can be included.

Since the growth of a tree, extending over many seasons, shows the same general features as that of a herb, living for only a few weeks, we may guess that this pattern is inherent in plant growth rather than the outcome of seasonal changes in growing conditions. The truth of this deduction can be demonstrated by growing plants under conditions which are artificially kept constant, when the same growth pattern is again obtained. Evidently it is a general rule that for a time the growth capacity of a plant increases and then, well before death, declines.

Although it can be useful, and has the merit of leaving the plant undamaged, height is on the whole an unsatisfactory measure of growth. Only the overground part of the plant is measured and no account is taken of thickness, degree of branching, or spread. Clearly, measurement of the height of its overground parts will not give a useful measure of the growth of a carrot plant (*Daucus carota*), for example, nor, if it were used to compare growth in full light and in near darkness, would measurement of height alone bring out the obvious difference between the growth of the thin drawn-out plants produced under the latter conditions and that of the sturdy much-branched ones in the light. Some more direct measure of the total amount of plant material is desirable to give a less misleading estimate of growth.

Volume might be used, but is not easily measured and has rarely been used in practice; weight is more satisfactory. Although it is more troublesome to determine, dry weight (that is to say, the weight of the residue left after all free water has been removed by heating to 100° C. or by some other means which does not cause decomposition of the organic matter) gives results which are more easily interpreted, and has been more often used than fresh weight in growth studies. The disadvantage of fresh weight as a measure of plant growth is that the major part of it, about 75 per cent, is due to water, and considerable amounts of this may be lost or gained independently of growth, e.g. in the course of a hot dry day plants may decrease in fresh weight even though by other criteria they continue to grow. Dry weight may be misleading in a similar sort of way, since it includes the weight of salts absorbed by the plant from the soil, and this does not necessarily bear any direct relationship to the amount of growth. However, errors from this source are usually small, and there is no doubt that dry weight is the most useful of the simply determined measures of growth.

Since it results in the destruction of the plant as a living thing, growth can be followed by this method only by making successive determinations on a number of similar plants. If the plants were genetically identical, and if all were grown under *exactly* similar conditions, it would only be necessary to take one plant at a time in order to obtain a growth curve as smooth as that in Fig. 1. Went (1953) showed that if seeds of a well-established, i.e. genetically uniform, variety of pea are sown in a uniform manner in a uniform material and germinated and grown under conditions which are really the same for all of them (in an ordinary greenhouse lighting varies greatly from place to place and draughts produce considerable local variations in temperature and humidity), then the plants are extraordinarily uniform, all being of similar height and with the same number of leaves, each orientated in the same way. A row of such plants is as regular as a parade of soldiers. With such material, single plants taken at intervals would suffice to give a good growth curve. However, sufficiently uniform growth conditions are difficult and costly to attain, even in experimental work, and, although all the plants used may be of the same variety, the variability in growth due to differences in environmental conditions is nearly always large. Under natural conditions, of course, variation is even greater, and there is a wide scattering of individual results about the ideal curve, just as in Fig. 3. To minimize the effects of variation it is necessary to take several plants at a time, chosen at random, so that representative average values may be obtained.

The sort of results obtained by the dry-weight method are illustrated in Fig. 4. Extensive data obtained for maize at the end of the last century were intensively analysed by

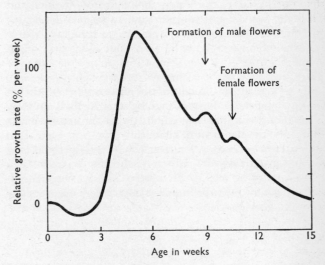

Fig. 4. Growth in dry weight of the maize plant. (After Briggs, Kidd, and West, 1920.)

Briggs, Kidd, and West (1920), and this figure gives an idealized curve based on their results. There is a general resemblance to the curves based on height measurements, but some new features are also apparent.

In the first three weeks, during which the seed germinates and the shoot appears above the soil surface, there is actually a loss of weight. Initially the seed contains stores of food material, and, while some of this is transformed into the living substance of the seedling, some is used up in the process of *respiration*, which is an inevitable accompaniment of the transformation, for which it provides the necessary energy. More will be said about respiration later; for the moment it is only necessary to say that the law of the conservation of matter is obeyed and that the missing material is liberated in the forms of water and the gas carbon dioxide, neither of which will be included when the dry weight of the seedling is taken. This loss of weight points to the imperfection of dry weight as a measure of growth, for while the loss is taking place the young plant is developing and increasing in size, and it would be quite unjustifiable to say that the word 'growth' does not describe what is happening.

Shortly after the shoot emerges into the light this trend is reversed and the dry weight of the plant begins to increase. Where the material for this increase comes from is not at all obvious and is a question which baffled the acutest minds before the development of chemistry as a science provided the concepts necessary for the answer. The account of a famous experiment by an early chemist, van Helmont (? 1577–1644), is well worth quoting in full as an example of the beginnings of the inquiries which were eventually to solve the problem:

> I took an earthen vessel in which I put 200 pounds of soil dried in an oven, then I moistened with rain-water and pressed hard into it a shoot of willow weighing 5 pounds. After exactly five years the tree that had grown up weighed 169 pounds and about 3 ounces. But the vessel had never received anything but rain-water or distilled water to moisten the soil when this was necessary, and it remained full of soil, which was still tightly packed, and, lest any dust from outside should get into the soil, it was covered with a sheet of iron coated with tin but perforated with many holes. I did not take the weight of the leaves that fell in the autumn. In the end I dried the soil once more and got the same 200 pounds that I started with, less about 2 ounces. Therefore the 164 pounds of wood, bark, and root arose from the water alone.*

The fact that the soil lost so little clearly disposed of the idea, originating with Aristotle, that the substance of plants is derived exclusively from the soil. Since the willow tree was

* Quoted from Sir E. John Russell, *Soil Conditions and Plant Growth*, eighth edition, 1950.

weighed in the fresh condition, not dried, the greater part of it was actually water, but van Helmont's conclusion that the whole of the 164 pounds arose from water alone was incorrect because he was not aware of the possibility of material derived from the air contributing to it.

This possibility was envisaged by Stephen Hales, Rector of Teddington and one of the greatest of plant physiologists, who in 1727 wrote of plants as 'very probably drawing through their leaves some part of their nourishment from the air' and came near to putting his finger on the essential factor for this process when he surmised, 'May not light also, by freely entering the expanded surfaces of leaves and flowers, contribute much to ennobling the principles of vegetables?' However, Hales did not establish these points conclusively, and the next step was the demonstration that plants give off something to the air when illuminated. The gas which we now call oxygen was found to be given off from plants by Priestley in 1772. Ingen-housz, in 1779, showed that light was essential for this oxygen production and that it occurred only in the green parts of plants. After Senebier (1782) had found that another requirement for the production of oxygen was the presence of the gas carbon dioxide, Ingen-housz (1796) suggested that plants obtain carbon, which by this time was known to be an important constituent of plant material, by decomposition of carbon dioxide from air with concomitant liberation of oxygen.

This was the first description of the process which we now know of as *photosynthesis*. More will be said about this later, but for the present it may be simply defined as the manufacture of organic materials from carbon dioxide and water by green plants in the light. This much can be deduced from observations on the growth of plants by the dry-weight method. If a plant is kept in the dark, or in the light but in air from which carbon dioxide has been removed, it will not show any increase in dry weight, thus showing that light and carbon dioxide are necessary for photosynthesis. The beginning of increase of dry weight in seedlings may be observed to follow on the emergence of the shoot into the light and its turning green. It is possible to produce mutant strains of maize entirely lacking green pigment; such plants do not photosynthesize and do not gain in dry weight unless provided with suitable organic foods such as sugars. That water contributes to the dry matter formed in photosynthesis is more difficult to prove, but it can be done by comparison of the weight of carbon dioxide used with the sum of that of the oxygen given off and that of the dry matter formed. The former is less than the latter, and water seems to be the only other substance available in sufficient quantity to the plant to make up the balance. Since hydrogen and oxygen, the elements of water, are also important constituents of the organic matter of plants, this seems a reasonable assumption.

The significance of the two-ounce loss in weight of soil which van Helmont found at the end of his experiment must not be overlooked. Some of the loss may have been due to decomposition by micro-organisms of organic matter in the soil, but part of it, at least, could have been accounted for as a gain in ash content of the willow shoot. Although most of the dry matter of a plant consists of organic compounds, largely built of the elements carbon, hydrogen, and oxygen, obtained from air and water, other elements, present in smaller proportions, play an indispensable part in the life of a plant. These mineral elements, which remain behind as ash when the organic material of the plant is burnt away, are obtained by the plant from the soil.

Seven mineral elements – potassium, magnesium, calcium, nitrogen, phosphorus, sulphur, and iron – are indispensable and needed in comparatively large amounts for plant growth. Gardeners, of course, know that some of these elements must be provided in fertilizers if their plants are to thrive, but proof that they are essential calls for a more refined technique than that of growing plants in soil, which is an uncontrollable mixture that always contains at least small amounts of the elements in question. Provided that their roots are well aerated, plants can be grown very well in water containing only mineral salts in solution. They will not grow for long in pure water. This technique of growing plants without soil, 'hydroponics', is quite extensively used commercially for valuable glass-house crops. From the scientific point of view it is important in providing a means for the exact investigation of the mineral requirements of plants. By using different combinations of salts, the effect of omitting a particular element can be observed, and in this way it has been shown that the seven elements mentioned above are essential for the growth of every kind of plant that has been tested.

In addition, by using highly purified materials and taking special precautions to prevent contamination, it has been found that certain other elements – boron, manganese, molybdenum, zinc, copper, and possibly some others – are also essential, but only in minute traces. The optimum concentration of a 'trace element' for plant growth is usually of the order of one part per ten- or hundred-million of solution, higher concentrations than these generally being poisonous rather than beneficial. It may be noted that some of the most abundant elements, such as aluminium and silicon, do not appear to be essential for plants. Another point is that the possibility of growing plants satisfactorily in solutions containing only purified mineral salts demonstrates that plants are not dependent on the soil as a source of organic materials. The parts which certain of the mineral elements play in the life of plants have been identified (see p. 143), but it is worth noting that we are still almost completely at a loss to account for the importance to plants of the major nutrient element, potassium.

Plants therefore grow by taking in and converting materials very different from their own substance. In this respect they differ radically from non-living things such as crystals, which are also spoken of as being able to 'grow'. A crystal grows in size by adding to itself chemically similar material from its surroundings; this is a process of accretion rather than of *assimilation* such as occurs in plant growth. The chemical processes, by which the simple molecules of the raw materials are built up in assimilation to the complicated molecules which form the fabric of the plant, are diverse and complicated. This is something which will be gone into later, and for the moment it is sufficient to note that, however quiescent the lily of the field may appear, intensely active toiling and spinning goes on inside it at the molecular level. The term *metabolism* is used to denote the complex of chemical activity which goes on in a living organism.

For a time dry matter is accumulated by a plant at an ever-increasing rate. This happens because the material which is manufactured is not inert but is itself capable of manufacturing more material. In this respect the growth of a plant somewhat resembles the growth of a sum of money on which compound interest is being paid. A difference is that, interest being payable at stated intervals of time, the increase of money takes place in steps, whereas the 'interest' on plant material is paid continuously during growth so that the curve of increase is smooth. The 'rate of interest', that is the rate of growth per unit of plant material, gives a much better idea of the growth activity than does the actual amount of material added in a given time per plant. Mathematically, the 'rate of interest' may be defined as R in the expression $dW/dt = RW$, in which W is the dry weight of the plant at any given time and dW its increase in dry weight in the time dt.

The expression becomes more useful when integrated

$$\log_e \frac{W}{W_0} = RT \quad \text{or} \quad \frac{\log_e W - \log_e W_0}{T} = R$$

W being the final dry weight after growth for a period of time, T, at the beginning of which the dry weight was W_0. R is called the *relative growth rate* and represents the efficiency of a plant as a producer of new material. For a plant such as maize the relative growth rate does not stay constant. If it is calculated for successive short periods it is found to vary in the manner shown in Fig. 4, rising to a peak at about five weeks after sowing, then declining. The decline is not steady, but may be interrupted by subsidiary peaks as growth is renewed in flowering and fruiting. It should be noted that the amount of new material produced by a plant depends both on relative growth rate and on the amount of growing material, so that actual growth is greatest after relative growth rate has already begun to decline.

A description of growth purely in terms of height or dry weight clearly leaves out a great deal of importance. It takes no account of the various changes in form which invariably accompany the growth of any plant. Changes in proportion of stem, leaf, and root, in leaf shape, in production of tubers and other storage organs, in flowers and fruit, are ignored, and the same value of height or dry weight may represent quite different types of growth. For a more complete picture it is necessary first of all to know something of plant structure and then to discover what growth implies in terms of this structure.

All plants, with the exception of some seaweeds and fungi, are built of units known as *cells*. These vary enormously in size and shape; some may be well over 1 millimetre in their longest dimension and thus be visible to the naked eye, but usually they are from 0·01 to 0·1 millimetre in diameter and can be seen only under the microscope. One of the most easily studied types of cell is that which makes up the delicate skin or *epidermis* on the surface of an onion (*Allium cepa*) bulb scale (Fig. 5). This is a representative plant cell except that it contains none of the green pigment which is necessary for photosynthesis. The most obvious feature is the wall, a thin cellulose envelope which is distended by its less conspicuous fluid contents. Cells are usually seen and depicted in section, but it must not be forgotten that they are three-dimensional objects. The onion epidermis cells are approximately polyhedral, each being gently rounded on its free, outer surface, and having flattened areas of contact with its neighbours, to which it is fastened by a substance which cements the walls together. Cells joined together form a *tissue*, the epidermis being a tissue. The living material, the *protoplasm*, lines the inside of each cell envelope. It is a viscous fluid containing numerous fine particles and globules, and during life shows more-or-less active streaming movements. Each cell contains a *nucleus*, a differentiated part of the protoplasm specially concerned with the transmission of heritable characters, which may lie against the wall or be suspended in the middle of the cell by fine strands

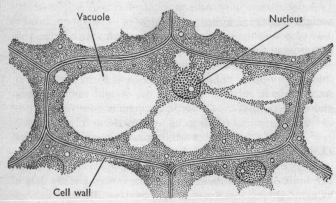

Fig. 5. A cell from the epidermis of an onion bulb scale as seen in optical section (× 700).

of protoplasm. A cell may divide, the nucleus dividing into two and new sections of cell wall being formed between the daughter nuclei. Much of the volume of a cell is taken up by one or more *vacuoles*, spaces within the protoplasm containing sap, that is water with various mineral and organic materials dissolved in it.

For the moment, however, we are concerned not with details of cell structure but with the interpretation of growth in terms of cell behaviour. It may be most helpful here to begin by considering a plant in which growth is not complicated by the aggregation of cells into tissues. On the whole, the plants discussed in this book will be of the kind which are most familiar, the flowering plants. However, since for experimental purposes it is often desirable to use material which is as free as possible from complications of form and life-history, much of our knowledge of plant physiology has been obtained with the simplest plants, the algae, a group which includes the seaweeds and their microscopic relations, and it will be necessary to mention these occasionally. Like flowering plants, algae are photosynthetic and, basically, their life-processes seem similar in spite of the differences in structural complexity. Mosses, ferns, and their allies, which occupy a position intermediate between the algae and the flowering plants in the evolutionary scale, appear to conform fairly closely to the physiological pattern of flowering plants but have been comparatively little investigated from this point of view. Fungi, which are not photosynthetic, are usually classified as plants, but in several respects their physiology is different from that of green plants and they will be mentioned hardly at all in what follows.

The individual of the green alga, *Chlorella*, consists of a single, nearly spherical cell, about five-thousandths of a millimetre in diameter, having essentially the structure just described and in which all the life processes take place. When a cell of *Chlorella* is placed under suitable conditions it will grow, that is it will expand in volume and the dry weight of material which it contains will increase, but this does not go on indefinitely, for sooner or later it will divide. Of the daughter cells thus produced, each leads an independent existence and in turn grows and divides. This process of cell division involves complicated chemical and structural changes within the cell, and we are still a long way from a full understanding of its mechanism.

Besides considering the growth of individual cells we can consider the growth of a *Chlorella* population. Starting from one cell we will get successively 2, 4, 8, 16, etc. cells as division proceeds, that is to say, numbers increase stepwise in geometrical progression. In actual practice, with a large number of cells divisions are nearly always out of step so that the increase appears continuous. Such growth in cell numbers gives a smooth curve of ever-increasing slope if a graph of cell numbers is plotted against time. This *exponential* type of growth can be described by the expression $n = n_0 e^{kt}$, where n and n_0 are the cell numbers per unit volume of the water in which growth is occurring at the end and beginning respectively of the growth period t, e is the base of natural logarithms, and k the relative growth factor. This is analogous to the expression already given for the growth of a multicellular plant (see p. 24) and can be converted to the form:

$$k = \frac{\log n - \log n_0}{t}$$

Unlike R, the relative growth rate of a flowering plant, which does not usually stay constant for any appreciable period, k may remain constant for a relatively long period in the growth of *Chlorella* and similar unicellular organisms, implying cell divisions at regular intervals of time. This can be shown by plotting a graph with logarithms of cell numbers (instead of the actual cell numbers) against time, when, for a population growing under suitable conditions, a straight line will be obtained (Fig. 6). If, instead of cell numbers, dry weight of material per unit volume of water is taken, the growth of *Chlorella* is found to follow a similar law but a slightly different value for k may be obtained. This simple mathematical relationship results because in *Chlorella* a large and nearly constant proportion of the material produced in photosynthesis is used to form more material directly capable of growth. *Chlorella* shows in a particularly clear way the characteristic capacity of protoplasm for self-replication.

When *Chlorella* grows exponentially cell numbers build up very rapidly, and it will be clear that this type of increase cannot go on indefinitely. Most usually it ceases because the supply of some raw material for growth becomes exhausted, or because the cell population becomes so dense as to prevent light penetrating far into it, with the result that photosynthesis is limited. Sometimes, in the course of growth, waste products accumulate until eventually their concentration is sufficient to poison the cells. Whatever the cause growth sooner or later slows down and the population becomes stationary. Cells which have thus passed into a nondividing condition are not always able to begin dividing again if transferred back to conditions favourable for growth. There may be a period of readjustment, the 'lag-phase', before exponential growth begins again. The whole sequence of phases in this growth cycle is represented in Fig. 6.

A population of *Chlorella* may be thought of as a plant in which the cells are all similar and have no attachment one

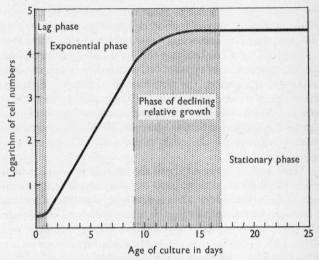

Fig. 6. The growth of the unicellular alga *Chlorella* in culture; the logarithm of cell numbers per unit volume of culture medium plotted against time.

to another. In such a population there is increase in dry matter accompanied by increase in cell numbers, and it shows a phase of rapid growth followed by a slowing down in growth. In this respect it resembles a maize plant, for example, which starts from a single cell, the fertilized egg, and grows into an aggregate of many millions of cells. The difference is that in the maize plant the cells become specialized to perform different functions and arranged into an organized whole. Thus the functions of absorption of water and mineral salts and of photosynthesis are carried out in maize in quite different types of cell, found respectively in the roots and leaves. Because the cells of root and leaf are of necessity separated in space, but nevertheless remain dependent on each other, there have to be other types of cells, in the stem and elsewhere, specialized for transporting materials between them and for providing mechanical support. Yet other cells become devoted to the storage of food materials. In some of these specialized cells, i.e. some of those serving for conduction or mechanical support, it is the wall which is important, and the protoplasm within it dies as soon as it has built up this wall to the required form and thickness. Other types of cell retain their living contents and, perhaps always, the potentiality of growth, but most often, having once been differentiated, neither increase in size nor divide. Growth is then itself restricted to specialized tissues located in particular places in the plant, the growing points, such as are obviously present at the extremities of shoots and roots.

Much can be deduced about the manner in which growth takes place from microscopical examination of longitudinal sections, i.e. thin slices taken lengthwise, like that of the root growing-point shown in Fig. 7. A millimetre or two behind the tip is a tissue, made up of small, thin-walled cells with dense protoplasmic contents, in which cell division is largely concentrated. This mass of dividing cells, which is called a *meristem*, is pushed forward through the soil as the cells which it produces add to the root behind it. The cells which are produced on its forward face form a cap of tissue which protects the delicate meristem in its rough passage. This root cap is worn away as rapidly as it is formed, its cells becoming mucilaginous and eventually disintegrating, so providing a lubricant for the advancing root-tip. The cells which are to form the permanent root tissues gradually cease to divide and begin to enlarge, mainly in the direction of the length of the root. The zone of maximum elongation thus lies some way behind the root-tip, as can be easily demonstrated by marking off a root in millimetres with

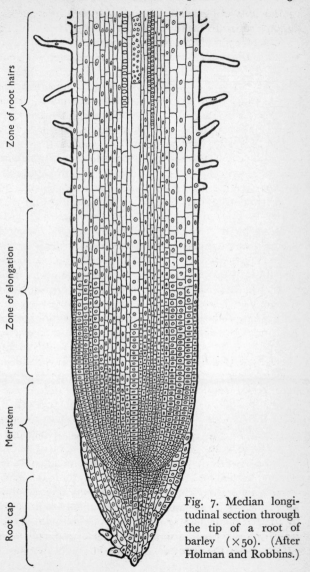

Zone of root hairs

Zone of elongation

Meristem

Root cap

Fig. 7. Median longitudinal section through the tip of a root of barley (×50). (After Holman and Robbins.)

Indian ink and leaving it to grow, when the marks will become separated as shown in Fig. 8.

Apart from the increase in their volume, which may be as much as thirty-fold, the most obvious change in the cells at

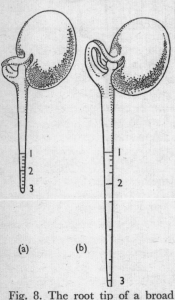

this stage is that their protoplasm becomes less dense as large vacuoles form in it. Once enlargement has taken place, cells become differentiated to perform particular functions and their walls become thickened. Fig. 7 shows the epidermal cells of the root becoming modified into root hairs, which are specially concerned with water absorption, and the central cells becoming modified as a *vascular strand* in which transport of water and dissolved substances takes place. Since the root is colourless and is usually in the dark anyway, it cannot manufacture the organic substances that it requires by photosynthesis, and these must be brought from elsewhere, so that it would be expected that the laying down of an efficient trans-

Fig. 8. The root tip of a broad bean seedling marked off with Indian ink (a). After a period of growth the marks became separated as in (b), showing that elongation is mainly confined to a region just behind the tip. (After Sachs, 1887.)

porting system as soon as possible would be important. Farther back along the root than this, lateral (branch) roots are formed by meristems produced by the division of groups of mature cells just outside the vascular strand. These lateral roots grow in a similar manner to the main root.

Growth of the shoot takes place in essentially the same

way as in the root. The meristem at its tip cuts off cells on its
lower side only – there is nothing analogous to the root cap –
and meristems arising behind the tip develop into leaves and
branches. This mechanism provides mainly for growth in
length but not for the considerable increase in girth which
is obviously necessary for mechanical reasons, if no others,
in the larger plants. In the dicotyledons and conifers, the
plant-groups to which the biggest trees belong, increase in
girth is achieved by means of a secondary meristem, or
cambium, which takes the form of a continuous cylindrical
sheet of dividing cells within stem or root. The cells of the
cambium cut off daughter cells both to the inside and outside. The cells formed on the inside become mainly modified
for water transport and mechanical support and constitute
the permanent tissue familiar as wood and more precisely
known as *xylem* (Plate 4).

Because the cambium is inactive during the winter and
since the cells which it produces vary somewhat according
to season, the wood of trees in temperate climates is laid
down in distinct layers, appearing as concentric rings in a
cross-section of the stem, each ring usually representing a
year's growth. The cells cut off from the outer surface of the
cambium include ones which become specialized for the
transport of organic substances and form the tissue known
as *phloem.* This tissue is inevitably torn as the stem expands,
and it cannot be permanent like the wood. Together with
the protective cork, which is produced by another secondary
meristem, it makes up the bark of the tree. It is the tearing
of the delicate tissue of the cambium which enables the bark
to be stripped so easily from an actively growing twig in the
spring. In the group of the monocotyledons, which includes
the grasses and palms, secondary thickening does not usually
occur.

The specialization of cell function found in the flowering
plants inevitably makes the process of growth much more
complicated than it is in a *Chlorella* population. In *Chlorella*
the stages in the sequence of photosynthesis, increase in cell
material and cell division, take place within a single cell and

are fairly closely related to one another. As a result, the general features of growth can be adequately described by simple mathematical expressions. In the more elaborate kind of plant, however, these various functions are performed by different cells; the proportion of photosynthetic tissue in a plant may vary within wide limits, and the material which it manufactures can be diverted from the production of protoplasm to the production of non-growing storage materials and greatly thickened cell walls; the proportion of dividing cells does not bear any fixed relationship to the amount of living material. Consequently, the mathematical description of growth is more complicated and, as we saw on p. 24, the relative growth-rate does not usually stay constant in maize or similar plants for any appreciable time. There is a further respect in which the structure of a flowering plant results in growth of a different pattern from those shown either by a *Chlorella* population or by an animal. Growth in a *Chlorella* population under the usual laboratory conditions takes place largely in the exponential phase (see p. 29), and a final cell population is reached which may remain stationary for some time. Growth in many animals is similarly concentrated in the embryonic phase and results in a mature individual, the size and number of constituent cells of which remain constant for a substantial proportion of the life span. In contrast, a flowering plant retains embryonic (= meristematic) tissues throughout its life, and is never mature in the sense that it achieves a final size and can then survive for a relatively long period without any further growth.

A major problem is that of discovering the way in which the complex structure of a flowering plant arises in the course of growth. In the beginning, the plant is a single undifferentiated cell, nearly spherical in shape, embedded in the tissues of an ovule of a flower of its parent. The first step in differentiation is the establishment of *polarity*, that is, the determination of the axis of the new plant and which end of it is to be the shoot. In the plant which develops on germination the axis established in the embryo gives rise to lateral growths, leaves, and branches, and the various parts assume the shapes and sizes characteristic for the particular kind of plant. We still know very little of how this is accomplished. The apical meristem (Plate 5) of the shoot seems to be of especial importance in determining form as well as in providing for growth in length. It is self-determining, for if it is cut away from the rest it can still regenerate into a complete plant under suitable conditions.

As organs are formed, their cells differentiate to form specialized tissues. Here, position is all-important. Thus cells become xylem when they are produced by division on the inside of the cambium, phloem if produced on the outside. Nevertheless, using special culture techniques, Steward and his collaborators (1958) have succeeded in regenerating whole plants from single cells from carrot phloem, thus showing that in spite of having been differentiated, these cells retain the potentiality of developing into any kind of tissue. Presumably, although it has not yet been demonstrated, living cells from xylem and other kinds of tissue may do the same. Thus it seems to be the environment resulting from the interactions of the surrounding tissues which evokes in a particular cell one kind of specialized development among the several of which it is capable.

The form characteristic of a particular species is attained by growth taking place to a greater extent in some directions than in others. The way in which this happens may be illustrated by the *Begonia* leaf studied by D'Arcy Thompson (1942). Growth in a leaf of this sort may be regarded as being made up of two components, increase in size taking place radially about the point where stalk and blade join and increase in size in directions transverse to these radii. In this particular leaf (Fig. 9) the heart-shape arises because radial growth is not uniform, being less, for example, along the radius *C* than along the radius *A*. The asymmetry of the leaf arises because growth transverse to the radii is greater on the right-hand side of the leaf than on the left. The position of the lines in Fig. 9 has been chosen so that *Oa* is the same length as *Oa'*, *Ob* as *Ob'*, and *Oc* as *Oc'*, i.e. the pairs of lines represent corresponding amounts of radial growth. The lines having been fitted in this way, measurement of the angles shows that *AOa'*, *AOb'*, and *AOc'* are in the same proportions as *AOa*, *AOb*, and *AOc*. Thus growth in the radial directions was similar on either side of the leaf, but that transverse to it was uniformly greater (almost twice) on the right-hand side than on the left-hand side.

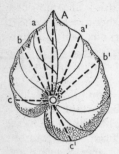

Fig. 9. Leaf of *Begonia daedalea* (after D'Arcy Thompson, 1942). For explanation see text.

In a similar way a difference in leaf-shape between two related species might simply depend on the relative amounts of growth in the two directions being different. Ultimately such differential growth is genetically determined, but the nature of the mechanisms which connect the final growth with the inherited code in the cell nuclei can be envisaged only in general terms. That there is ample opportunity for non-genetical factors to exert their influence is evident in the way in which leaf-shape, for example, in a single species varies according to the environment. A striking example of this is provided by the water plant, *Sagittaria sagittifolia*, the leaves of which are ribbon-like when submerged, ovate when floating, and arrow-shaped when borne above the water (Fig. 10). Here it is the external environment which is most important, but the internal conditions in the plant also have their effects, since there are always more-or-less distinct differences in the shapes of leaves borne at different positions on the same plant.

Although a plant may sometimes continue vegetative growth indefinitely, producing nothing but leaves, branches, and roots, flowering and reproduction normally occur sooner or later. This involves drastic changes in the form of growth. The first visible sign, to be seen if the growing-point is dissected out and examined with a lens, is an alteration in the shape of the apical meristem, which becomes more

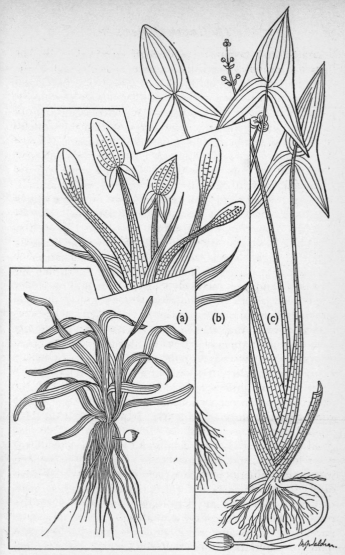

Fig. 10. The arrow-head (*Sagittaria sagittifolia*): (a) totally submerged plant with ribbon-like leaves only; (b) plant showing
transitions from ribbon-like to aerial arrow-head type leaves;
(c) plant with aerial leaves only. (After Arber, 1920.)

elongated and begins to produce flower initials, special centres of growth which will eventually develop into flowers. A second phase is the maturation of the parts of the flower and the differentiation of the reproductive cells themselves. Within the *anthers* are produced the pollen grains, which give rise to the male cells, the sperms. Within the ovule is developed the embryo sac, which contains the egg. Following pollination egg and sperm fuse, and the embryo of a new plant develops from the fertilized egg. The ovule with its contained embryo develops into the seed, which usually becomes stocked with food reserves, and other structures develop into the fruit, in which the seed is contained. Physiologically, flowering and fruiting are distinct processes. Flowering is a transitory phase which involves the differentiation of highly specialized cells and striking changes in form but no massive redeployment of material. Fruiting, on the other hand, is of relatively long duration and resembles vegetative growth in requiring large supplies of food materials to maintain it.

It is obvious that the various growth processes taking place in a plant are closely linked with each other. In other words, a plant grows as a single unit and not as a collection of independent parts. To some extent this correlation may depend on straightforward nutritional relationships. Shoot and root grow in proportion, for example, and one would guess that this depends to a considerable extent on their mutual dependence; the shoot supplying the organic material which the root, not being photosynthetic, is unable to make for itself, and, in return, obtaining from the root the water and mineral salts to which it does not itself have direct access. Similarly, the retardation of vegetative growth that occurs when a plant is fruiting is probably largely the result of the diversion of the available food materials to the developing seeds and fruits. However, there is certainly more to correlation than this. So long as the terminal growing-point of a shoot is active the lateral buds below it remain dormant, but if the growing-point is cut off or ceases to function for any reason a lateral bud develops and continues the growth of the shoot. This illustrates in a particularly clear way the tendency of correlation to restore the former condition of a plant after an interference. However, the point to be emphasized just now is that this inverse correlation between the development of terminal and lateral growing-points does not depend simply on the diversion of food materials from one to the other. The inhibitory effect on lateral buds of the terminal growing-point can be imitated exactly by use of a single chemical substance, auxin. If the terminal growing-point is cut off and a trace of this substance is applied to the cut end of the shoot its lateral buds remain dormant as if the tip were still there. As we shall see later, auxin is a substance of general importance in growth correlation, but other substances have their effects also, and the interaction of the various factors is often complicated.

Finally, we must take into account the close adjustment which the growth and development of a plant shows to its particular environment. Growth, being dependent on water and light and a suitable temperature, shows seasonal variations corresponding to those of climate. But apart from these major effects on the amount of growth, there are close adaptations of the direction and form of growth to the local physical and chemical conditions. An everyday example of this is the way in which the stem and leaves of a potted plant standing in a window take up attitudes which result in the interception of the maximum amount of light. Similar reactions are shown by plants growing under natural conditions. The leaves on the lower branches of a forest tree become arranged in a mosaic in which there is little shading of one leaf by another and in which the angle of each leaf is such as to make the best of the available light (see Plate 1). A recently transplanted shrub usually looks awkward at first, and it is only after fresh growth has allowed some adjustment to the local conditions that it begins to look at home. Similarly, below ground growth is closely adapted to local peculiarities; thus, other things being equal, roots grow towards a supply of water. Such responses are particularly striking when seen speeded up as a motion picture; growth of potato (*Solanum tuberosum*) sprouts towards a chink of light, for example, then gives an extraordinary impression of the plants' awareness of their surroundings and of animal purposefulness in the struggle for existence.

Development of form, as well as direction of growth, shows definite relationships to environment. The opening of buds and the production of flowers and fruit occur at definite times of the year in response to particular environmental circumstances. It is not simply that, as a result of the direct effects of factors such as the seasonal increase in temperature and light, a plant reaches the stage of growth at which it is able to flower in a particular month. In spite of unseasonable weather and the vagaries of cultivators, most plants can be relied upon to flower at pretty much the same time each year – the confidence with which nursery catalogues give the flowering dates of trees and shrubs to the nearest week has a great deal of justification. Flowering in most plants is more than a matter of reaching a certain size; it requires special conditions of temperature and illumination which have little effect on the amount of vegetative growth. Many varieties of *Chrysanthemum*, for example, require a short day, that is, about 9 hours of illumination in 24, for flowering, and in long days, say of 18 hours illumination, will not flower however long they are left under these conditions (Plate 22). The effect is clearly not just a matter of the production of a certain amount of material by photosynthesis; to mention one only of the many complications involved, a brief exposure to light of low intensity – quite insufficient for a significant amount of photosynthesis – given in the middle of the dark period produces a very marked retardation of flowering in chrysanthemums grown under short days.

These effects are all manifestations of a property common to living things in general, that of response to stimulus, or 'irritability' as it is sometimes called. A response to stimulus is an alteration in a vital process usually out of all proportion or in no way clearly related to the change in environmental conditions which induces it. Further, it is often such as to promote the well-being of the organism. Thus a light contact between the tendril of a sweet pea (*Lathyrus odoratus*) and a solid support, such as a stick, is sufficient stimulus to cause the side of the tendril away from the support to grow more rapidly than that in contact with it, so that the tendril coils round the stick. This response is of obvious advantage to the plant as a whole, since it enables it to maintain an upright position and so obtain the light necessary for photosynthesis.

The response does not always take place in the part of the plant by which the stimulus is received. Thus it is the tip of a growing stem which is most sensitive to unequal illumination, but the growth response, which results in the bending of the stem towards the source of the light, takes place some way below the tip. So to the problems of how the stimulus is perceived and how the response is brought about there must be added that of how instructions are transmitted about the plant.

Plant growth is thus an extremely complex thing. Nevertheless, the many questions which can be asked about it may be grouped under a few major heads. First, there is the problem of increase in substance; how the simple inorganic materials – carbon dioxide, water, and mineral salts – are absorbed and converted into the various and often complex organic substances which make up the body of a plant. Secondly, it may be asked how these substances become organized into living protoplasm, cells, tissues, and organs having specialized functions. In a plant having specialized parts, materials must be exchanged between these parts and their activities must be co-ordinated so that a third problem is that of how a plant is able to behave as a functional whole. Fourthly, there is the relation of plant to environment, how variations in external conditions have their effects on the amount and form of growth. The arrangement of the rest of this book follows this subdivision of the subject.

PART I

INCREASE IN SUBSTANCE

. . . an enchanted dupe I sat, my heart the tree heart, coursing sweet green sap, sweet fire within my veins. I knew its secret name, its drift of years; I felt my thick mindless roots clutch the live earth, digging through earth and stone groping for water. I heard each leaf grow out, an unfurling pennant in strong search of that other rain, the light. I strained my branches, a twist earnestly playful, insinuating into emptiness the flourish of my life.

HAN SUYIN
(*A Many-Splendoured Thing*)

CHAPTER 2

The Gathering of Raw Materials and Energy from Air and Light

THE chief means whereby plants increase in substance is the process known as photosynthesis. Before going into the details of this it is as well to be clear about its significance and importance. All living things, plant and animal, the martyr at the stake as well as the firewood, contain materials which can be made to yield heat or other form of energy by chemical change such as burning in oxygen. Such materials have high potential chemical energy, and contrast with those of the inorganic world, which are preponderantly of low potential chemical energy and incombustible. Substances of high potential chemical energy are continually being broken down in living organisms, liberating energy and giving products of low potential chemical energy, this breakdown being inseparable from the maintenance of active life. The chemical products may be reassimilated, directly or indirectly, and their atoms incorporated once more in living matter, but the energy which has been released cannot be recovered once it has been dissipated. As a result, every organism requires a supply of substances of high potential chemical energy for the maintenance of its life. Animals, fungi, and other organisms which do not photosynthesize are dependent on other organisms for their supply of these substances. Green plants, on the other hand, are able to build inorganic substances into substances of high potential chemical energy by absorbing light energy and transforming it into chemical energy in the process of photosynthesis.

The conversion of light energy into chemical energy is not in itself particularly remarkable, and generally occurs to some extent whenever light falls on a substance which absorbs it. Usually, however, the products of higher energy content which result are extremely unstable and decompose immediately, dissipating their energy as heat. Thus one of the most familiar instances of the chemical effect of light, the fading of dyed textiles in sunlight, is one in which decomposition occurs. The unique feature of photosynthesis is that such back-reactions are largely avoided and the energy fixed is accumulated in the form of stable compounds.

As the major process producing substances of high potential chemical energy, photosynthesis is of first importance for the maintenance of life on earth. The familiar text 'All flesh is grass' is true in a literal sense. Rabinowitch (1945) has put the same point thus: 'The reservoir of life is fed by a single channel, through which matter is pumped up from the low-lying sea of the stable inorganic world, to the high plateau of organic life; it finds its way back in hundreds of streams or meandering rivulets, which set in rotation, as they hurry down towards the sea, thousands of little wheels of life.' The capacity of this single channel is enormous; exact estimates are difficult, but it is probable that the total yield of photosynthesis by land plants and the microscopic algae of the oceans is at least 14×10^{10} tons of organic matter per year. The annual outputs of the world's chemical, metallurgical, and mining industries add up to less than one-hundredth of this in weight, and the energy fixed in photosynthetic products corresponds to the output of something like two thousand million large power stations.

As we have already seen, the most obvious indications that photosynthesis is taking place are that one gas, carbon dioxide, is absorbed by the plant, while another, oxygen, is given off. The oxygen, like the carbon dioxide, is an inorganic substance of low potential chemical energy; the products of high potential chemical energy are organic substances, the appearance of which is not always easy to demonstrate. However, using a mature leaf, from a runner bean (*Phaseolus multiflorus*), for example, it is easy to show that the organic substance starch is formed in quantity as a result of photosynthesis. The leaf, while still attached to the plant, is covered with a stencil so that parts of it are exposed to sunlight while others are kept in darkness. After some hours the leaf is detached and boiled in alcohol to remove the pigments, which might otherwise make it difficult to see the results of the test, then treated with iodine, which gives a dark blue colour with starch. Those parts of the leaf exposed to the light and able to photosynthesize are found to contain abundant starch, whereas the shaded parts contain little, if any. If the amounts of carbon dioxide used and the amounts of oxygen and organic material produced in the light by a green plant are measured they are found to correspond fairly well with the following chemical equation:

$$CO_2 + H_2O \rightarrow (CH_2O) + O_2 \qquad (1)$$
$$\text{carbon dioxide} + \text{water} \rightarrow \text{organic matter} + \text{oxygen}$$

In this, (CH_2O) is a non-committal formula for organic matter, which may be, but is not necessarily, starch or some other carbohydrate. A more detailed study of this process may be begun by seeing how its rate is affected by putting the plant under various conditions.

The rate of photosynthesis might be measured in terms of consumption or production of any of the four substances represented in equation 1. However, there is so much water about in a plant that it is difficult to detect the small changes in its amount, less than 1 per cent, which are caused by photosynthesis. Organic matter, or, what is nearly the same thing, total dry matter, may be determined, but changes in amounts of either of the two gases are more conveniently measured and are more often used in practice. It is awkward to use whole plants in studies of the rate of photosynthesis,

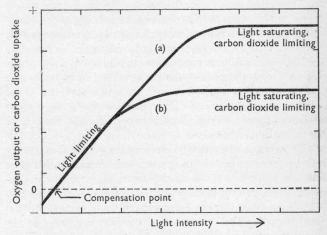

Fig. 11. The relation of rate of photosynthesis to light intensity; (a) at high and (b) at low carbon dioxide concentration.

and leaves or unicellular algae, such as *Chlorella*, are generally used as subjects for experiment.

As would be expected, the rate of photosynthesis depends on the intensity of the light reaching the plant. The relationship between rate and intensity, which is illustrated in Fig. 11, is not, however, altogether simple. Very weak light produces no observable amount of photosynthesis, and it is only when the intensity is increased to a certain value that the gas exchanges characteristic of the process begin. This happens when the synthesis of organic matter just balances the breakdown by respiration. For this reason this point is called the *compensation point*. Above the compensation point increase in intensity at first produces proportional increase in photosynthesis, but at moderate intensities the amount of photosynthesis for a given increase in illumination begins to fall off, and at high intensities the rate no longer increases and becomes independent of light intensity. Here, photosynthesis is said to be *saturated* with respect to light. The intensity required to produce saturation varies according to what the other conditions are, as we shall see, but for single leaves or thin suspensions of *Chlorella* it is always reached well below the intensity of full sunlight. It should be noted, however, that for whole plants even full sunlight may not give the maximum possible rate of photosynthesis, since, although the uppermost leaves may be light-saturated, those lower down, which they shade, will still be light-limited. In leaves or algal cells exposed to very high intensities there may be actual damage, so that the rate of photosynthesis decreases.

The average carbon dioxide content of air is 0·03 per cent by volume, but it can rise to as much as 0·10 per cent near the ground at night. The relationship of rate of photosynthesis to carbon dioxide concentration is of the same form, providing other conditions are suitable, such as that for light intensity. The carbon dioxide compensation point, at 0·01 per cent, lies rather close to the average concentration in air; saturation is reached at a concentration several times this average concentration, and high concentrations have a poisonous effect. However, these values again depend on the level of other factors, especially the intensity of light, and, conversely, the carbon dioxide concentration affects the response to other conditions, including light intensity. The sort of interaction which takes place is indicated in Fig. 11. At low light intensities, in the region in which photosynthesis is proportional to intensity, alteration in carbon dioxide concentration has no effect unless extremes are reached. As light saturation is approached, however, carbon dioxide concentration becomes more important and the maximum rate attainable becomes higher the more carbon dioxide is supplied. Putting it the other way round, at low carbon dioxide concentrations light intensity, unless very low or high, has no effect on the rate of photosynthesis, but when carbon dioxide is at a saturating concentration light becomes rate-determining.

That this should be so may seem obvious. However, in the more ample days at the beginning of this century the idea of the 'bottleneck' was evidently less familiar, to plant physiologists at least, than it is now. Investigations of the effects of a particular factor on plants were made with little regard for the possible importance of the level of other factors, and results were accordingly difficult to interpret. F. F. Blackman (1905) thus made an extremely important forward step when he enunciated the 'principle of limiting factors' as follows: 'When a process is conditioned as to its rapidity by a number of separate factors, the rate of the process is limited by the pace of the "slowest" factor.' In Fig. 11 light is represented as being limiting on the left-hand side of the diagram while carbon dioxide supply is limiting on the right-hand side. However, following Blackman, other people have shown that the principle does not apply rigidly and that in intermediate ranges increase in any of several factors may cause an increase in the rate of a physiological process. This is evident from Fig. 11; the lines do not have sharp breaks where light intensity ceases to be limiting and becomes saturating, as would be expected if the principle applied strictly, and, in the range where the line bends over, increase in either light or carbon dioxide will produce an increase in the rate of photosynthesis. Nevertheless, the principle of limiting factors remains a good general guide to the behaviour of plants as well as many other things.

Besides light intensity and carbon dioxide, many other factors, such as availability of water, temperature, colour of light, presence of poisons, and accumulation of products, have their effects on the rate of photosynthesis. The water content of healthy photosynthetic tissues is always high and well in the saturating concentration range, so that, although it is one of the raw materials for photosynthesis, changes in its concentration would be expected to have no direct effect on this process in practice. However, a leaf that is beginning to wilt may photosynthesize at only half the rate of a turgid one, and a leaf that is quite flaccid is usually nearly inactive in photosynthesis. A water loss sufficient to result in wilting is small in terms of the total water content of the leaf, about 10 per cent for most thin-leaved species, and is not enough to reduce the water concentration to a directly limiting value for photosynthesis. The effect, like many others that might be mentioned, is an indirect one, depending on the structure of the photosynthetic system. To get any farther in understanding photosynthesis we must look more closely at this structure.

Underlying all the wonderful variety of the plant kingdom there is one common feature of design: the form of the plant body is always such as to provide a large surface area in relation to its volume. Whereas animals take their food in concentrated, usually solid, form, plants, whether photosynthetic or dependent on pre-formed organic substances, obtain the materials that they require for growth from dilute solution, and the amount which can be taken in in these circumstances is proportional to the area of the absorbing surface. A nearly spherical unicellular plant such as *Chlorella*, say 6 μ* in diameter, has a high surface/volume ratio, 10,000 square centimetres for every cubic centimetre of cell substance. If through growth it doubles its diameter this ratio falls to 5,000 to 1, because volume is proportional to the cube of linear dimensions, whereas the surface is proportional to the square. The bigger the cell, therefore, the less efficient it becomes in exchanging substances with its environment, and the slower its growth-rate must be in consequence. A *Chlorella* cell the size of a tennis ball would have only 1 square centimetre of surface area per cubic centimetre and could be expected to grow at only $\frac{1}{10000}$ of the rate of a real *Chlorella*.

For plants which float freely in water the best way to keep a high surface/volume ratio is to remain small. The floating

* A micron or μ is 0·001 millimetre or about 0·00004 inch.

plant-life of the oceans is the most abundant form of life on earth, yet consists entirely of microscopic unicellular forms. However, in this book we are mainly concerned with plants which have become adapted to life on land, and for these there are serious disadvantages in being small. A free-floating unicellular plant is surrounded by water, which normally contains ample amounts of carbon dioxide, and a modest ability to float or swim ensures that the remaining major requirement for photosynthesis, light, can be attained. For land plants, on the other hand, it is necessary to be fixed in one spot (John Wyndham's triffids in gaining the ability to lumber about had to adopt the un-plant-like habit of taking nourishment in concentrated form), and be big enough to maintain a position in the light and at the same time reach down to a fairly permanent supply of water. The carbon dioxide supply in air is rather more tenuous than that in water, so it remains highly important that a large surface area should be available for its absorption, and it is also important, of course, that a large area should be presented to the light. The structure of a successful land plant must thus somehow combine large size with a high surface/volume ratio.

A large surface relative to bulk may be produced by elaboration of external form. A sphere has the least possible surface area for a given volume, and any departure from this shape produces an increase in surface/volume ratio. Subdivision and flattening, as in branches and leaves, increase surface area enormously and are generally carried as far as is compatible with adequate mechanical robustness. For ordinary plants the limit seems to be reached at about 30 square centimetres of surface per cubic centimetre of tissues – a distinct improvement on the tennis ball, but nowhere near *Chlorella*. However, this is only external surface, and the internal structure of a multicellular plant is such as to provide a large area of cell surface over which absorption of carbon dioxide may take place.

Fig. 12 gives some idea of the internal structure of a leaf such as one from an apple tree (*Pyrus malus*). The upper and

lower surfaces are covered by single layers of flattened
epidermal cells. These cells are colourless and largely protective in function. Their outer walls are rendered more or
less water- and gas-tight by wax and a continuous covering
of *cutin*, a resistant fatty material. The only holes in the

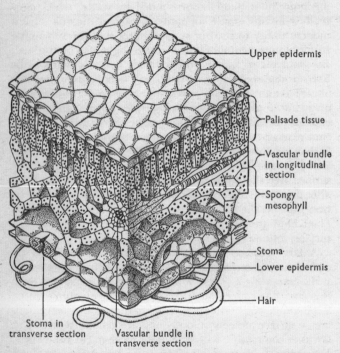

Fig. 12. Magnified three-dimensional view of a square cut from an
apple leaf (× 100).

epidermis are the *stomata* (singular *stoma*, a slit-like opening
between two *guard cells*), which in an apple leaf are confined
to the lower surface. Because of the special form of the guard
cells, stomata can open and close. Below the upper epidermis
are two layers of elongated cells arranged at right-angles to
the surface. These cells, which from their appearance are

called *palisade cells*, are circular in cross-section and are not tightly packed so that air is free to circulate between them. Below the palisade cells is a tissue of irregularly shaped cells which contains large air-spaces and which is known as the *spongy mesophyll*.

Altogether the air-spaces of a leaf make up from 8 to 70 per cent of its volume. Both palisade and spongy mesophyll cells contain green pigment. This pigment is not distributed uniformly throughout each cell, but is confined to small, uniform, discoid or ellipsoid bodies known as *chloroplasts*. The number of chloroplasts per cell varies from a few to a hundred or more. Small as they are – the largest diameter is usually about 4 μ – they have an elaborate submicroscopic structure (Plate 7) and house the complete mechanism of photosynthesis. This is indicated by the fact that starch produced in photosynthesis is formed within the chloroplasts, and has been proved by the recent demonstration by Arnon (1955) that chloroplasts isolated from the rest of the protoplasm are still capable of producing sugar by photosynthesis. Also visible in leaf sections are *vascular strands*. These contain xylem and phloem and thick-walled fibres, and provide both for the transport of water and other materials to and fro from the leaf tissues and for mechanical support. It is these vascular strands which are left behind as a fine lace-like 'leaf skeleton' when the softer tissues have rotted away.

We must now consider this structure from the point of view of carbon dioxide absorption. The main path of entry of this gas into the leaf is through the stomata. This has been demonstrated using leaves, like those of the apple, in which the stomata, being all on one surface, can be blocked with petroleum jelly or similar substance, leaving the other surface, without stomata, clear for the gas to penetrate if it can. Leaves with stomata blocked are found to absorb little, if any, carbon dioxide as compared with untreated leaves; the cutinized epidermis is nearly impervious to this gas. At first sight this restriction of entry to the stomata would seem to offset the effects of the high surface/volume ratio achieved by the special shape of the leaf. The individual stomatal pore is minute, the average diameter being about 10 μ, and although there may be thousands of stomata per square centimetre, the total area of their openings amounts at the most to 3 per cent of the surface area of the leaf. Nevertheless, leaves do absorb large quantities of carbon dioxide during photosynthesis. They can do so because gases diffuse through a barrier with a sufficient number of small holes in it almost as rapidly as if the barrier were not there.

This was first demonstrated experimentally in the classic work of Brown and Escombe (1900) at Kew, although the theoretical basis had been worked out by the physicist Stefan some twenty years earlier. It is found that whereas diffusion over an extensive area is proportional to area, over a limited area it becomes proportional to the linear dimensions of the cross-section through which the molecules pass. The reason for this is not difficult to understand. Diffusion occurs because the molecules in a gas or liquid are in random movement. If we think of a small part of a large plane area through which diffusion is taking place, although the diffusing molecules actually come at all angles the average paths of diffusion can only be at right-angles to the plane (Fig. 13a). With a small hole in an impervious barrier, on the other hand, a much larger effective space supplies the diffusing molecules and diffusion can take place along the

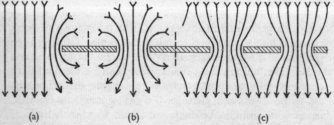

(a)   (b)   (c)

Fig. 13. Lines of flow of gas molecules during diffusion from a high concentration (above) to a low concentration (below): (a) unrestricted and around an edge; (b) through a small isolated hole; (c) through small closely spaced holes.

paths shown in Fig. 13b. Since the majority of diffusing molecules slip round the edge, as it were, diffusion is proportional to the length of edge presented by the hole, and so is proportional to its diameter. The total amount of edge presented by the open stomata of a leaf is sufficient to enable diffusion to take place almost as rapidly as if the epidermis were not there; it could not, of course, be more rapid than this. If holes are so numerous as to be close to each other there will be interference (Fig. 13c). Stomata are generally about 10 diameters apart, a spacing at which interference begins to be appreciable if they are fully open.

Having entered through the stomata, carbon dioxide is able to diffuse freely within the leaf because the air-space system is continuous. This may be readily demonstrated with an onion leaf: a piece of glass tubing is pushed into the cut end of the leaf and bound firmly into position, then, if the leaf is immersed in water and one blows gently through the tube, bubbles of air will issue from the stomata. Each cell has direct access to air, and together the internal cell surfaces of a leaf provide a large area for the absorption of carbon dioxide. The ratio of internally exposed cell walls and external leaf surface has been found to be between 7 and 31. Thus an average leaf has a total surface area of the order of 600 square centimetres per cubic centimetre and achieves a very fair solution of the problem of combining large size and a high relative surface area.

When the carbon dioxide reaches the wet cell wall it dissolves and thence diffuses in water to the chloroplasts, the site of photosynthesis. Although this last part of the journey is short, a matter of a micron or so, it is the slowest, for diffusion in water takes place at only $\frac{1}{10000}$ of the rate of that in air. This means that if the intercellular air-space system became filled with water, as one might expect in wet weather, the supply of carbon dioxide from the atmosphere would be virtually cut off. This untoward happening is prevented by the structure of the stoma; the walls of the guard cells are not only covered with wax, which makes them unwettable, but in addition are so shaped as to make the entry of water impossible unless it is forced in under pressure. It will be seen from Fig. 14 that ridges project from the guard cells so that the stomatal pore does not have parallel sides but widens suddenly after the narrow entrance. This means that, if the stoma is covered by a rain-drop and water begins to enter the pore, any penetration involves a relatively considerable expansion of its surface, which will be opposed by surface tension.

Leaves must also be considered as light-absorbing organs. The wave-length range within which light can be utilised for photosynthesis happens to correspond roughly with that visible to the human eye, i.e. radiations of wavelength from

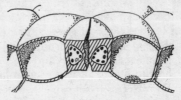

Fig. 14. Magnified three-dimensional view of a stoma and adjacent cells cut transversely (×500). (After Meyer, Anderson, and Böhning, 1960.)

about 800 mμ (1 millimicron = 0·001 μ = 10 Ångström units) at the red end of the spectrum to 400 mμ in the violet. Light reflected or transmitted by a substance cannot produce chemical change in it, so it is among the pigments of the leaf that we must look for the absorbing substance or substances, since materials are white or colourless because they reflect or transmit all the light which falls on them. The association of green pigment with photosynthesis has already been mentioned, and it is reasonable to suppose that it is this which absorbs the light needed for the process. The green of the chloroplasts is due to the presence in them of four principal pigments, *chlorophylls a* and *b*, which are green, and *xanthophyll* and *carotene*, which are orange yellow. The two chlorophylls are never found in flowering plants except in chloroplasts. The two orange-yellow pigments may occur elsewhere in cells, but then have no direct part in photosynthesis.

Substances appear coloured because they absorb light of different wavelengths to different extents, their colour being that of the light least absorbed. Thus the chlorophylls absorb violet and red light most and green light least. The orange-yellow pigments absorb the blue and violet. This can

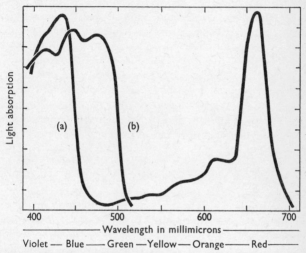

Fig. 15. Spectral absorption curves of chlorophyll *a* (a) and β-carotene (b).

be given precise expression as a *spectral absorption curve*, in which the proportion of light absorbed is plotted against wavelength (Fig. 15). The extent of absorption of light by a pigment solution also depends on its concentration and on the distance which the light travels through it. This has the result that if the solution is concentrated enough and the path of light through it sufficiently long there will be virtually complete absorption, even though the specific absorption for the particular wavelength is low. Thus a strong chlorophyll solution appears black, absorbing even green light almost completely.

The amount of light which is received by a plant depends very much on its general form, and much of the detail of leaf form and arrangement is of functional significance in the diffusion and interception of light as well as being aesthetically pleasing to human beings. A conical shape is generally most advantageous for a plant, since it presents a large light-absorbing surface and results in minimum shading of the lower leaves. Small leaves or large dissected ones are of advantage because they allow part of the light to pass without interruption to the foliage below, which might otherwise be in continuous shadow. The orientation of the individual leaves is particularly important. A leaf facing the light source, i.e. at right-angles to the rays, intercepts the maximum amount; one edge-on, i.e. parallel to the rays, receives the minimum, and in between the amount is proportional to the sine of the angle which the rays make with the leaf.

From what was said on p. 46 about light saturation and the bad effects of high intensities it will be realized that in full sun it may be to the plant's advantage to have its leaves edge-on to the rays. This happens very obviously in *Silphium laciniatum*, the compass plant of the prairies, which has its leaves turned edgeways due north and south, thus avoiding getting the midday sun at full strength but making the most of the less intense light available at the beginning and end of the day. It is to be noted that plants such as maize and sugar-cane (*Saccharum officinarum*), which are among the photosynthetically most efficient, have their light-absorbing surfaces nearly vertical, which has a similar effect. Some plants are capable of adjusting the orientation of leaves fairly quickly in response to changes in the intensity and direction of light. Leaves may turn on their stalks so that they face a light source of moderate intensity but present themselves edgewise to bright sunshine. The French bean (*Phaseolus vulgaris*) is an excellent example of this; in the morning and evening and in dull weather the young leaves are spread so as to intercept as much light as possible, but at midday in intense sunlight each leaflet turns edge-on to the light.

Of the light falling on a leaf some may be reflected and that which penetrates may be absorbed or transmitted unabsorbed. The relative proportions of reflected, absorbed, and transmitted light vary, not only with wavelength (Fig. 16) and the angle at which the light strikes the leaf but also

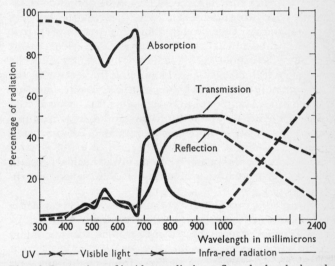

Fig. 16. Proportions of incident radiation reflected, absorbed, and transmitted by a green leaf, in relation to wavelength. (After Tranquillini, 1960.)

with the kind of leaf. It is a matter of common observation that leaves of some species are shiny or whitish while others have a matt surface and are deep green in colour. There is also the contrast between, for example, the delicate translucency of young beech foliage and the opacity of an old leaf of laurel (*Prunus laurocerasus*).

The degree of reflection depends on the smoothness of the epidermis and the size and form of hairs, if present. It may be to the plant's benefit if the intensity reaching its photo-synthetic tissues is reduced by reflection of some of the light falling on the leaf surface. Furthermore, the light reflected may fall elsewhere on the same plant, perhaps on less brightly illuminated leaves, and so not be lost for photosynthetic purposes. It is generally the case that leaves of species which usually grow in full sunlight have high reflectivity, whereas leaves of shade-plants reflect very little.

Light penetrating a leaf may be absorbed by the chloroplasts, which correspond to a rather concentrated solution of the pigments, since a single chloroplast absorbs from 30 to 60 per cent of the light which falls on it. A further feature favouring absorption is that light is not transmitted directly through a leaf but is reflected and refracted backwards and forwards at the interfaces between air-spaces, cell walls, and protoplasm. The path of light through a leaf is thus several times the actual thickness of the leaf, and the opportunities for absorption are correspondingly increased. Because of this even green light is eventually absorbed to a considerable extent, and the absorption spectrum of a living leaf (Fig. 16) is much flatter than that of a solution of extracted pigment (Fig. 15).

The capacity to absorb light of the leaves of a particular species can vary quite considerably. Shade-leaves are larger, and so intercept more of the available light, than sun-leaves of the same species. They are thinner than sun-leaves, but the chloroplasts are larger, and on a fresh-weight basis there may be twice as much pigment, so that the percentage light absorption is also increased. Besides these fixed adaptations there are responses which may occur quite rapidly and enable a plant to adapt itself to some extent to the intensity of light which it receives. Chloroplasts can change their shape, becoming nearly spherical in light of low intensity, whereas in bright light they become flattened and orientated so that the light strikes only their edges. Not only this, but they may move within the cell, gathering on the illuminated face in moderate light but lining up on the side walls in strong light (Fig. 17). This movement of chloroplasts has an appreciable effect on the amount of light transmitted: a leaf kept in the sun for a few hours may let through as much as one-third more light as a similar leaf kept in diffuse light.

Light may be absorbed by leaf pigments other than those in the chloroplasts, for example by the red pigments of the

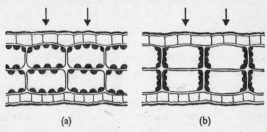

Fig. 17. Sections of frond of ivy duckweed (*Lemna trisulca*) to show arrangement of chloroplasts in diffuse daylight (a), and direct sunlight (b). (After Stahl.)

copper beech and of the red and purple maples (different species of *Acer*). Light thus absorbed is not available for photosynthesis, and its energy appears in the leaf as heat. Varieties containing red pigments are consequently photosynthetically less efficient than are green varieties and are liable to leaf-scorch in full sun. Solar radiation, of course, always contains a large proportion of infra-red, which is unavailable for photosynthesis and which if absorbed gives rise to thermal energy. Leaves, however, contain few substances absorbing infra-red of the particular wavelengths (Fig. 16) which predominate in the sunlight reaching the earth's surface (this is why vegetation appears white in infra-red photographs) and so do not heat up in full sunlight as rapidly as they might otherwise.

Two other necessities for efficient photosynthesis are a good water supply and means for exporting the photosynthetic products to other parts of the plant. As we have seen, the vascular tissue of a leaf is well developed, and its ramifications are capable of conducting water throughout the photosynthetic tissue. However, it is of little use to consider a leaf by itself in this connexion, and this brings us to the water economy of the plant as a whole, a subject which is dealt with in the next chapter. The removal of photosynthetic products from the leaf is also something which is largely determined by the behaviour of the plant as a whole, but at this point it may be noted that the accumulation of these products in the leaf reduces its capacity for photosynthesis. If a leaf is detached, and thereby prevented from exporting material, its rate of photosynthesis declines as sugars and starch accumulate in it. It is a consequence of the chemical law of mass action that the rate of a reaction should decrease as the concentration of its products increases, but it is doubtful whether the performance of a detached leaf depends exclusively on this simple relationship. Mechanical disruption of the photosynthetic apparatus may play a part as well, for chloroplasts sometimes become greatly distended by starch formed within them. In a leaf attached to the plant, photosynthetic products are moved out via the vascular strands, but, nevertheless, under good conditions for photosynthesis products accumulate and the rate of photosynthesis correspondingly declines.

CHAPTER 3

A Digression on Water Economy

THE efficiency of leaf structure for photosynthesis is not achieved without cost. A large expanse of moist cell surface exposed to the air provides an excellent means of absorbing carbon dioxide, but is inevitably equally efficient in evaporating water. As a result, although the amount of water actually consumed in photosynthesis is quite small, the process can usually be carried on only at the expense of a considerable water loss through evaporation. In the course of a summer day a tree such as a beech may lose an amount of water equal to nearly five times the fresh weight of its leaves, and for an acre of beech-wood this will mean a loss of something like 3,400 gallons per day. Since under normal conditions plants maintain their water content and do not wilt, this means a correspondingly large intake. In fact, in temperate countries about as much water is absorbed and evaporated by plants as runs down to the sea in rivers. Nevertheless, plant growth is commonly limited by lack of water, even in a notoriously damp climate such as that of Britain. Penman (1958) has shown that crops in south-east England would benefit from irrigation at least in eight years out of ten. It is not surprising, then, that much of the structure and function of land plants seems to be concerned with the delicate business of achieving maximum photosynthesis and at the same time keeping water loss at a minimum.

The process of evaporation from plants is given the special name *transpiration*, but this must not be taken as implying that it is fundamentally different from the physical process of evaporation as it occurs, for example, when washing is hung out to dry. There are differences, but these seem to arise only from the greater complication of plant structure as compared with that of man-made materials. Evaporation

occurs when a molecule of water acquires sufficient energy
to break away from the constraint of its fellows in the liquid
phase and to diffuse freely in the gaseous phase. The higher
the temperature of the water, the more rapidly its molecules
will move and the higher will be its rate of evaporation.
Since it is those molecules possessing energy above the
average which succeed in escaping, continued evaporation
lowers the average energy of the molecules in the liquid, i.e.
decreases its temperature, if no energy is supplied from outside. The rate of evaporation thus depends on the rate of
heat-flow into the water which is evaporating. At the same
time as molecules are leaving the liquid others diffusing in
the air above it may strike its surface and be unable to leave
it again.

The net rate of evaporation depends on the extent to
which the number of molecules leaving the liquid exceeds
that rejoining it. At any given temperature air can contain
only a certain proportion of water molecules. At this saturation point the numbers of molecules passing in the two
directions will be equal and the net rate of evaporation will
be zero. Immediately above liquid water exposed in the
open air there forms a layer of saturated air, which acts as a
diffusion barrier, grading into incompletely saturated air
farther away. At constant temperature the rate of evaporation depends on the steepness of this diffusion gradient. Air
movement, by carrying the diffusing water molecules away
from the surface, in effect steepens the gradient and so increases evaporation.

For the moment we will confine attention to transpiration
as it takes place from a leaf with open stomata. Leaf cuticle
is rather impermeable to water, and less than 10 per cent of
the loss of water from a leaf takes place through it unless it
is unusually thin. Water vapour must thus be exchanged
largely by way of the stomata, and from what has already
been said about diffusion through these it will be appreciated that this need not result in much restriction of transpiration.

The general effects of environmental conditions on transpiration and on evaporation from an inanimate system such as blotting-paper soaked in water are, as we should expect, similar. The rates of both depend on the dryness of the air, that is, on the steepness of the diffusion gradient. This relationship is expressed in Fig. 18, which shows, however, not dryness but relative humidity (the usual measure of the water content of the air; it is the amount of water vapour which the air actually contains expressed as a percentage of that which it would contain if saturated at the

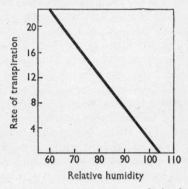

Fig. 18. Relation of transpiration rate to relative humidity of the atmosphere.

same temperature). An anomalous point will be noticed: if the graph is continued down it cuts the relative humidity axis beyond the 100 per cent point, which implies that evaporation can take place from a leaf into an atmosphere which is more than saturated with water vapour. The reason for this is that in a living leaf there is a continuous slow release of energy sufficient to keep its temperature a fraction of a degree above that of its surroundings. Water molecules thus still leave the leaf cells faster than they are replaced from the air, but since the air is saturated, this means that water must condense from it somewhere else. A difference of a fraction of a degree between the leaf and its surroundings is sufficient to account for the discrepancy shown in Fig. 18.

Absorption of radiant energy may also cause leaf temperature to rise, and thus increase transpiration. As we have seen, absorption of the infra-red, which would have the biggest heating effect, is small, but, nevertheless, leaves in bright sunshine sometimes attain temperatures as much as 15° C. above their surroundings. A rise in air temperature without an increase in leaf temperature decreases transpiration, since the vapour pressure of the water in the air is increased and the diffusion gradient correspondingly decreased. The effect of wind on evaporation depends on the size and shape of the object from which evaporation is taking place as well as on the speed of air movement. As would be expected, transpiration may be increased several-fold when leaves are exposed to wind because of the steepening of the diffusion gradient. On the other hand, most of the heat gained by the leaf by absorption of light is dissipated by transfer to the surrounding air, and hence air movement will tend to keep leaf temperature down so that transpiration is reduced. The effects of wind on transpiration are consequently complicated, and until more is known of the aerodynamics of leaves precise description is impossible.

As a result of transpiration, the cells of a leaf lose water. To understand how this loss is made good we must first of all consider the plant cell as an *osmotic* system. The process of *osmosis* is essentially one of diffusion and, in fact, the laws which govern it have a basic similarity to those which govern the behaviour of gases, which also depends on the random movement of molecules. In any solution the molecules of both solute (e.g. sugar), and solvent (e.g. water), are in random movement. Suppose two compartments, separated by a partition which is permeable to both sugar and water, in one of which is put water alone and in the other of which is put sugar solution. Both sides of the partition will be hit and penetrated by diffusing molecules, but at first sugar molecules will come from only one side, so that there will be a movement of sugar from one compartment to the other until equal numbers of sugar molecules strike either side of the partition and net movement of sugar ceases.

Water molecules will move in the opposite direction, because at first more will strike the partition on the side with water only than on the other side, where the water is, so to speak, diluted with sugar. In technical terms there is a *diffusion pressure deficit* of water in the compartment containing the sugar solution. In these circumstances diffusion will equalize the concentration of the solution on either side of the partition.

Osmosis occurs when the partition, instead of being permeable to both solvent and solute, can be penetrated by the solvent only; such a partition is called a *semipermeable membrane*. Here, as before, the diffusion pressure of water is greater on the side of the partition on which there is water only than on the other side, so that there is a net movement of solvent into the solution. The sugar must stay in the compartment into which it was put. If nothing happens to interfere, osmosis goes on until the solution reaches infinite dilution. Now suppose that the compartment containing the solution is closed with a piston. As osmosis goes on, the volume of the solution increases and the piston will be pushed out. However, if pressure is applied to the piston, osmosis can be prevented and the volume kept constant. What happens is that pressure increases the energy of the molecules, so that, although there are relatively fewer of the solvent molecules on the solution side of the partition, they move faster, and so in a given time equal numbers strike both sides of the membrane, with the result that no net movement of solvent takes place. In the familiar demonstration of osmosis a piston is not used, but osmosis takes place into a funnel, the mouth of which is closed by a semipermeable membrane, until the pressure of the solution rising up the vertical stem of the funnel is sufficient to balance the diffusion pressure causing the solvent to enter. The pressure required just to prevent the osmosis of solvent into a solution in this way is known as the *osmotic pressure* of the solution, and is dependent on the concentration of the solute in it.

A plant cell consists of a semipermeable membrane, the

protoplasm, surrounding a solution of salts and organic substances, the vacuolar sap, which is sufficiently concentrated to have an osmotic pressure of between 5 and 30 atmospheres. If the cell is placed in water osmosis occurs, and water would go on entering until the cell burst were it not for the restraint of the wall. The cell wall is freely permeable to water and most solutes, and is elastic, so that as the cell increases in volume it becomes stretched and exerts an inwardly directed pressure on the protoplasm, like the case of a football on the inflated bladder. These osmotic relations can be expressed thus:

$$S = (P_i - P_o) - T \qquad (2)$$

where P_i is the osmotic pressure of the vacuolar sap and P_o that of the solution external to the cell (which will be zero if this is water only), T the *turgor pressure*, which is the inwardly directed pressure of the cell wall, and S a measure of the capacity of the cell to absorb water. S has usually been called *suction pressure*, a self-contradictory term that is best left to die; the more modern term, *diffusion pressure deficit*, is more cumbersome, but does less violence to our concept of the underlying mechanism. The manner in which these quantities vary in relation to each other is shown in Fig. 19. Notice that S is zero when the cell is fully *turgid*, that is, when the turgor pressure balances the osmotic pressure tending to force water into the cell. If the cell is placed in a solution having a greater osmotic pressure than the vacuolar sap, water passes out of the cell, the contents shrinking away from the wall, and the cell is then said to be *plasmolysed*. A plasmolysed cell transferred to water has a maximum diffusion pressure deficit.

The situation is not really so simple as this in an intact plant, because then a cell is not subjected to the restraint of just its own wall but also to the pressure from the cells which surround it. Quite considerable *tissue tensions* may develop as a result of this. Take a fresh dandelion (*Taraxacum officinale*) flower stalk and slit it lengthways, and the strips will immediately curl outwards (Plate 11 shows a similar effect with pea stems); this happens because the turgid inner tissue was held under compression by the more inextensible outer tissues. With the release from this constraint, that is, with the reduction of T in equation 2, the diffusion pressure deficit, S, of the inner cells will increase correspondingly. Tissue tensions are the main source of mechanical rigidity in herbaceous plants – it will be scarcely necessary to remind the reader of the limpness of a drying lettuce leaf – and they

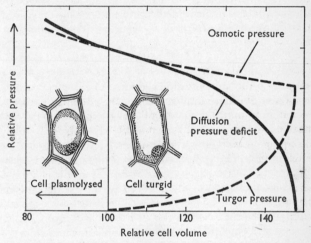

Fig. 19. Interrelations of osmotic pressure, diffusion pressure deficit, turgor pressure, and volume of a cell. (The graph after Bennet-Clark, 1958.)

are also often made use of in seed-dispersal mechanisms. The balsam, *Impatiens noli-tangere*, is an example that is probably familiar, but the squirting cucumber, *Ecballium elaterium*, is more spectacular. The pulpy interior of this fruit develops a high osmotic pressure and takes in water until a pressure of as much as 3 atmospheres is developed inside the elastic casing. Thus charged, it requires only a slight disturbance to set the contrivance off; the fruit stalk comes out like a stopper, and the pulp with its contained seeds is squirted to a distance which Overbeck (1930) reported to be as much as 13 yards.

It should be pointed out at this stage that osmotic forces may not be the only ones bringing about water movement in and out of cells. The evidence for active 'pumping' of water is much clearer for animals than plants, and it seems that in a tissue such as that of the human kidney, active transport of water completely overrides the osmotic factors affecting its distribution. There are many indications that something needs to be added to the simple osmotic picture of water movement in plants, but there is no really conclusive evidence as to what this is. One example only can be given: Bennet-Clark (1948) plasmolysed cells in a solution of potassium chloride, then transferred them to a sugar solution having the same osmotic pressure. The osmotic properties of a solution are independent of the chemical nature of the solute, so that this change might be expected to have no effect on the amount of water in the cells. Actually there was quite a marked increase in cell volume, indicating water uptake. On transferring back to potassium chloride solution the cells reverted to their original size. It is not certain what the mechanism of this is; perhaps it depends on changes in electric charges across the cell membrane, but it might also be the result of the free space in the protoplasm (see p. 145) being different for sugar and potassium chloride. Active transport of water, if it occurs, would certainly involve expenditure of energy. It is, in fact, observed that rate of water transport in tissues is sometimes correlated with the rate of respiration, that is, of the energy-producing processes.

However, we must return to the transpiring cells of the leaf. Evaporation takes place from the wet cell walls, in which the water is held in capillary spaces too small to be seen with the ordinary microscope. As the water retreats in these submicroscopic pores the effect is to decrease its diffusion pressure. The adjacent cells are then no longer in osmotic equilibrium with the water surrounding them, water diffuses out, and their diffusion pressure deficit rises. Since the cell walls of leaf cells are fairly rigid, that is to say, inelastic, the turgor pressure falls rapidly and the rise in diffusion pressure deficit is consequently steep. A diffusion pressure gradient is thus quickly set up in the leaf tissue, and water will move towards the evaporating surfaces from regions of higher diffusion pressure. It has been a matter for debate for a long time whether this movement takes place mainly in the cell walls or mainly through the protoplasts. The question seems to have been settled by experiments such as those of Ordin and his fellow workers (1956) employing isotopically labelled* water, so that its diffusion into ordinary water can be followed. Study of the diffusion of labelled water in plant tissues shows that it takes place as a uniform wave irrespective of cell walls, protoplasm, or vacuoles. The water-conducting structures of the leaf veins contain water with relatively little dissolved material in it, and therefore have a high diffusion pressure. As a result, diffusion of water takes place into the leaf tissues and more flows along the veins from the stem and roots to replace it. This flow of water through the plant is known as the *transpiration stream*.

The structures through which water is conducted in the xylem deserve closer examination than we have given them so far. There are two main kinds of water-conducting unit, *tracheids* and *vessels*, in flowering plants, but only tracheids are found in the wood of conifers. Both of these structures are derived from cells which lose their living contents at maturity. Tracheids are cigar-shaped with thickenings of the wall in the form of rings, 'spirals' (more correctly called

* A chemical element may exist in different forms, or *isotopes*, having the same chemical properties but differing atomic weights. Isotopes may occur naturally, and can also be produced artificially, as in the atomic pile. Some isotopes are unstable, or *radioactive*, and can be detected with a Geiger counter or by their effect on a photographic plate (see Plates 8 and 9). Others are stable and can be determined only by some such means as a mass-spectrometer. If a substance is 'labelled' or 'tagged' by incorporating in it an isotope which does not occur naturally or one which normally occurs only in small proportions its molecules will behave in a living organism in a similar fashion to unlabelled molecules of the same substance, but their movement and fate may be followed by means of the label. For more on radioactive isotopes, see J. L. Putman, *Isotopes* (Penguin Books, 1960).

helices), or more elaborate structures, which give mechanical strength while leaving thin areas of wall offering a minimum of resistance to the passage of water in and out. Tracheids may be up to 1 centimetre in length and are clearly well suited for the conduction of water. Vessels (Plate 4 and Fig. 37) are even more suitable. The vessel segment is a barrel-shaped piece of thickened wall formed from a cell the end walls of which have disappeared. Series of vessel segments arranged end to end form tubes which may be as much as half a millimetre in diameter and up to several metres long.

It can easily be demonstrated that most of the water transport in a stem takes place through the tracheids and vessels. If a cut shoot is put with its end in a suitable dye solution, e.g. eosin, the solution will be drawn up the xylem as transpiration goes on, and the cell walls with which it comes into contact will be stained. Eventually, even the minutest veins in the leaves become picked out in red, and examination of sections under the microscope shows that it is the walls of tracheids and vessels which have become stained. Another way to show the same thing is to block the tracheids and vessels of a cut shoot with gelatine or low-melting-point wax. This prevents water movement, and the shoot will wilt as a result. However, the walls of xylem cells have submicroscopic pores in them, like the walls of the photosynthetic cells of the leaf, and a certain amount of water transport within them is possible when the spaces enclosed by them are blocked (see p. 86).

As transpiration goes on and water is withdrawn from it, tension develops in the xylem. This can be shown by allowing a young plant to wilt, then cutting its stem under eosin solution. The red solution is drawn into the xylem, downwards as well as upwards, moving many centimetres in a few seconds as the tension is released and the walls of the vessels and tracheids relax. No such entry of eosin solution is found if the experiment is repeated with an unwilted, well-watered plant. If a cut shoot is attached to a glass tube full of water with its lower end dipping in mercury the mercury will be drawn up the tube as transpiration goes on and tension develops. The same thing happens if a porous pot filled with water is substituted for the shoot. Whereas a positive pressure increases the diffusion pressure of water, a tension, or negative pressure, decreases it, having the same osmotic effect as a dissolved substance. The diffusion pressure deficit which develops in transpiring leaves is thus transmitted down the xylem into the roots. The root tissues, which we may suppose to be turgid, i.e. with a high diffusion pressure, will thus lose water to the xylem and a diffusion gradient of water will be set up from the soil water on the outside of the root to the xylem in its core (Plate 3).

A root can thus be looked on as a simple osmotic system, with its tissues acting as a semipermeable membrane through which water diffuses into the xylem from the soil solution, which, because it has only a small concentration of dissolved matter in it, normally has a high diffusion pressure. It is particularly important to realize that the osmotic pressure of the contents of individual cells is irrelevant in this picture. It is a gradient of diffusion pressure which determines the movement, and water may pass from a dilute solution in the soil to another dilute one in the xylem through cells in which the sap is concentrated, so long as the osmotic pressure of this sap is balanced by tissue tension. It is, however, an over-simplification to look on the root tissues as a uniform semipermeable membrane, for the *endodermis* (Fig. 20 and Plate 3), a continuous layer of cells surrounding the vascular strands, consists when mature of cells with walls impregnated with fatty substances, and movement of water through it is restricted to a few *passage cells* which are not waterproofed in this way. An endodermis is almost universally present in roots, and it evidently has some important function in controlling water movement. This function may be to ensure that the tissues are truly semipermeable, for the endodermis has the appearance of a device to ensure that all water taken in by the root passes through the protoplasm of the passage cells. Were it not for this, a great deal of water movement, carrying dissolved substances with it, could take place via cell walls which are not semipermeable.

The diffusion pressure deficit in the xylem of the root is not only a result of negative pressure. The water in the xylem usually has some dissolved material in it, and normally has a greater osmotic pressure than the water in the

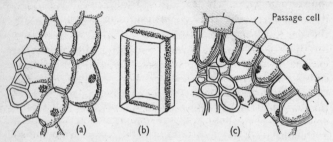

Fig. 20. The endodermis of the root: (a) part of the endodermis as seen in a transverse section of the absorbing region of a root; (b) three-dimensional diagram of a single endodermal cell showing the arrangement of the band impregnated with fatty substances; (c) the endodermis of an older root, most of the cells with thick impervious deposits on their inner and radial walls, but one thin-walled passage cell shown. (After James, 1936.)

soil. Consequently, even in a plant which is not transpiring, water tends to be absorbed by the root, and positive pressures may develop in the xylem as a result. When this happens, drops of water may be forced out of the leaves, a phenomenon known as *guttation*. Grasses and herbaceous plants usually do this in the early hours of morning, but it can be brought about at more convenient times for observation if a vigorously growing potted plant is prevented from transpiring by being put in a water-saturated atmosphere under a bell-jar. Guttation occurs at the tips and on the margins of leaves in regions of specially low resistance to water movement, where vascular bundles end in a tissue of thin-walled cells, and incompletely differentiated and permanently open stomata provide pores for the escape of the liquid to the outside.

If the stem of a vigorously growing plant is severed just above ground level, similar absorption of water by the roots will result in 'bleeding' of sap from the xylem. Large quantities of sap may be lost in this way. The stump of a sunflower plant has been found to produce over a litre of sap, a volume three times that of its roots, in thirteen days. This is not an extreme example, for the volume of sap lost in twenty-four hours often exceeds the volume of the roots of the bleeding plant. If a vertical tube is attached to a bleeding stump a column of sap will rise in it until the pressure exerted by this column balances the diffusion pressure, causing water to enter the root. Usually it is most convenient to measure this *root pressure* by means of a mercury manometer attached to the stump. Stephen Hales, who coined the term 'root pressure', described this method in 1727 and recorded pressures of over one atmosphere developed by a grape-vine (*Vitis vinifera*). This is an average value; root pressures of six or seven atmospheres have been reported more recently by White (1942) for tomato (*Lycopersicon esculentum*).

Root pressures seem to be largely an osmotic phenomenon for they are abolished if the roots are watered with a solution having an osmotic pressure equal to or greater than that of the sap in the xylem, just as we should expect if the root tissues were functioning as a semipermeable membrane in an osmometer. This is not to say that we know everything about the process; the continued passage of water into the xylem would be expected to wash out dissolved substances, so that the diffusion pressure deficit should gradually fall and root pressure drop to zero. In fact, root pressure and bleeding may be maintained for long periods. It seems that the solute concentration is maintained by the living cells of the roots secreting salts, sugars, and other substances into the xylem, and thus keeping up its diffusion pressure deficit, but the way in which this is done is not at all clear.

Root pressure is affected by oxygen supply and by poisons to an extent which would not be expected if the root tissues were behaving purely as an osmotic system, for these factors affect the release of energy in the respiration of the living cells rather than the semipermeable properties of the protoplasm. This has been put forward as evidence that root pressure depends on an active pumping of water into the xylem by living cells. However, oxygen supply and poisons would also have a marked influence on the secretion of soluble substances into the xylem, which would certainly depend on respiration, and it seems most reasonable to think that root pressure is purely a matter of diffusion pressure gradients, with the proviso that these are nevertheless maintained by the activity of the living cells.

It is clear that the root system of a plant must be capable of absorbing water at a high rate from the reservoir of the soil. This water is not freely flowing and cannot just be sucked up in bulk; uptake depends on an enormous area of contact between the roots and the water films around the soil particles. Unless one goes to great trouble to excavate the root system of a plant and wash out its tiniest ramifications in an undamaged condition, it is difficult to appreciate its extent (Fig. 21). Pavlychenko (1937) found that a two-year-old plant of the grass, *Agropyron cristatum*, had 315 miles (over 500 kilometres) of roots occupying a cylindrical mass of soil 1·2 metres in diameter and 2 metres deep. A root system of this extent, which is not at all unusual, provides an enormous area for water absorption. Not all of this area is, of course, equally useful for absorption. The older parts have a corky covering which greatly restricts water intake (but evidently does not prevent it entirely, because many evergreen trees survive and evidently transpire during the winter, when the entire root system is like this). However, many studies have shown that maximum absorption occurs in the growing parts, especially in the zone with root hairs, but to a rather small extent in the actual meristematic region. Root hairs, which are seen to good advantage when mustard and cress are grown on wet flannel, have thin walls, and their presence increases the surface area of the root from three to twelve times, as well as increasing the volume of soil which is tapped. Brouwer (1954) and other people have

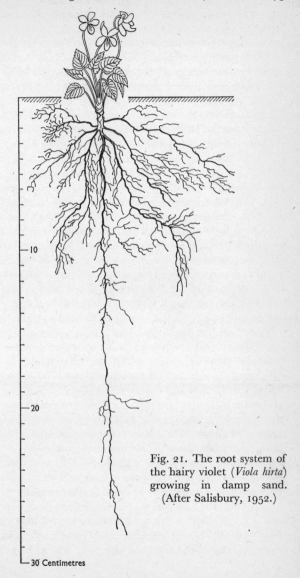

Fig. 21. The root system of the hairy violet (*Viola hirta*) growing in damp sand. (After Salisbury, 1952.)

10

20

30 Centimetres

found that the zone of most rapid absorption tends to shift up the root as the rate of transpiration increases; this may be because tissues become more permeable to water as the cells become less turgid.

The water in soil is held mainly by *capillary* forces in the smaller spaces and as films covering the soil particles, the larger spaces draining free of water comparatively rapidly. This capillary water is freely available to roots, but, when it is exhausted, that which is left *adsorbed* in the clay and humus is held by rather stronger physical forces against removal by roots, and permanent wilting of the plant sets in. There is little movement of capillary water in soil. Contrary to the generally held view that water rises in soil, much as it might do in a wick, experiments show that there is little upward movement of this sort, and that when moist soil is placed in contact with dry soil little redistribution of water takes place. Roots move to the water, rather than vice versa, and continued uptake of water by a plant largely depends on active root growth. The *Agropyron* plant referred to in the previous paragraph, for instance, must have increased its root system by many miles a week during the growing season.

We must, therefore, visualize a plant as expanding farther and farther into a soil mass, with its growing roots leaving behind them soil sucked dry of its available moisture. Livingston (1927) pictured roots as continuously sewing the soil mass through and through, picking up moisture as they come to it. This is perhaps not a hit or miss process; roots may have a tendency to grow towards moisture, a response known as *hydrotropism*, although the evidence for this is not altogether conclusive. Thinking in these terms it is easy to visualize the uncomfortable situation of a pot-bound house-plant and the silent but intense competition which goes on between the root systems of neighbouring plants.

Although the roots are responsible for the bulk of a plant's water supply, there are other means which are sometimes used and which may enable survival under drought conditions. We have already seen that leaf cuticle is rather impermeable to water and that the structure of the stomata is such as to prevent the entry of liquid water into the interior of the leaf. It is not, therefore, surprising to find that the leaves of most species are capable only of slow absorption from rain or dew deposited on their surfaces. The process is one of diffusion, and the amount taken in depends on the permeability of the epidermis to water and the diffusion-pressure deficit of the tissues inside it. There is some evidence showing that plants in dry situations are able to absorb dew deposited on their leaves to a sufficient extent to have a beneficial effect on growth.

At times when transpiration exceeds the capacity of the roots to absorb water some tissues, generally those which are least active and contain the lowest concentrations of dissolved substances, lose more water than others. In effect, the plant uses such tissues as water reservoirs and maintains the turgor of the active photosynthetic and growing tissues at their expense. The water in the older parts of tree trunks, in old leaves, and in fruits may be drawn on in this way. It may be replaced when the water balance becomes favourable again, but if much is withdrawn the part will die. Cacti and other succulents living in desert conditions have extensive tissues consisting of large cells with large vacuoles, thin walls, and little protoplasm, which can lose a large proportion of their water without damage.

So far, we have regarded transpiration as an unavoidable process of evaporation, but one might expect that plants would have some means of directly controlling a process which can be so detrimental to them. Comparison of the rates of transpiration and of evaporation from a free water surface or porous surface saturated with water suggests that there is some means of control. Before considering this it should be pointed out that, whereas the measurement of rate of evaporation is fairly straightforward, measurement of the rate of transpiration is not. The most satisfactory measurements can be made with potted plants, water loss from which can be followed over a long period of time by direct weighing. Certain precautions are necessary: the pot and soil surface must be covered with a waterproof material to prevent evaporation from them and, of course, any water added to the soil must be allowed for. The plant is not under natural conditions, and unless particular care is taken, its water absorption may be quite different from that of a plant growing unrestrictedly in the ground. All the same, this method is far superior to any other.

The apparatus known as a *potometer* measures the water intake of a cut shoot, the behaviour of which may be very different from that of an intact plant. Furthermore, as will be realized from what has just been said, water intake is not necessarily equivalent to water loss in transpiration. Any method of measuring the amount of water vapour lost by a shoot necessitates enclosing it in some way, and this at once alters the conditions affecting evaporation. This illustrates very well the point that any experiment with a living thing inevitably interferes with its natural activities and renders it to some extent abnormal. However, measurements of transpiration which are believed to reflect fairly well what happens with a plant under natural conditions have been made, and show that on a still, cloudless day the transpiration of a plant well supplied with water follows much the course we should expect, increasing in the morning with the power of the sun, reaching a peak just after midday, and decreasing to a minimum during the night. Air movements, clouds, and other things will, of course, cause irregularities in the course of events, but, providing that ample water is available, transpiration and evaporation follow roughly parallel courses. When water is scarce, however, the fall in transpiration rate usually begins in the morning while evaporation rate is still increasing (Fig. 22). Something evidently occurs in the plant to reduce transpiration under conditions of water shortage.

To the unsophisticated it seems obvious that the stomata should be the means whereby this control is exerted. Most of the water loss from leaves takes place through the stomata and these openings are made so that they can be shut. Nothing could be clearer. However, the plant physiologist has learnt to be suspicious of arguments like this; the design of a plant structure often provides valuable clues as to its functions, but these clues can be misleading, and science demands direct proofs that the supposed functions are actually performed. Obtaining direct proof of the role of stomata in the control of transpiration has, however, not been at all straightforward. Mathematical considerations

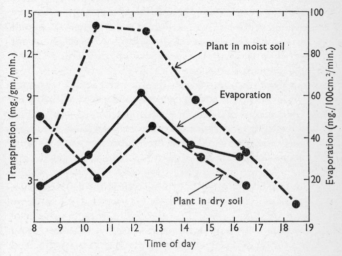

Fig. 22. Course of transpiration from plants of field southernwood (*Artemisia campestris*), growing in dry and moist situations, during a sunny day. A curve for evaporation is given for comparison. (After Bosian, 1933.)

put forward by Jeffreys (1918) showed that in a plant such as the sunflower the stomata are so closely crowded that they must close until their pore diameters are $\frac{1}{50}$ of that in the fully open condition before diffusion of water vapour through them is appreciably reduced. Actual observations on rate of transpiration and stomatal aperture made by many workers led to a similar conclusion, and Knight (1919) summed up a general opinion among physiologists when he said that 'the stomata themselves cut but a poor figure in the array of regulating influences' for transpiration.

Various other means of control have been suggested, but we need not consider them here, for nothing in science is final, and more recently this conclusion regarding stomata has had to be revised. An argument put forward by van den Honert (1948), which has done much to bring about this change, is a refinement of the argument from design, but is nevertheless rather convincing. The movement of water through a plant resembles the flow of current through a wire in that its rate, dm/dt, is proportional to the potential difference, $P_1 - P_0$ (i.e. voltage in electricity, diffusion pressure gradient in water movement), and inversely proportional to the resistance, R; that is to say it follows an analogue of Ohm's law. When a steady state is established the flow of water in each part of the system must be the same. The situation can then be represented by the following equation, which although not quite valid for the transpiration stream, is sufficiently accurate for present purposes:

$$\frac{dm}{dt} = \frac{P_1 - P_0}{R_r} = \frac{P_2 - P_1}{R_x} = \frac{P_3 - P_2}{R_l} = \frac{P_4 - P_3}{R_g} \qquad (3)$$

where R_r, R_x, etc., are the resistances offered respectively by root, xylem, leaves, and gaseous diffusion in the air. The diffusion pressure gradient between soil water and the cells of the leaves, $P_3 - P_0$, is at the most 50 atmospheres. Since water passes from a solution into an unsaturated atmosphere by a diffusion process, it is possible to express $P_4 - P_3$ in terms of diffusion-pressure deficit too. When the atmosphere is 90 per cent saturated with water vapour its diffusion pressure deficit is 140 atmospheres and when it is half saturated, as it often is in an English summer, its diffusion pressure deficit is about 924 atmospheres. From this it follows that the resistance to water movement from leaf to air must be correspondingly great. Thus, when the air is half saturated

$$\frac{50 - 0}{R_r + R_x + R_l} = \frac{924 - 50}{R_g}$$

and R_g is 17·5 times as great as the resistance offered by the plant. It follows that the resultant rate of movement of water is largely determined by this larger resistance, between the leaf cells and the atmosphere, and that a change in the smaller one, between leaf cells and soil, will have very little effect. This is to say that stomata are situated just where they can be most effective in controlling the rate of water movement.

It has also become evident that experimental results seeming to show that stomata are ineffectual in controlling transpiration are not always what they are purported to be. Direct measurement of stomatal aperture with a microscope is tedious, and most investigators have preferred to use a convenient instrument known as a *porometer*. This measures stomatal aperture indirectly in terms of the resistance to flow of air through the leaf. It necessitates the enclosure of a small area of leaf surface under a small cup, and it had been assumed, apparently justifiably, that the behaviour of stomata under the cup is similar to that of those elsewhere. It is now known that this is not necessarily true; as will be explained more fully later (p. 167), stomatal movement is affected by many factors, among which is carbon dioxide concentration. The carbon dioxide supply within the porometer cup is usually limited and soon exhausted by photosynthesis, and in these circumstances stomata open fully, whereas those outside, with normal carbon dioxide supply, may behave quite otherwise. So it has happened that porometer measurements have sometimes shown stomata to remain fully open while transpiration rate has been varying, whereas in fact the majority of the stomata on the plant were probably behaving quite differently and very possibly in a manner which would account for the changes in transpiration rate.

As a result of recent experimental work, particularly that of Stålfelt (1932) and Bange (1953), it is now agreed that stomatal control of transpiration is important, at least under conditions favouring high rates of evaporation, in wind, for example. As Fig. 23 shows, at low rates of evaporation in still air the stomata have to be nearly closed before there is any appreciable reduction of transpiration. This is in agreement with the mathematical predictions of Jeffreys. In wind, however, the stomata exert considerable control over transpiration even when they are wide open. This seems reasonable. The resistance to water movement between the wet cell walls in the leaf and the atmosphere can be separated

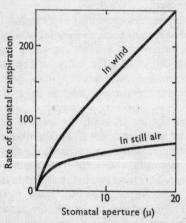

Fig. 23. Relationship between stomatal transpiration and stomatal aperture in a *Zebrina* leaf in still air and in wind. The curves are theoretical ones corresponding well with observed values. Notice that stomatal control of transpiration is greater in wind and that in still air the stomatal aperture has to be less than 3 μ wide before control is appreciable. (After Bange, 1953.)

into two components, the resistance to diffusion through stomatal pores and the resistance to diffusion through the water-vapour-saturated layer of air next to the leaf surface. In completely still air this second resistance will be great, and will consequently control the rate of water movement so that the stomata can exert little effect. In moving air this layer will be largely swept away, and its resistance will be lowered so that the first component becomes rate-determining. This first component of resistance depends on stomatal aperture, and so the controlling power of the stomata will become appreciable. Internal factors seem to play little part in controlling the rate of transpiration, for, as Gregory and his associates (1950) have shown, if stomatal control is eliminated, leaves may lose a large proportion of their water without any reduction in the transpiration rate. So, after all, it seems to be the stomata which exert the main controlling influence on transpiration, at least in certain circumstances. There remain the questions of what determines stomatal movements and of whether these always take place so that water is conserved when it is in short supply. Discussion of these problems is best deferred to a later chapter (see p. 167).

Finally, in this survey of the water relations of plants we come to a question which is frequently put to the plant physiologist, but to which he still does not have a completely satisfying answer – how does sap get to the top of tall trees? With herbaceous plants and even shrubs there does not appear to be any difficulty in accounting for the movement of water from roots to leaves. The water moves under the combined action of root pressure and evaporation from the leaves. In water plants, in which transpiration is abolished, root pressure alone causes an appreciable movement of water through the vascular system. With trees, which if they are redwoods (*Sequoia sempervirens*) may be as much as 340 feet high, the problem of the movement of sap is more acute because of the relatively large expenditure of energy which is needed to raise water to such heights. Root pressure cannot account for the rise, since coniferous trees, which are among the tallest, usually do not show this, and the possibility of a pumping action by the living cells seems to be ruled out, because the transpiration stream in a tree continues even if a considerable length of its trunk is killed. In a porous material, such as wood, water may rise by capillarity, as it does in a piece of blotting-paper one end of which is dipped in water, but such a rise cannot be of more than a few inches and is not a continuing flow. The only explanation to which there does not seem to be any insuperable objection is that given by the *cohesion theory*, which was first propounded by Dixon and Joly in 1894.

Water is fluid because its molecules slip round each other easily, which is quite a different thing from the molecules being easily separated from each other. Actually water molecules have a strong mutual attraction, so that, if liquid water completely fills a container, the walls of which it wets easily (which implies a strong attraction between the water molecules and those on the solid surface), it is capable of withstanding considerable tension before it ruptures and a cavity is formed in it. Normally it is not evident that water has a tensile strength, because nearly always it has in it particles of dust, or it is contained in a vessel which is not perfectly clean, so that there is unwettable material from which it can be pulled away so that cavities form. It is for this reason that a suction pump cannot raise water more than about 33 feet. This is the height of the column of water which can be supported by atmospheric pressure, any further tension causing the column to break so that a vacuum forms above it. If the water were perfectly pure and the pump and its tubing perfectly clean and constructed of some perfectly wettable material, then this rupture of the column would not occur so soon and water could be raised to a much greater height than 33 feet.

The cohesion theory supposes that something of this sort happens in plants. The energy for raising the water is the heat absorbed from the environment in transpiration, and the diffusion-pressure deficit which develops in the tissues of transpiring leaves corresponds to the pump, withdrawing water from the xylem and causing a tension to develop in it. It is supposed that, even when the diffusion-pressure deficit amounts to several atmospheres, the water columns in the xylem do not break and that the tension is transmitted all the way back to the roots. The cell walls of the xylem are perfectly wetted by water, and dust or other extraneous solid matter which might cause breaks is excluded so long as the tissues are undamaged.

The tensions which develop in the xylem of transpiring

trees cannot be measured directly, but there is much indirect evidence showing that they are sometimes great. If,
for example, the xylem of a tree-trunk is exposed by carefully peeling away the bark and then punctured, air will be
drawn in rapidly, as shown by the loss of translucency above
and below the puncture. If it is arranged that a dye solution
is drawn in instead of air it is possible to measure the rate of
movement of sap in the xylem. A method of doing this without damaging the plant, used by Huber and Schmidt (1937)
is to heat the water in the xylem locally by means of a heating element applied to the trunk and to measure the time
taken for the heated water to reach a thermocouple placed
some distance above the heating element. The rate of movement varies greatly, being least at night and greatest when
transpiration is rapid. In conifers, which, it will be recalled,
have no vessels in their xylem, the maximum observed rate
is about 1·5 metres per hour, but in plants with large vessels
rates of over 100 metres per hour have been recorded. If the
resistance to flow offered by the xylem is known it is possible
to calculate from such measurements the magnitude of the
tensions developed. Such calculations indicate, in agreement
with other evidence, that these tensions may often be as
much as 20 atmospheres.

Dixon believed that water columns could withstand tensions of 200 atmospheres without breaking. Although the
value is still uncertain, it seems from more recent work that
the breaking tension is unlikely in practice to be more than
30 atmospheres. This is still sufficient to provide for the
ascent of sap in the tallest trees, but it yet has been ques-
tioned whether the unbroken columns of water required by
the cohesion theory are always present in transpiring trees.
It appears that stretched water columns in wood break
rather easily and that normally a high proportion of vessels
contain air rather than water. The crucial experiment might
seem to be one in which overlapping saw-cuts are made
close together and from opposite sides through a tree-trunk
so as to break all the water columns. That after this treatment water continues to move up the stem of a tree and that

the leaves may remain unwilted seem to show that unbroken water columns are not necessary for the maintenance of the transpiration stream. However, when a break occurs in a stretched water column the air bubble will expand to fill the whole of the cavity of the tracheid or vessel but no farther; the physical forces operating in the submicroscopic pore system of the cell walls keep them filled with water and prevent the passage of air into adjacent cell cavities.

Thus, although the coarse-pore system of the wood is completely blocked by air bubbles, continuity may still be maintained through the submicroscopic pore system of the wall material. Blockage of the coarse-pore system will, of course, entail an increase in the resistance to the passage of water through the wood, but reference to equation 3 (p. 80) will show that this need result in little reduction of rate of flow of water, since there will be a corresponding increase in the diffusion-pressure deficit gradient in the xylem. Scholander and his colleagues (1957) have demonstrated that this sort of thing does indeed happen in the grape-vine, which can transpire quite rapidly even when the xylem vessels are almost completely blocked with air.

The xylem newly formed by cambial activity is completely filled with sap, and in some species, such as birch (*Betula* spp.), root pressure is sufficient to force sap into older, air-filled xylem and make the water columns in it once more continuous. Thus ample means of conducting the large amounts of water required by expanding shoots in the spring are available. As the season advances soil water becomes exhausted and an increasing proportion of the xylem becomes blocked, with air following breakages of water columns caused, for example, by sudden stresses in high winds. It seems likely that at the top of a tall tree in summer the leaves are generally in a state of incipient wilting, with transpiration just balanced by the water that can be drawn up through such continuous water channels as remain. As already mentioned (p. 48), leaves in this condition are capable of little photosynthesis, and thus cannot contribute to the growth of the tree. The height of a tree is thus perhaps largely dependent on the efficiency of its xylem in maintaining intact water columns.

Transpiration is an inevitable concomitant of photosynthesis in a land plant – in unscientific terms, a necessary evil. Nevertheless, it may not be wholly disadvantageous to a plant. Evaporation absorbs heat, and thus transpiration has a cooling effect which may sometimes be important in preventing damage to the leaf tissues. The transpiration stream also plays an important part in the movement of materials within plants, as we shall see in a later chapter (p. 184).

CHAPTER 4

The Chemical Machinery – Respiration and Photosynthesis

WE now turn from the problems associated with the absorption by plants of the principal raw materials needed for growth to those of how these materials are built up into plant substance.

First it will be as well to consider the general chemical nature of plant material. An analysis of the amounts of the various chemical elements in plants, for example that for maize given in the table on p. 89, shows that relatively few of the ninety-two naturally occurring elements are present in appreciable amounts in plants, three of them – carbon, hydrogen, and oxygen – making up something like 90 per cent of the total dry weight. This is in agreement with the idea that most of the raw material for plant growth is derived from air and water. The remaining elements, which mostly remain as ash when the organic, carbon-containing materials are burnt away, are present in relatively small amounts whether weights or relative numbers of atoms are considered.

Plant material, of course, is not a single chemical substance but a complicated mixture. Most of the fresh weight is due to water, but foremost among the remaining components of most higher plants is cellulose, the principal constituent of the cell walls. This, on the average, makes up about one-third of the dry weight. Cellulose, the chemical nature of which will be described below (p. 91), is composed of carbon, hydrogen, and oxygen in the proportions $7 \cdot 2 : 1 : 8$ by weight – nearly the same as in the analysis given in the table on p. 89, i.e. $7 \cdot 2 : 1 \cdot 03 : 7 \cdot 34$. The living material of the plant, the protoplasm, has protein as the principal component of its dry matter, with lesser proportions of nucleic acids, fats, carbohydrates, and mineral salts.

TABLE

Average elemental composition of the dry material of five mature maize plants grown at Manhattan, Kansas. (Data of Latshaw and Miller, 1924.)

Element	Weight (grams)	Percentage of total	Relative number of atoms
Oxygen	371·4	44·43	4,640
Carbon	364·2	43·57	6,060
Hydrogen	52·2	6·24	10,440
Nitrogen	12·2	1·46	174
Phosphorus	1·7	0·20	11
Potassium	7·7	0·92	39
Calcium	1·9	0·23	9
Magnesium	1·5	0·18	12
Sulphur	1·4	0·17	9
Iron	0·7	0·08	2
Silicon	9·8	1·17	70
Aluminium	0·9	0·11	7
Chlorine	1·2	0·14	7
Manganese	0·3	0·03	1
Undetermined elements	7·8	0·93	

Proteins are organic compounds having large complex molecules containing carbon, hydrogen, oxygen, nitrogen, and, sometimes, sulphur. These molecules are built up of repeating units, groups of atoms, called amino-acids. Amino-acids, of which there are about twenty different kinds commonly found in protein (Plate 6), are organic acids in which one hydrogen atom is substituted by the amino-group, $-NH_2$. The simplest is glycine, or amino-acetic acid, $CH_2(NH_2)\cdot COOH$. Since amino-acids have both acidic, $-COOH$, and basic, $-NH_2$, groups, they are able to combine with each other, thus forming peptides, e.g.:

$$CH_2(NH_2)\cdot COOH + CH_3CH(NH_2)\cdot COOH$$
$$\text{Glycine} \qquad + \qquad \text{alanine}$$
$$\rightarrow CH_2(NH_2)\cdot CO\cdot NH + H_2O \quad (4)$$
$$CH_3CH\cdot COOH$$
$$\rightarrow \text{glycyl-alanine} \quad + \text{ water}$$

Proteins are peptides in which several hundred amino-acid residues are joined together.

Most of the nitrogen of the plant is in the form of protein, but some is present as nucleic acids. These, as their name implies, are especially characteristic of the nucleus. Nucleic acids contain phosphorus in addition to carbon, hydrogen, oxygen, and nitrogen, and are also built up of units, the nucleotides. There are usually only four different nucleotides in a nucleic acid molecule. Each nucleotide is itself built up of a nitrogenous base combined with a pentose sugar and phosphoric acid. The nucleotides are joined together in the nucleic acid molecule thus:

nitrogenous base–pentose–phosphate

nitrogenous base–pentose–phosphate

nitrogenous base–pentose–phosphate

Some nucleotides occur free, not combined in nucleic acids, and, as we shall see, have extremely important roles to play in the chemistry of the cell.

Fats are compounds of an alcohol, usually glycerol, $CH_2OH\cdot CHOH\cdot CH_2OH$, the substance familiar as 'glycerine', with fatty acids, e.g. oleic acid, $C_{17}H_{33}\cdot COOH$. Simple fats thus contain only the elements carbon, hydrogen, and oxygen, but their more complex derivatives contain nitrogen and phosphorus as well and are important plant constituents. Fats are characteristically insoluble in water but soluble in organic solvents such as ether and benzene.

Carbohydrates are compounds containing only carbon, hydrogen, and oxygen, the hydrogen and oxygen usually being present in the same proportions as in water – hence the name. The simplest carbohydrates are the sugars, and the simplest sugar, glyceraldehyde, $CH_2OH\cdot CHOH\cdot CHO$, which is related to glycerol, has three carbon atoms, and is hence called a triose. The more familiar glucose has six carbon atoms, i.e. it is a hexose, and commonly exists in a form with the molecule joined up with itself to make a nearly flat ring:

$$CH_2OH$$

Other simple sugars of importance in plants are the pentoses (5 carbons), which, as we just saw, are components of the nucleotides, and the septoses (7 carbons). Sugars are able to join together through their ^-OH groups. Cane sugar, sucrose, is a compound sugar of this sort, being a *disaccharide* composed of glucose combined with another hexose, fructose:

glucose residue   fructose residue

Polysaccharides have long chains of sugar residues joined in this fashion. Starch and cellulose are important polysaccharides, both built of glucose residues. The structure of starch may be represented thus:

with the chains, which may be branched, up to 300 units long. Cellulose has the structure:

The chains of cellulose are unbranched and up to several thousand units long. It will be noticed that, whereas in starch the glucose units all lie in the same relative position, in cellulose they are joined differently so that every other unit is turned the other way up. As a result, although these two substances are each built of nothing but glucose, they have rather different properties. Starch occurs in plants in characteristic grains and is readily broken down into glucose, whereas the long balanced chains of cellulose form fibres well suited for structural purposes and are chemically rather inert.

Besides cellulose, plant cell walls contain pectic substances. Pectic acid itself consists of chains of galacturonic acid units, galacturonic acid being a derivative of the hexose sugar, galactose. Pectic acid occurs in cell walls as a mixture of calcium and magnesium pectates in association with polysaccharides built of galactose and of arabinose, a pentose sugar. Pectins are cementing materials, fastening the cells in a tissue together. They may be extracted from tissues with boiling water, forming a solution which gels – this being the basis of jam making.

It will be noticed that a general feature of all the various types of large complex molecules found in living organisms is that they are built up of simple units arranged according to a more or less regular pattern.

Despite its quiescent appearance, a growing plant is the seat of intense chemical change. This becomes obvious when isotopically labelled substances are supplied to plants. For example, by supplying carbon dioxide labelled with radiocarbon it can be demonstrated that, in the light, carbon from this source can be built up by the plant into quite complicated substances, such as fats or sugars, within thirty seconds. This is amazing when it is considered that it involves chemical reactions which proceed at an infinitesimally slow rate under otherwise similar conditions outside the plant. Thus the sugar glucose, which is one of the early products of photosynthesis, is not formed in the absence of living organisms however long a solution of carbon dioxide in water is allowed to stand. It can be made from carbon dioxide and water by purely chemical means, but only by the use of temperatures and reagents which would rapidly destroy living protoplasm. Glucose has been made from carbon dioxide and water in the test-tube under conditions compatible with life (see p. 124), but only by means of particular substances extracted from plants. Substances of this sort, having pronounced powers of making chemical reactions go more quickly, are known as *enzymes*.

An enzyme may be defined as a complex organic *catalyst* produced by a living organism, a catalyst being a substance which has the property of accelerating a chemical reaction without itself undergoing any permanent change. To this we may add that all known enzymes are proteins; that most are destroyed rapidly at the temperature of boiling water; and that most are highly specific, acting on only one chemical substance, which is known as the *substrate* of the enzyme. For example, the enzyme β-amylase, which catalyses the removal of successive pairs of glucose units from the starch chain, thus converting it into the disaccharide maltose, will not attack cellulose even though this somewhat resembles starch in structure. The breakdown of starch to sugar by an unheated malt extract, one of the most familiar of enzyme actions, was studied as long ago as 1833 by Payen and Persoz. The name diastase, which they gave to the active preparation which they obtained, is still used, but it is now known that at least two enzymes, of which β-amylase is one, are involved. Dixon and Webb (1958) have listed 650 different enzymes that have been obtained from plants, animals, and bacteria. This is not a large number considering the multifarious chemical activities that are exhibited by living organisms, and it is certain that there are many more to be identified. It seems likely that most of the protein in a cell is enzymically active. The mechanism of enzyme action cannot be gone into here, but it can be said that it does not appear to depend on anything beyond the powers of the chemist to explain. There is good evidence that enzymes combine with their substrates, and this may be visualized as producing a strain in the substrate molecule which makes it susceptible to a particular kind of conversion.

The modern era in the study of enzymes began when Buchner (1897) showed that a juice may be obtained from yeast by grinding and high pressure, which, although completely devoid of living cells, has powers of fermenting sugar similar to those of the original living material. Boiled, this juice loses its powers of fermentation and, as we now know, it contains such of the yeast enzymes as are water soluble and not destroyed during the extraction process. Expressed as a chemical equation, the essential process which has made yeast the most appreciated of micro-organisms is:

$$C_6H_{12}O_6 \rightarrow 2C_2H_5OH + 2CO_2 \qquad (5)$$
$$\text{glucose} \rightarrow \text{alcohol} + \underset{\text{dioxide}}{\text{carbon}}$$

Study of this process soon showed that it is not simple but takes place in a number of steps each catalysed by a special enzyme. Our present rather detailed knowledge of these steps has been obtained in part by separating the enzymes, which can be done by making use of their slightly differing properties, e.g. the differing extents to which they are thrown out of solution by salt solutions or alcohol, so that their actions can be studied individually. For example, alcohol dehydrogenase, the enzyme which catalyses the final reaction producing alcohol:

$$CH_3 \cdot CHO + CoI \cdot H_2 \rightleftharpoons C_2H_5OH + CoI \qquad (6)$$
$$\text{acetaldehyde} + \underset{\text{co-enzyme}}{\text{reduced}} \rightleftharpoons \text{alcohol} + \text{co-enzyme}$$

has been isolated in crystalline form. For its action it requires a hydrogen donor, a reducing substance which will readily give up hydrogen. The immediate hydrogen donor for alcohol dehydrogenase is a specific organic substance, co-enzyme I, also known as diphosphopyridine nucleotide (DPN). This is required only in minute traces, since it acts as a carrier of hydrogen from other substances, a single molecule accepting and passing on as many as 1,000 pairs of hydrogen atoms per minute. In this way its function is catalytic, but, because it is not a protein and is not effective by itself, it is called a co-enzyme rather than an enzyme. Alcohol dehydrogenase catalyses the reaction equally well in either direction, hence the arrows in both directions in equation 6, the direction in which the reaction proceeds depending on the concentration of the substrates and products. As enzymes go, it is not highly specific, since it works with alcohols and aldehydes other than ethyl alcohol and acetaldehyde.

Another line of attack on the mechanism of fermentation has been by the use of substances which will stop the chain of reactions at some specific point, so that some intermediate compound, which is used up as fast as it is formed when the complete machinery is in action, accumulates in sufficient quantities for chemical identification. Acetaldehyde, which normally is present only in minute traces in fermenting mixtures, has been identified as an intermediate by use of sodium bisulphite. Bisulphite combines with acetaldehyde and removes it from the reaction chain so that it accumulates in large amounts instead of the usual end product. Other substances, known as *inhibitors*, which stop the action of particular enzymes, have been used in a similar way.

The picture of alcoholic fermentation by baker's or brewer's yeast which has been built up in this fashion has some fourteen steps, each catalysed by a special enzyme, and is represented in simplified form in Fig. 24. Such complication in the apparently simple splitting of glucose into four fragments seems at first sight unnecessary and meaningless, but becomes intelligible when the process is considered not just as a chemical reaction but as a life process of the yeast. This involves a rather important fact which is not apparent from equation 5, namely that the alcoholic fermentation of glucose, a substance of high potential chemical energy, releases free energy, about 72,000 calories per gram molecular weight (180 g) of the glucose. As a result of this, if fermentation is carried out in large vessels, so that heat losses by radiation are small, the temperature of the liquor may rise sufficiently high to kill the yeast. Although much of the energy released in fermentation appears as heat, some is used in the yeast cells for processes such as the building up of complex substances – being colourless and not photosynthetic, yeast cannot use light energy to do this. The

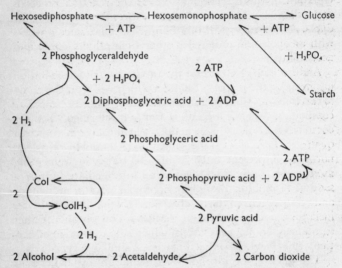

Fig. 24. Simplified scheme showing the reactions in the breakdown of carbohydrate in yeast fermentation. H_3PO_4 = phosphate, ADP = adenosine diphosphate, ATP = adenosine triphosphate, CoI = co-enzyme I, $CoIH_2$ = reduced co-enzyme I, ⇌ denotes a reversible reaction.

complicated nature of fermentation evidently depends in part on the manner in which the energy transfers are accomplished. Living organisms are often likened to machines, and there is certainly a rough analogy between the parts played by fermentation in yeast and the combustion of petrol in a car, but, unlike a car, a yeast cell is constructed of much the same sort of material as that which it uses for fuel. If energy were released from the glucose molecule in one step as heat, as the energy of petrol is released in the cylinders of the internal-combustion engine, it would not

only be of little use for the vital processes of the cell but
might also damage the cell structure. As it is, the splitting of
glucose in a roundabout manner by a number of reversible
steps enables the release of energy to be controlled and the
energy to appear partly in a form in which it can be used in
chemical synthesis and other cell processes.

The first step in the discovery of how this is accomplished
was made by Harden and Young (1905) when they found
that fermentation by yeast juice can take place only in the

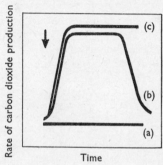

Fig. 25. The effect of phosphate on the fermentation of glucose by
yeast juice. (a) with no addition but glucose; (b) with a small
amount of inorganic phosphate added at the time indicated by the
arrow; (c) as b, but with the addition of an enzyme which breaks
down organic phosphates liberating inorganic phosphate. (After
Harden and Young.)

presence of inorganic phosphate and that this is converted
into organic form during the fermentation (Fig. 25). Later,
Lipmann (1941) showed that certain organic phosphates
have a considerable amount of potential chemical energy
associated with the linkage between the phosphate group
and the rest of the molecule. Adenosine triphosphate
(generally known by the initials ATP), which is apparently
universally present in living organisms, is evidently the most
important of such substances. Adenosine is a nucleotide,
like those found in nucleic acids, but details of structure need
not concern us here, for the important property is that it can

lose one of its phosphate groups, forming adenosine diphosphate, ADP, and inorganic phosphate, P_i, and releasing energy:

$$ATP \rightleftharpoons ADP + P_i + 9,000 \text{ calories} \qquad (7)$$

If we now turn to the scheme for alcoholic fermentation (Fig. 24) we see that it involves various organic phosphates, including ATP. The process begins with the transfer of phosphate groups from ATP to the sugar and the splitting of the sugar phosphate into two 3-carbon fragments, i.e. two molecules of phosphoglyceraldehyde. The principal energy-yielding process of fermentation lies in the *oxidation* of phosphoglyceraldehyde to phosphoglyceric acid. It should be remembered here that oxidation can consist in the removal of hydrogen as well as in the addition of oxygen, and that, in fact, most biological oxidations are of this sort:

$$AH_2 + B \rightleftharpoons A + BH_2 \qquad (8)$$

where A, the hydrogen-donor, is oxidized and B, the hydrogen acceptor, is reduced. In fermentation the energy liberated in the oxidation of the aldehyde group to the acidic group does not appear as heat, but is used to form another organic phosphate linkage so that the product, diphosphoglyceric acid, has about the same potential chemical energy as the initial substrate:

$$CH_2O \textcircled{P} \cdot CHOH \cdot CHO + \quad P_i \quad + \quad CoI \rightleftharpoons$$

$$\underset{\text{aldehyde}}{\underset{\text{phosphoglycer-}}{}} \quad + \quad \underset{\text{phosphate}}{\underset{\text{inorganic}}{}} + \quad \underset{\text{enzyme}}{\underset{\text{co-}}{}}$$

$$CH_2O \textcircled{P} \cdot CHOH \cdot COO \textcircled{P} + \quad CoI \cdot H_2 \qquad (9)$$

$$\underset{\text{acid}}{\underset{\text{diphosphoglyceric}}{}} \quad + \quad \underset{\text{co-enzyme}}{\underset{\text{reduced}}{}}$$

$\textcircled{P}$ in this equation standing for the high-energy phosphate group. From diphosphoglyceric acid one phosphate group is immediately transferred to ADP to give ATP:

$$CH_2O \textcircled{P} \cdot CHOH \cdot COO \textcircled{P} + ADP \rightleftharpoons$$

$$CH_2O \textcircled{P} \cdot CHOH \cdot COOH + ATP \qquad (10)$$

Later on, the second phosphate group is transferred to ADP so that in the fermentation of one molecule of glucose two molecules of ATP are used up and four produced – a net gain of two. In this way, about 18,000 calories of the 72,000 liberated by the fermentation of a gram-molecule of glucose is stored in the form of ATP. We will see later how this stored energy can be used in energy-consuming reactions. Finally, in the fermentation process one of the end products, carbon dioxide, is produced by the splitting of pyruvic acid, and the remaining fragment of this, acetaldehyde, is reduced by the hydrogen produced earlier in the sequence and carried by co-enzyme I, to give alcohol, the other final product.

Alcoholic fermentation is a form of *respiration*, a term which, although originally used to denote the breathing movements of animals, is now used by biochemists as a general name for the processes, of which breathing is but a symptom, whereby the potential chemical energy of organic compounds is released in living organisms. As a respiratory process fermentation is inefficient, for most of the potential energy of the sugar consumed remains in one of the products, alcohol. Complete oxidation of sugar releases much more energy, roughly 700,000 calories per gram-molecule, as compared with 72,000:

$$C_6H_{12}O_6 + 6O_2 \rightarrow$$
$$\text{glucose} + \text{oxygen} \rightarrow$$

$$6CO_2 + 6H_2O + 700,000 \text{ calories} \qquad (11)$$
$$\text{carbon dioxide} + \text{water}$$

This type of respiration, depending on the oxygen of the air, is called *aerobic*. Fermentation, which does not require free oxygen, is *anaerobic* respiration. On the whole, anaerobic respiration is characteristic of bacteria and other microorganisms. Yeast itself is capable of aerobic as well as anaerobic respiration and, in fact, grows rather poorly in the complete absence of oxygen. Green plants normally respire aerobically and cannot survive for long under anaerobic conditions.

Green plants are, nevertheless, capable of carrying out a process closely resembling yeast fermentation, and this fact has proved to be important for the understanding of their aerobic respiration. This is the justification for devoting so much space to yeast, which, although it may at a stretch be called a plant, is non-photosynthetic and thus outside the scope of this book. The sequence of reactions in yeast fermentation, indeed, appears to be of nearly universal occurrence in living organisms. Yeast happens to be good experimental material, and since it is of economic importance, biochemists have naturally devoted a great deal of attention to it. However, detailed investigations on vertebrate muscle have shown that an almost identical process goes on in this tissue, and less extensive evidence shows that it takes place in bacteria and in green plants too. This is only one instance illustrating one of the most striking findings of biochemistry, that the essential chemical basis of life, on this planet at least, is always the same.

If deprived of oxygen, tissues of flowering plants will respire anaerobically for a time, sugar being broken down and alcohol and carbon dioxide being produced, until they become damaged and eventually die. It can be shown that this anaerobic respiration is taking place in the plant cells themselves and is not merely due to yeasts or bacteria that happen to be in or on the tissues. In intact plant tissues the amount of alcohol appearing does not always correspond with equation 5 (p. 94), and other products, such as acetaldehyde, which appears, for example, in apples stored in an atmosphere of carbon dioxide, may be formed instead, but press juice from peas, potato, and beet (*Beta vulgaris*) has been found to ferment sugar, with the production of carbon dioxide and alcohol in the expected ratio. It has also been shown that enzymes similar to those concerned in yeast fermentation are present in flowering plants.

There is also evidence to show that breakdown of sugar in this way, *glycolysis* as it is called, does not happen only under anaerobic conditions but goes on when the plant is in air and actually forms an integral part of normal aerobic respiration. Inhibitors such as iodoacetate and fluoride, which are believed to act specifically on enzymes of the fermentation series, appreciably reduce aerobic respiration. They may not stop aerobic respiration entirely, because there exists an alternative pathway for the breakdown of sugars, via the pentose cycle (see p. 122). On the other hand, if inhibitors for enzymes catalysing the later stages of aerobic respiration, e.g. cyanide (see p. 103), are used, alcohol may be produced by fermentation even though oxygen is in ample supply. From this it seems that in aerobic respiration sugar is first broken down by the glycolytic pathway and that it is the products of this process which are oxidized to carbon dioxide and water. Alcohol itself is not readily oxidized by tissues of flowering plants, and it seems that, when it is part of the aerobic process, glycolysis stops at pyruvic acid (see Fig. 24). This is confirmed by the fact that, if glycolysis is inhibited with iodoacetate or fluoride, aerobic respiration can still take place at its normal rate if this intermediate, pyruvic acid, is supplied.

Pyruvic acid, then, may be regarded as the fuel for the second stage in aerobic respiration. In this stage a mechanism depending on a cycle of organic acid transformations, which was first discovered in animal tissues by Krebs and others, seems to operate. The first step (Fig. 26) is that the pyruvic acid is split to give carbon dioxide and a 2-carbon fragment which combines with oxaloacetic acid (4-carbons) to give citric acid (6-carbons). Citric acid then undergoes a series of transformations, in the course of which two more carbons are lost as carbon dioxide and six hydrogen atoms are removed, giving back oxaloacetic acid (4-carbons) again. The net result of one turn of this cycle is thus that one molecule of pyruvic is completely decomposed to carbon dioxide and hydrogen.

This hydrogen, it must be emphasized, does not appear as the element, but is attached to hydrogen-carriers. It is eventually disposed of by combination with the oxygen of the atmosphere to form water, which final step in aerobic respiration is catalysed by enzymes called oxidases. One oxidase system is that which depends on cytochromes, hydrogen-carriers chemically related to the haemoglobin of blood. These are pigments the colour of which changes slightly, enough to be observed with a spectrometer, according to whether they are oxidized or reduced, a feature which enables the changes which they undergo to be followed in

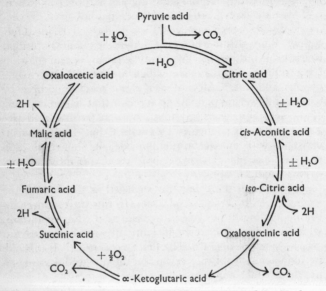

Fig. 26. Simplified scheme showing the reactions of the Krebs or organic acid cycle. ⇌ denotes a reversible reaction. (After James, 1955.)

living material. Thus, if a yeast suspension is vigorously aerated the absorption spectrum observed is that of oxidized cytochrome, but if it is allowed to become anaerobic the spectrum becomes that of reduced cytochrome. Cytochromes accept hydrogen from many different sources, including co-enzyme I, a reaction catalysed by cytochrome reductase, then hand it on to molecular oxygen, producing water, a reaction catalysed by cytochrome oxidase:

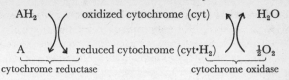

$$AH_2 \qquad \text{oxidized cytochrome (cyt)} \qquad H_2O$$

$$A \qquad \text{reduced cytochrome (cyt·H}_2) \qquad \tfrac{1}{2}O_2$$

cytochrome reductase   cytochrome oxidase

Cytochromes seem to be of universal occurrence in living organisms, with the exception of certain bacteria which are only able to respire anaerobically, and it seems that they are the chief oxidase systems in animal respiration. Cytochromes are inhibited by traces of cyanide – which is the reason for this substance being so deadly a poison.

Besides cytochromes other oxidase systems, using ascorbic acid (vitamin C), phenolic substances, or other hydrogen-carriers, are to be found in plants. It seems that the cytochrome system is the most important one in the respiration of very young tissues, but opinions differ as to its role in adult tissues, in which the rate of respiration is much slower; there is some evidence indicating that in old tissues the hydrogen is carried through one of the other oxidase systems.

These transfers of hydrogen are the energy-yielding reactions in aerobic respiration, and are coupled with the formation of ATP in the same sort of way as they are in fermentation. It is not yet settled how many molecules of ATP are thus produced per molecule of glucose used. A reasonable estimate is thirty-four, which implies that, of the energy released, 306,000 calories, or 44 per cent, may be stored in a form in which it may be used in cell maintenance and growth.

The rate of respiration in plant organs is usually low, so that heat production is insufficient to raise the temperature more than a few tenths of a degree Celsius (Centigrade) above that of their surroundings. Nevertheless, in rapidly respiring material, such as germinating seeds, the heat output is considerable, as may be demonstrated by putting the seeds in a vacuum flask and measuring the temperature rise. A particularly striking instance of heat production in respiration is afforded by the developing inflorescence of cuckoo-

pint (*Arum maculatum*), which has been found to rise as much
as 27·7° C. above the temperature of the surrounding air;
the hot-house conditions so provided may well be an
attraction to the flies upon which the plant depends for
pollination.

The biochemical detail given in the preceding pages is
necessary for an understanding of what respiration is and
does, but it is apt to be confusing, and it may be as well to
summarize at this point. Sugar, which for convenience we
may take as the starting-point for respiration (although
other substances, such as fats or proteins, may sometimes be
the actual materials consumed), is first of all broken down,
without the intervention of oxygen from the air, to give
pyruvic acid. In the absence of air this substance is converted to alcohol and carbon dioxide. Alternatively, pyruvic
acid may enter the Krebs cycle, in which it is broken down
to carbon dioxide and hydrogen, which is transferred to
carrier substances. This hydrogen can be further transferred
by oxidase systems to atmospheric oxygen, if this is available, with the formation of water. This is probably the chief
pathway for aerobic respiration; there are others, but these
involve the same general principles and need not be considered here. The potential energy of sugar is released when
it is broken down and oxidized, but the reactions of respiration are such that it does not all appear as heat, which cannot be used in the cell for building other substances of high
potential chemical energy or for performing mechanical or
osmotic work, but is stored in a readily available form as
potential chemical energy in organic phosphates such as
ATP. Instead of a crude shattering of the molecule, which
would release energy in unmanageable and damaging
amount, there is a delicate juggling, one part of the molecule being changed at a time so that it is dismantled completely and in a smooth and controlled manner. Besides
making energy available, this also provides a variety of
intermediates which, as we shall see, do not necessarily get
consumed in respiration but may be drawn off and used to
build proteins, fats, or other materials required by the cell.

An important question which arises out of this is how is it that these various reactions occur in orderly sequence? We do not find this order in a mere mixture containing the enzymes, accessory substances, and substrates for respiration, and respiration soon ceases in a cell which has been killed, even though killing does not necessarily inactivate the individual enzymes concerned. Furthermore, in the words of James (1953), 'the probable reactions that do not occur are perhaps as significant as the improbable ones that do'. That is to say, from what we know of the substances and enzymes present in cells we should expect a great many reactions to go on which in fact do not take place to any appreciable extent, at least until the cells are killed. For example, phenolic substances are rapidly oxidized by oxidase action to give coloured products in many plant tissues once these are damaged – the browning of a cut apple is a familiar instance of this – but somehow this is prevented so long as the tissue is intact. The answer to the problem evidently lies in the fine structure of protoplasm being such as to prevent some reactions by keeping enzymes and substrates apart and to promote others by bringing the participants together.

The enzymes concerned in glycolysis seem to occur in free solution in the protoplasm and, as we have seen, operate in extracted juice in much the same way as they do inside the cell. Here the sequence of reactions is determined by purely chemical factors. The enzymes of aerobic respiration, however, are confined in minute particles, less than 1 μ in diameter, called *mitochondria*, which can be separated from a mush of disintegrated cells by centrifuging under special conditions. The electron microscope shows that mitochondria have a double membrane, the inner of which is folded so as to give a large internal surface. It may be imagined that the enzymes are disposed on this surface in order, so that the product leaving one enzyme immediately comes into contact with the next enzyme in the sequence. Isolated mitochondria are capable of producing ATP if they are allowed to oxidize a suitable substrate such as pyruvic acid, but cannot do this if they are broken into fragments.

The rate of respiration is probably governed by different limiting factors in different species and according to circumstances, but it seems that often the controlling factor is the supply of substances such as ADP available to accept the high-energy phosphate groups which it produces. If ADP is regenerated rapidly from ATP as a result of the use of the latter in synthesis, respiration can proceed correspondingly rapidly, but if the rate of ATP utilization is low, then there will be little ADP, and this will be the bottle-neck in respiration. Alternative explanations are possible, but it seems that this latter situation is found in a nitrogen-starved plant, in which, of course, protein synthesis is brought to a standstill by lack of an essential ingredient. The rate of respiration is low, but is increased dramatically if a readily available source of nitrogen, such as ammonia, is supplied and the synthesis of nitrogenous substances which follows uses up ATP (Syrett, 1953). Similarly, dinitrophenols, inhibitors which break the coupling between oxidation and formation of high-energy phosphate and so remove the limitation by ADP, have the effect of increasing the rate of respiration as measured in terms of carbon dioxide output. This means of inducing an organism to burn up its substance without producing energy in a form which can be used for synthesis has been exploited in the use of these dangerous poisons in slimming and in weed killing.

The release of energy from organic substances which we have just been discussing is something which occurs in all living organisms. Now we must consider more closely the energy transformation which is the unique feature of plants – the transformation of light energy to potential chemical energy which takes place in photosynthesis.

There is much to show that photosynthesis is not a simple process but consists of at least two main steps. One indication of this is that if light is supplied to a plant in short intense flashes, lasting something like $\frac{1}{100000}$ of a second, separated by dark periods, a higher photosynthetic yield for a given amount of light is possible than if light of the same intensity is given, under otherwise similar conditions, in one uninterrupted period of illumination. This suggests that there are at least two separate reactions, one for which light is necessary and another, the slower under the particular conditions used, which can go on in the dark. The dark reaction is often called the Blackman reaction, after F. F. Blackman, who first demonstrated its existence. When light is given continuously the rate of photosynthesis is limited by the dark reaction. When this reaction is given time to catch up with the faster light reaction, then a greater amount of photosynthesis is possible.

It has, in fact, proved possible to separate, in a strictly physical sense, the photosynthetic mechanism into two distinct parts, one of which carries out the light reaction and the other of which carries out reactions independent of light. The first important step towards this achievement was made by Hill and Scarisbrick (1940) when they showed that chloroplasts can be isolated, more or less free from other cell material, from ground-up leaves, and that when illuminated these isolated chloroplasts can reduce certain substances and produce oxygen. Carbon dioxide itself was not reduced by Hill and Scarisbrick's preparations, but the capacity for reduction and evolution of oxygen in the light, which has come to be called the Hill reaction, was shown to be related to photosynthesis, since a variety of treatments had similar effects on both processes. Apparently these isolated chloroplasts contained a part of the photosynthetic mechanism producing reducing power, i.e. hydrogen donors, by splitting water by means of energy derived from light. The reactions may be envisaged as:

$$4 H_2O \xrightarrow{\text{light energy}} 4 [H] + 4 [OH] \qquad (12\ a)$$

$$4 [OH] \rightarrow 2 H_2O + O_2 \qquad (12\ b)$$

$$4 [H] + 2A \rightarrow 2 AH_2 \qquad (12\ c)$$

where the square brackets denote that H and OH are in some sort of combination and A is the substance reduced (often called the Hill reagent). Some substances active as Hill reagents, e.g. ferricyanide and benzoquinone, are not known to occur naturally in plant cells, but co-enzyme II, otherwise known as triphosphopyridine nucleotide (TPN), is a naturally occurring Hill reagent.

At about the time of the discovery of the Hill reaction it was becoming evident that organic phosphates are of particular importance in the energy transactions of living organisms, and it was naturally supposed that they might be concerned in photosynthesis. Transient increases in ATP in green cells following illumination were reported, and it was also found that the early products of the photosynthetic fixation of carbon dioxide were compounds containing phosphate groups, but real understanding of the part played by phosphate was first provided by Arnon in 1954, when he reported that isolated chloroplasts, in addition to carrying out the Hill reaction, can also synthesize ATP in the light from ADP and inorganic phosphate (P_i). It could be, of course, that this ATP formation is secondary, arising from the aerobic respiration of some product of the Hill reaction, but this possibility has been disproved by the preparation of isolated chloroplasts having no appreciable capacity for respiration but which are able to produce ATP rapidly in the light in the complete absence of oxygen, or in the presence of respiratory inhibitors, provided that certain catalysts, vitamin K and flavin mononucleotide, are supplied. This *photosynthetic phosphorylation* may be represented thus:

$$ADP + P_i \xrightarrow{\text{light energy}} ATP \qquad (13)$$

Arnon and his collaborators have gone on to show that preparations of isolated chloroplasts can be obtained which are able to synthesize sugar from carbon dioxide in the light. This capacity for complete photosynthesis depends on the water-soluble chlorophyll-free fraction of the chloroplasts. If this is extracted, the insoluble remainder containing the chlorophyll is still capable of the Hill reaction and photosynthetic phosphorylation but not of photosynthesis of sugar. This situation is represented diagrammatically in Fig. 27. There is some evidence that the production of the hydrogen donor, which appears to be co-enzyme II, and ATP are linked reactions:

$$2\text{CoII} + 2\text{ADP} + 2\text{P}_i + 4\text{H}_2\text{O} \xrightarrow{\text{light}}$$
$$2\text{CoII}\cdot\text{H}_2 + 2\text{ATP} + \text{O}_2 + 2\text{H}_2\text{O} \qquad (14)$$

In the absence of a Hill reagent to accept hydrogen from reduced co-enzyme only ATP is formed, as in equation 13.

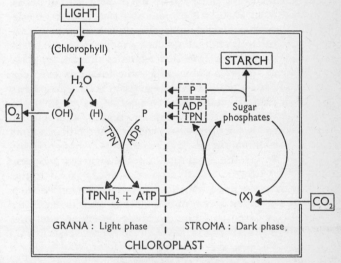

Fig. 27. Photosynthesis by isolated chloroplasts; in the light reaction, catalysed by 'grana', oxygen is evolved and assimilatory power, in the form of the hydrogen donor, reduced co-enzyme II (TPNH_2), and high-energy phosphate (ATP), generated; in the dark reactions these are used by the enzymes in the 'stroma' to assimilate carbon dioxide. See also Plate 7. (After Arnon, 1959.)

The essential part of photosynthesis lies in the reactions associated with the chlorophyll-containing insoluble part of the chloroplast, for it is in these that the transformation of light energy into potential chemical energy in the form of reduced co-enzyme II and ATP takes place. These two compounds may, indeed, be regarded as the real products of photosynthesis. What happens in between the absorption of light energy and their appearance is still something of a mystery.

When radiant energy is absorbed by a substance one or more of various things may happen. The absorbed energy may be added to the already existing thermal energy of the substance, that is, increase the rate of the random movement of whole molecules. Such absorption is ineffective in photosynthesis. With visible light the most important effect occurs within the atoms making up the substance. Each atom consists of a positively charged nucleus around which are held a number of negatively charged electrons moving in orbits which tend to be as close as possible to the centre. The energy of light is not indefinitely divisible, but is distributed in *quanta*, definite indivisible 'packets' of energy behaving in certain respects like particles. On absorption of a quantum of light by a molecule an electron may be displaced to an outer orbit and the potential energy of the molecule rises accordingly. If the quantum absorbed carries sufficient energy the electron is displaced to such an extent that it escapes from the molecule altogether. This is the *photoelectric effect*, on which the action of photoelectric cells depends. An electron displaced to a higher energy level sooner or later reverts to its original position and the energy is released in various ways. The energy may be used to produce chemical change, that is, the effect is *photochemical*. Or the energy may be re-emitted as light. If this happens almost instantaneously after the act of absorption it is called *fluorescence*. Chlorophyll fluoresces both *in vitro* and *in vivo*, and the extent to which it does so *in vivo* provides some guide to the amount of energy being consumed by photochemical reactions. If the latter are slowed down or prevented fluorescence increases accordingly.

Another possibility which should be noted is that the energy may be transferred to an adjacent molecule. The physics of this is abstruse, and it will suffice to say that it can take place between pigment molecules of different kinds, provided that they are in close proximity, and that it does not depend on the re-absorption of energy emitted as fluorescence. It is now well established that transfer of this sort occurs in photosynthesis. For example, light of a wavelength which is absorbed principally by xanthophyll and scarcely at all by chlorophyll may be just as effective in photosynthesis as light of a wavelength that is almost exclusively absorbed by chlorophyll. Since there are good reasons for believing that chlorophyll *a* is the key substance in the photochemical reaction of photosynthesis, this indicates transfer of energy from the xanthophyll to chlorophyll *a*. Further evidence that this can occur is provided by the observation that light energy absorbed by xanthophylls can reappear as fluorescence of a wavelength that is characteristic of chlorophyll *a*. Such transfer has been demonstrated in a variety of different kinds of plant, but seems to be of especial biological advantage in algae, e.g. red seaweeds, growing in deep water. Green light, which penetrates farthest in clear water, is not well absorbed by chlorophyll (see Fig. 15), but is absorbed by special accessory photosynthetic pigments which these algae possess, and is thus made available for photosynthesis.

Whether energy is received directly as light or by transference from another pigment molecule it is evidently the chlorophyll *a* molecule which plays the key part in transforming it into potential chemical energy. The displacement of an electron to a higher energy level by absorption of a light quantum excites the whole molecule so that it may undergo chemical change in any part. A theory originated by van Niel (1941) is that this change is one which results in the splitting of the water molecule, H_2O, into [H] and [OH] radicals as in equation 12a. Franck (1955) has suggested a mechanism whereby the activated chlorophyll *a* molecule might accomplish this, and evidence that water molecules do actually interact chemically with chlorophyll *a* during photosynthesis has been obtained by Vishniac and Rose

(1958) using water labelled with the radioactive hydrogen isotope, tritium. They found that if labelled water is supplied to photosynthesizing chloroplasts the label is incorporated into the chlorophyll so that this becomes appreciably radioactive within a minute or so. In the dark, on the other hand, chlorophyll does not become radioactive even if the chloroplasts are left for long periods in the labelled water. Furthermore, it can be shown that the labelling is on just the carbon atom in the chlorophyll molecule which Franck's hypothesis requires. (Incidentally, it is worth mentioning that if photosynthesizing cells are given carbon dioxide labelled with radiocarbon there is no incorporation of the label into the chlorophyll in short-term experiments. This is further evidence that the fixation of carbon dioxide is quite separate from the photochemical reaction.)

On the hypothesis that the splitting of water is the crucial reaction, it is supposed that the [H] gives rise to hydrogen-donors which can be used for the reductions in photosynthesis. Recombination of [H] and [OH] to give water would yield energy which might be used for the formation of high-energy phosphate groups, as when ATP is formed by photosynthetic phosphorylation (equation 13). The [OH] fragments which are left over when the [H] portions are used for reduction must be disposed of if photosynthesis is to continue. In the higher plants this problem has been solved by means of a mechanism which eliminates oxygen in its molecular form. This may occur via the formation of a peroxide, perhaps hydrogen peroxide, H_2O_2, but more probably an organic peroxide, which subsequently decomposes liberating oxygen, the net effect being that represented by equation 12b. Photosynthetic bacteria, which never evolve oxygen, must use another sort of disposal mechanism. The green sulphur bacteria, for example, carry out a form of photosynthesis in which hydrogen sulphide is apparently the source of hydrogen rather than water:

$$CO_2 + 2H_2S \rightarrow (CH_2O) + H_2O + 2S \qquad (15)$$

carbon dioxide + hydrogen sulphide $\rightarrow$ carbohydrate + water + sulphur

Van Niel's theory supposes that the apparent hydrogen-donor is here merely providing a means of getting rid of the oxidizing fragment of the water molecule:

$$2[OH] + H_2S \rightarrow 2H_2O + S \qquad (16)$$

Another suggestion about the nature of the primary photochemical process has recently been put forward by Arnon (1959). He supposes that absorption of a quantum of light energy results in the displacement of an electron from the chlorophyll molecule. The chlorophyll molecule thus becomes able to act as an electron acceptor, and if it were to take back the electron directly the energy would be re-emitted as light, i.e. fluorescence would occur. Alternatively, the electron might be captured by some other electron acceptor which would thereby become reduced.* From this acceptor, which is probably vitamin K or flavin mono-nucleotide, the electron might be returned to the 'hole' in the chlorophyll molecule via a series of electron acceptors, the oxidation of which could be used to drive the synthesis of ATP. In other words, the electron (or hydrogen) transport is coupled to ATP formation in a similar way to that which exists in aerobic respiration. Cytochromes, similar to but not identical with those concerned in respiration, occur in chloroplasts and seem to be intimately concerned in photosynthesis, and could well be the hydrogen carriers involved. This scheme (Fig. 28a) provides an explanation of the *cyclic* type of photosynthetic phosphorylation (equation 13, p. 108), in which ATP is synthesized in the light with no consumption of external hydrogen donors. In some circumstances this may be the only photochemical process necessary for photosynthesis. *Chromatium*, a purple sulphur bacterium, seems to be able to carry out photosynthesis of this

* Reduction may be defined as the acquisition of one or more electrons by a molecule. Acquisition of electrons may enable a molecule to capture hydrogen ions, always available in aqueous systems because of the dissociation of water, $H_2O \rightleftharpoons H^+ + OH^-$, and thus to add on hydrogen. The reduction of fumaric acid to succinic acid, for example, may be regarded as taking place thus:

$$(CH \cdot COOH)_2 + 2H^+ + 2e \rightarrow (CH_2 \cdot COOH)_2 \qquad (17)$$

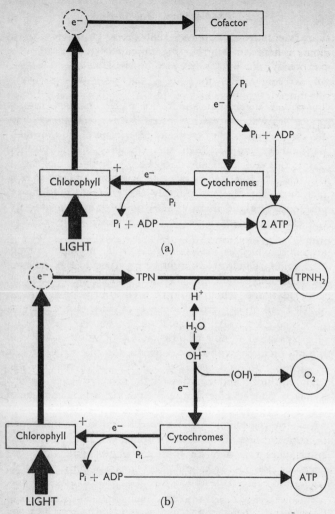

Fig. 28. Simplified schemes for cyclic (a) and non-cyclic (b) phosphorylation processes in photosynthesis according to Arnon (1960). e^- = electron, P_i = inorganic phosphate, ADP = adenosine diphosphate, ATP = adenosine triphosphate, TPN = co-enzyme II (triphosphopyridine nucleotide).

type. It is able to make reduced co-enzyme II, the hydrogen-donor necessary for the synthesis of organic compounds from carbon dioxide, from hydrogen in the dark. Given hydrogen gas, carbon dioxide, and light, it is able to produce organic substances by photosynthesis, but Arnon (1960) has shown that for the isolated photosynthetic mechanism of this bac-terium ATP and light are entirely equivalent. *Chromatium* is strictly anaerobic, and therefore cannot make ATP by the usual processes of aerobic respiration, but if it is supplied with this substance in the dark, it is able to manufacture organic materials similar to those which it normally makes in the light.

Photosynthetic bacteria such as *Chromatium* need to be supplied with a substance – hydrogen itself, hydrogen sul-phide, or an organic substance – which can be used as a source of hydrogen. Green plants possess a mechanism whereby they can get the hydrogen from water. Arnon's theory of how this is accomplished is summarized in Fig. 28 b. The electrons expelled from chlorophyll, together with hydrogen ion, H^+, produced by dissociation of water, are thought to be used to reduce co-enzyme II. The hydroxyl ions, OH^-, are used as a source of electrons to replace those lost from the chlorophyll, their transference being again accomplished by cytochromes and coupled with ATP formation. The [OH] radicals left after removal of the electrons react to given oxygen and water, as in equation 12b (p. 107). This scheme thus explains the *non-cyclic* type of photosynthetic phosphorylation, the simultaneous forma-tion of reduced co-enzyme II, ATP, and oxygen by isolated chloroplasts as represented in equation 14 (p. 109).

There are thus two plausible but rather different theories to explain the conversion of light energy to potential chemi-cal energy by chlorophyll. Only further investigation can decide between them. Whatever the mechanism, it is prob-able that it depends not only on the special properties of the chlorophyll molecule but also on its relations with other com-ponents, that is, on the structure of the chloroplast. Exam-ination of thin sections of chloroplasts with the electron microscope (Plate 7) has confirmed, what was already suspected from other evidence, that the essential structure is a laminated one, like a multi-decker sandwich. In this sandwich there are alternating layers of fatty material and protein-with-water, each about 0·0065 μ thick. Calculation shows that there is sufficient chlorophyll in a chloroplast to cover the interfaces between the layers on the assumption that the ring system of the chlorophyll molecule lies flat in the interface, with the phytol tail (see Fig. 29) projecting at right angles into the fatty layer. The chlorophyll molecules are fixed into this structure by some sort of chemical bonding; this is indicated by various facts, one being that it is difficult to extract chlorophyll from chloroplasts with solvents, such as dry acetone, which readily dissolve free chlorophyll. The long-chain molecules of the carotenoid pigments would fit in between the chlorophyll molecules, also at right angles to the plane of the layering (Frey-Wyssling, 1957; Wolken, 1959). Such an arrangement seems admirably suited to promote the transfer of energy between the various pigment molecules, on the one hand, and

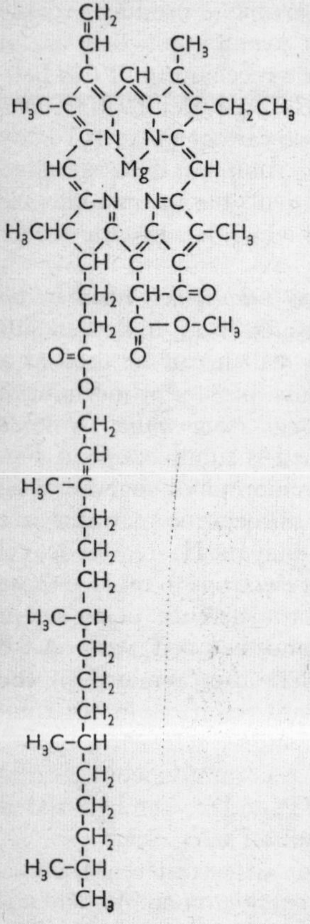

Fig. 29. The chlorophyll *a* molecule.

to allow the free diffusion of the water-soluble intermediates involved in the dark reactions, on the other. Chloroplasts can be broken down to a considerable extent and still retain some photochemical activity, but it appears that this is lost once the lamellar structure is entirely destroyed. Chlorophyll extracted from the chloroplasts appears to be incapable of sensitizing any process resembling photosynthesis.

The structure of the chloroplast is reminiscent of that of a semi-conductor, that is, a material in which migration of electrons is not confined to individual molecules but is possible within the crystalline structure formed by a number of molecules. These materials are playing an important part in modern electronics and are, in fact, used in the 'solar battery' of sputnik fame, which converts radiant energy into electrical energy. It has been shown by Arnold and Maclay (1959) that dried chloroplasts and films of chlorophyll and carotene do actually become semi-conducting on illumination. On the view that the chloroplast acts as a semi-conductor, the electron and the hole which it leaves might be separated and migrate over relatively large distances before being trapped by their respective acceptor substances (cytochrome can be looked on as an acceptor for holes). In this way several thousand chlorophyll molecules might serve one pair of acceptor molecules. There is, in fact, evidence for the existence of a photosynthetic unit in which light absorbed by several thousand chlorophyll molecules can be contributed to a single carbon dioxide reducing centre. Another consequence of the separation of electron and hole would be that they might be stored for appreciable lengths of time and that the process might be reversible. Evidence of reversal has, indeed, been obtained. By means of sensitive photomultipliers Strehler and Arnold (1951) were able to show that *Chlorella* emits light, feebly but definitely, for a second or two following transfer from light to dark. All plants seem to be capable of luminescence of this sort – but, of course, it is not detectable by the human eye.

The mechanism by which carbon dioxide is built up into organic compounds such as sugars can function, as we have seen, in the dark and is mechanically separable from the photochemical apparatus. To identify the intermediates taking part, and so determine the pathway of carbon fixation, an obvious way to proceed seems to be to compare analyses of plant material that has been kept in the dark for some time with those of similar material exposed to light for a brief period. However, the reactions proceed so rapidly and the intermediates are produced in such small amounts that classical methods of chemical analysis failed entirely to provide any consistent information. As a result, a theory which postulated formaldehyde as the key intermediate was able to hold the field for many years although unsupported by any direct evidence. Formaldehyde, CH_2O, seems an obvious intermediate, for not only is it the simplest substance containing carbon, hydrogen, and oxygen in the proportions in which they are found in carbohydrates but it is also known to condense under certain conditions to form sugars. If this were so the chemical pathways of production of sugar in photosynthesis would be of quite a different sort from those involved in, say, respiration, and photosynthesis would be marked out as something separate and distinct from other cell processes. Results of analyses for formaldehyde in illuminated plants have been inconclusive, and plants seem unable to assimilate it to produce sugars, as one would expect them to do if it were actually an intermediate. The formaldehyde hypothesis is now only of historical interest.

That we now have detailed knowledge of the path of carbon in photosynthesis is largely due to the brilliant exploitation by Benson and Calvin and their collaborators in California of the technique of chromatography combined with the use of radiocarbon as a tracer. Chemically the radioactive isotope of carbon, C^{14}, behaves in a similar way to the most abundant natural isotope of carbon, C^{12}, which is not radioactive. If the carbon dioxide supplied to a photosynthesizing plant contains radiocarbon the sequence in which radioactivity appears in compounds in the plant will indicate the path taken by carbon in the fixation process. As already indicated (p. 92), the radiocarbon finds its way rather rapidly into substances which are unlikely to be intermediates in this process, so that, if they are to be of any use, analyses must be made within seconds after the beginning of photosynthesis with the labelled carbon dioxide. Paper chromatography, which makes possible the separation and identification of numerous compounds present in small amounts in a mixture, provides the necessary supplement to the use of tracers. In this method a spot of the extract to be analysed is placed on a sheet of filter paper and a suitable solvent is allowed to travel along the paper by capillarity. The different substances present in the extract are carried along at different rates, so that they become separated out in distinct patches. Further separation may be achieved by causing a second solvent to pass along the paper in a direction at right angles to that of the first. The patches may be made visible by spraying the paper with a reagent that will give a colour with the substances being examined, or, if they contain radioactive isotopes, by making a photographic print from the paper. The paper with its separated patches of different substances is known as a *chromatogram*. The substances may be identified by their relative positions on the chromatogram and by extraction from the paper and analysis (see Plate 6).

The early products in the photosynthetic fixation of carbon dioxide have now been examined in a variety of different plants, including unicellular green algae, seaweeds, and flowering plants such as barley (*Hordeum vulgare*) and geranium (*Pelargonium zonale*), the results all being similar. Experiments are most conveniently carried out with unicellular algae, such as species of *Chlorella* or *Scenedesmus*. These are allowed to photosynthesize for a time in the presence of ordinary carbon dioxide, which is then swiftly replaced by labelled carbon dioxide. After a further short period of photosynthesis the algal suspension is run into boiling alcohol, which immediately stops all enzyme reactions and extracts the fixation products. Chromatograms of this extract are then made. It is in addition necessary to carry out a control experiment with the alga in the dark, since carbon dioxide can enter into biochemical reactions apart from those involved in photosynthesis. Dark fixation of carbon dioxide was first shown to occur in bacteria (Wood and Werkman, 1935), and is now thought to occur in all forms of life.

The reactions concerned are of this type:

$$CH_2{:}CO\,\fbox{P}\,{\cdot}COOH + C^{14}O_2 \rightarrow$$

phosphoenol-
pyruvic acid   +   carbon
           dioxide $\rightarrow$

$$HOOC^{14}{\cdot}CH_2{\cdot}CO{\cdot}COOH + \quad P_1 \quad (18)$$

oxaloacetic   +   inorganic
acid   phosphate

in which carbon dioxide is added to an already existing organic molecule, $\fbox{P}$ again standing for a high-energy phosphate group. This is the reversal of a type of reaction, already met with in connexion with fermentation and respiration, in which carbon dioxide is split off (see pp. 99 and 101). The same enzymes, in fact, catalyse the fixation or evolution of carbon dioxide according to circumstances. Since these reactions do not involve reduction, the energy changes are small and not comparable with those in the fixation with reduction which is the final outcome of photosynthesis. If radioactive carbon dioxide is supplied to plant material in the dark a chromatogram of an extract of the material shows several radioactive patches corresponding to various organic acids in which carbon dioxide has been incorporated as a result of the activity of Krebs cycle enzymes.

However, in the light the pattern of fixation is quite different, and radioactivity appears in a variety of compounds, including sugars and their phosphate derivatives and amino-acids. If the period of photosynthesis in the presence of radioactive carbon dioxide is as short as five seconds one particular labelled compound, phosphoglyceric acid, $CH_2O\,\fbox{P}\,{\cdot}CHOH{\cdot}COOH$, predominates. Radioactive phosphoglyceric acid is not formed in any appreciable quantity during dark fixation of carbon dioxide, and is thus specifically associated with photosynthesis. These results obtained by chromatography have been confirmed by isolation and identification by other methods, and there can now be no reasonable doubt that phosphoglyceric acid is the first stable intermediate in which carbon fixed in photosynthesis appears.

After chemical breakdown of the phosphoglyceric acid produced in photosynthesis with radioactive carbon dioxide, the fragments can be examined for radioactivity and the position in the molecule at which carbon has been incorporated can be established. Provided that the period of photosynthesis has been quite short, it is found to be in the acidic group. The radioactive substance thus has the formula,

$CH_2O\,\textcircled{P}\cdot CHOH\cdot C^{14}OOH$, and has apparently been

formed by addition of carbon dioxide to some substance already containing two carbon atoms. Intensive search has failed to show the existence of any such 2-carbon acceptor, but evidence has been obtained that phosphoglyceric acid is formed by addition of carbon dioxide to a 5-carbon substance, the phosphorylated pentose sugar, ribulose diphosphate, which subsequently breaks in two, giving two molecules of phosphoglyceric acid. In experiments in which the photosynthesizing plant is exposed to the radioactive carbon dioxide for longer than a few seconds it is found that all three carbons in the phosphoglyceric acid become labelled. This suggests that the ribulose diphosphate is itself formed from phosphoglyceric acid, and a cycle of conversions by which this is probably brought about has been worked out by Calvin and his collaborators.

Phosphoglyceric acid is an intermediate not only in photosynthesis but also in glycolysis (Fig. 24), and it seems that the first reaction in the photosynthetic cycle at least strongly resembles one which we have already discussed in some detail, working in reverse. By referring back to equations 9 and 10 it will be seen that for this reversal, i.e. for the production of phosphoglyceraldehyde from phosphoglyceric acid, a hydrogen donor and ATP are required. These are provided by the photochemical reaction. The hydrogen donor produced by the photochemical reaction is reduced co-enzyme II, whereas the hydrogen carrier in glycolysis is co-enzyme I, but it seems that an enzyme closely related to the one involved in glycolysis but adapted to work with co-enzyme II is present in green tissues.

A triose sugar phosphate, viz. phosphoglyceraldehyde, has now been produced, and from this a whole range of others sugars can be derived. Hexose may be produced by a reversal of the glycolytic reactions, and other sugars can be formed by interchange of parts, which takes place readily between sugar phosphates in the presence of the appropriate enzymes. Thus, hexose phosphate and triose phosphate exchange parts, giving pentose and tetrose phosphates:

$$C-C:O-C-C-C-C-\boxed{P} \;+\; \mathbf{C-C-C-}\boxed{P} \;\rightleftharpoons$$
$$C-C-C-C-\boxed{P} \;+\; C-C:O-\mathbf{C-C-C-}\boxed{P} \qquad (19)$$

Only the skeletons of the sugars are represented here, and the carbons of the triose are distinguished by being printed in heavy type. By such interchanges a cycle is possible whereby ribulose diphosphate is synthesized from phosphoglyceric acid and in turn, by addition of carbon dioxide, regenerates phosphoglyceric acid, the process being driven by reduced co-enzyme II and ATP produced by the photochemical reaction. The details of this cycle, which is represented in part in Fig. 30, need not concern us, but it should be noted that nowhere is there any intermediate of which one can say 'this is the final product of photosynthesis'; as will be seen later, organic matter can be withdrawn from the cycle at any point.

It should also be reiterated that this mechanism is something separate from the photochemical mechanism. This is well illustrated by an experiment of Arnon's (1959). A chloroplast suspension was illuminated in the absence of carbon dioxide, so that there was no raw material for carbohydrate synthesis; instead, large amounts of ADP, inorganic phosphate, and co-enzyme II were supplied. The result was the evolution of oxygen and an accumulation of ATP and reduced co-enzyme II. The green part of the chloroplasts was then removed by centrifuging, and carbon dioxide was

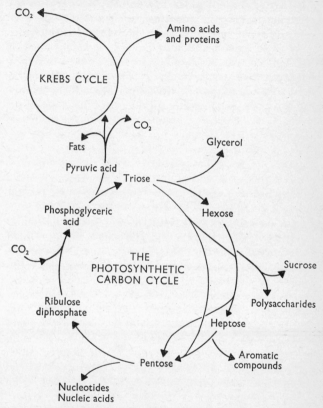

Fig. 30. Simplified scheme showing the reactions of the photosynthetic carbon cycle according to Calvin (1957).

supplied to the solution remaining. Using the ATP and reduced co-enzyme made when the light was on, the enzymes of the carbon fixation cycle now proceeded to assimilate the carbon dioxide in the dark, producing the same carbohydrates as are made in normal photosynthesis by whole chloroplasts or green leaves. Racker (1955) has shown that it is possible to produce sugar from carbon dioxide in an artificial mixture, containing a hydrogen donor, ATP, and the eleven enzymes postulated as necessary, but entirely free from chlorophyll or chloroplastic material. In fact, there seems to be nothing in the carbon-fixation cycle specific to green plants, nearly all the reactions involved in it being known to occur in non-photosynthetic organisms.

The whole complicated machinery of photosynthesis is capable of functioning with considerable efficiency in the conversion of light energy into potential chemical energy. As pointed out in Chapter 2, by no means all the light which falls on a leaf is absorbed and, if other things are limiting, full use cannot be made of what light is absorbed. In fact, if the potential chemical energy represented by the total yield of dry matter per acre of a crop plant such as wheat is compared with the energy received as sunlight by the same area during the growing season it is found that the net energy fixation is only a small fraction, less than 1 per cent of that received. Nevertheless, if young, actively growing, material is examined under optimum laboratory conditions with light intensity limiting, it is found that the efficiency of conversion of absorbed radiant energy into potential chemical energy is as much as 30 per cent.

However, it is more enlightening to consider the quantum requirement of photosynthesis rather than its efficiency expressed as a percentage. The energy carried by a quantum of red light of wavelength 660 mμ is such that the total provided by three quanta is just equal to that required for the reduction of one molecule of carbon dioxide to the equivalent of carbohydrate. Since one quantum absorbed by a molecule can produce only one chemical change in it, any energy in a quantum over and above that required for this change is necessarily wasted. Four atoms of hydrogen are required for the reduction of one molecule of carbon dioxide to the carbohydrate level, and it is to be expected that a quantum is required for the activation of each of these. In addition, energy is required for the production of ATP and, as we have seen, it is possible that several molecules of this may be produced as a single electron displaced from chlorophyll is returned along a series of electron acceptors.

The experimental determination of the quantum requirement is in principle a straightforward matter, all that is necessary being the accurate measurement of the amount of light absorbed by photosynthesizing plant material followed by estimation of the substance produced. Nevertheless, few experiments in plant physiology have aroused more acrimonious controversy than this. Warburg, who with Negelein reported the first measurements in 1923, has asserted that the minimum requirement is four – the very least, which as we have just seen, seems possible – or less. Emerson and many other workers, on the other hand, have maintained that the requirement is at least eight quanta, which corresponds to the efficiency of 30 per cent mentioned above. A major source of this uncertainty seems to lie in the use of gas exchanged during photosynthesis as a measure of the organic matter produced. This method is convenient but indirect and open to error because of the indefinite nature of the organic products of photosynthesis. Determinations made by the less equivocal method of measuring the energy retained and lost during a period of photosynthesis give the minimum quantum requirement as at least eight, and this value is now accepted by the majority of workers.

The relationships between the two major processes just described, respiration and photosynthesis, are of particular complexity. The final result of respiration is, of course, the exact opposite of that of photosynthesis (compare equations 1 and 11), a fact which bothers anyone who wishes to get a true estimate of the rate of photosynthesis. The convention has been to assume that the rate of respiration in photosynthesizing organs is the same as that in the same organs in the dark, so that to obtain the true rate of photosynthesis one has to add a correction for dark respiration to the apparent rate. This is certainly more convenient than exact.

Not only are the end products of one process the raw materials for the other, but, as we have seen, there are common intermediates, e.g. phosphoglyceric acid. If the two processes go on side by side it would be surprising if the rate of respiration were not affected to some extent by photosynthesis. The extent of interaction may hinge on how 'side by side' the two processes are, i.e. on the degree of spatial separation between the mechanisms responsible. The chloroplasts contain all that is necessary for complete photosynthesis, whereas the respiratory machinery is mainly housed in the mitochondria, and as a result of this separation there might be little interaction between the two processes. This idea is borne out by the results of some experiments with the alga *Chlorella*, carried out by Brown (1953), in which isotopic labelling was used to distinguish between oxygen taken up and oxygen given out. When the *Chlorella* was exposed to air in which the oxygen was labelled with the heavy isotope, O^{18}, it was found that uptake of the labelled molecules, i.e. uptake of oxygen in respiration, continued at the same rate in the light as in the dark, whereas unlabelled oxygen, liberated from water in photosynthesis, was evolved in the light (Fig. 31). Other algae, however, were found to behave quite differently. In the blue-green alga, *Anabaena*, for example, a similar experiment showed complete suppression of oxygen uptake in the light. This is in agreement with what we know of the cell structure of blue-green algae, for they do not have their photosynthetic apparatus enclosed in a membrane as do other plants, and there could thus be more free interchange between it and the respiratory machinery. In any case we do not know whether the hydrogen donors which are oxidized by the oxygen taken up come from the same source in the light as in the dark. It is conceivable that hydrogen donors from the photochemical reaction might be substituted for those produced by respiration, in the light. It seems likely that the relationship between the two processes varies greatly according to the physiological condition of the plant as well as according to the kind of plant.

Perhaps the most interesting point that has emerged from recent studies is that the key products of the photochemical process of photosynthesis and of respiration are virtually the

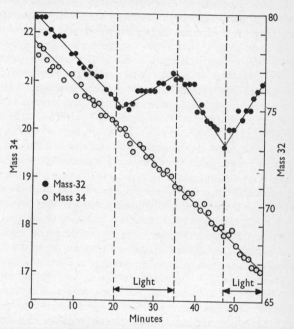

Fig. 31. Absorption and evolution of oxygen by the alga *Chlorella*, supplied with air enriched with the heavy oxygen isotope (O^{18}), as followed by means of the mass spectrometer. Molecules of mass 32 (ordinary oxygen, $O^{16}O^{16}$) decreased in the dark owing to respiration, but increased in the light owing to liberation in photosynthesis from water containing O^{16} only. Molecules of mass 34 ($O^{16}O^{18}$) decreased uniformly in light and dark owing to respiration. The intensities for the two light periods were different. (After van Norman and Brown, 1952.)

same, viz. hydrogen donor (reduced co-enzyme I or II) and ATP. Moreover, since the photosynthetic fixation of carbon dioxide and respiration intermesh through many common intermediates, they provide a similar range of carbon skeletons which can be used as building units for larger molecules. In the synthesis of organic matter in a plant, then, respiration and photosynthesis may play exactly interchangeable roles. This is well illustrated by some experiments of Maclachlan and Porter (1959) on starch synthesis in tobacco (*Nicotiana tabacum*) leaves. The synthesis of starch from glucose requires ATP (see p. 132), and in discs of tobacco leaves supplied with glucose solution this can be provided equally well by aerobic respiration or by photosynthetic phosphorylation, as shown by starch synthesis taking place in the light whether or not oxygen is supplied, but in the dark only if oxygen is present (Plate 10). The same conclusion is indicated by the fact that the abundances of the two cell structures concerned, mitochondria and chloroplasts, show an inverse relationship. Mitochondria are abundant in colourless cells but infrequent in cells with numerous chloroplasts.

With certain exceptions, which, although they may be extremely important in affecting the course of development (see Chapter 11), are of very minor quantitative importance, a plant is in fact capable of making all the vast range of organic compounds it requires either photosynthetically or in the dark using respiratory processes. In a germinating seedling respiration alone supplies the material and driving power for synthesis; later photosynthesis assumes the dominant role, with respiration important only during dark periods and in colourless parts such as roots. If photosynthesis is prevented by keeping the plant in the dark, or impossible because the plant is an albino, growth may still take place if a substrate for respiration, e.g. sugar, is provided. Borgström (1939) has been successful in getting pea plants to produce flowers and seeds when grown on sucrose in complete darkness.

CHAPTER 5

The Mechanisms of Synthesis

Now we must consider how the components of a plant are built using the raw materials and energy provided by photosynthesis or respiration. A plant contains a tremendous variety of different chemical substances. Each of the main groups of compounds – proteins, nucleic acids, fats, and carbohydrates – is represented by tens or hundreds of different substances, even in the same plant, and besides these there are hundreds of other, less tersely describable, substances which, although relatively small in amount, may be of literally vital importance. How does a plant manufacture this extraordinary variety of substances? In trying to answer this we must break the question up into several subsidiary ones: What are the units from which the substances are built, and how are they obtained? By what means are these units built into big molecules, and how is the energy necessary for this synthesis supplied? Another, less obvious, question is one which leads into one of the most exciting fields of contemporary biology: How does a plant, or indeed any living thing, achieve the specificity in synthesis upon which its individuality depends? The differences which exist between species and between individuals belonging to the same species must ultimately have a chemical basis and evidently depend on highly specific substances. How is it that a particular plant is able to synthesize the specific materials which make it, say, a Hybrid Tea rose of the variety Ena Harkness rather than the generally similar materials which go to make up a blackcurrant bush or the presumably even more similar materials which constitute the rose variety Mme Louise Laperrière?

A proper attempt to answer these questions would take us deep into biochemical and genetical matters which are outside the scope of this book, but an indication must be given of some of the general principles which can be discerned.

The diversity and complexity of plant chemistry depend on the unique ability of one element, carbon, to combine with itself indefinitely in various patterns, rather than on the combination of a large variety of different elements. Besides carbon, the compounds found in plants always contain hydrogen and usually oxygen. We have already seen how these elements are brought into combination in photosynthesis. The reactions by which the intermediate products of photosynthesis are interconverted are rapid and reversible, so that a flexible system exists from which material can be supplied in many different chemical forms. This system may also be fed with organic materials from other sources, since it shares common intermediates with the glycolytic and organic acid systems of respiration. The whole complex of intermeshing systems can be regarded as a 'metabolic pool', a universal melting pot, or a roundabout from which radiate the roads leading to the synthesis of protein, fats, carbohydrates, and other compounds, as well as the roads on which material is brought in from photosynthesis and respiration (Fig. 32). It does not matter that the amount of material in this pool at any one moment is small, it is the rate of turnover which determines the amount of materials which flow through it.

Starch may be taken as an example to show how carbohydrates with large molecules are synthesized and how the energy of ATP is utilized. The starch molecule is comprised of glucose units (p. 91), but there is no known mechanism for making starch directly from glucose itself or even from maltose, which consists of two glucose units already joined in the right way. β-Amylase (p. 93) breaks down starch into maltose, but no one has been successful in making it build starch from maltose, even though theory suggests that all enzyme reactions should be reversible. A possible starting material for starch synthesis is glucose-1-phosphate, which could be supplied directly from the photosynthetic carbon-fixation cycle. Phosphorylase, an enzyme first discovered in pea seeds and potato tubers by Hanes (1940) and now

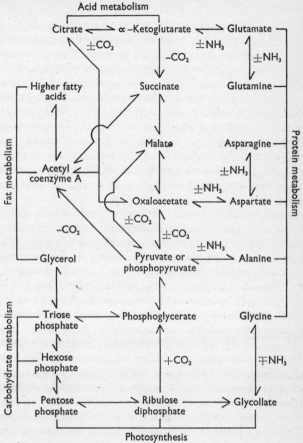

Fig. 32. Simplified scheme showing some interrelations between the components of the metabolic pool. (After Fogg, 1953.)

known to be commonly present in plant tissues, breaks down starch to produce glucose-1-phosphate and will, under suitable conditions, work in reverse to produce something like starch:

$$\text{starch} + n\text{-}P_i \xrightleftharpoons[\quad]{\text{phosphorylase}} n\text{-glucose-1-phosphate} \qquad (20)$$

The energy which is needed to join the glucose units together comes from the potential energy of the phosphate bond. In the presence of phosphorylase, ATP as the source of energy, and the appropriate enzymes for transferring the energy-rich phosphate group, glucose itself can be used as the raw material for the synthesis. It is interesting that there is a lag in synthesis by phosphorylase unless some starch is supplied to act as a primer. The 'starch' produced by purified phosphorylase is not identical with natural starch, consisting only of unbranched chains. A second enzyme, called the Q-enzyme, can introduce branch-point linkages, and in its presence something extremely like natural starch is formed.

In spite of this successful enzymic synthesis of a starch-like material in the test-tube, there are good reasons for thinking that starch is not made in this way in the living plant. The conditions in plant cells seem to be such as to favour starch splitting by phosphorylase rather than its synthetic activity and, furthermore, phosphorylase appears to be absent from the chloroplasts – just where starch synthesis goes on most vigorously. It seems that not a simple glucose phosphate but uridine diphosphate glucose, a nucleotide derivative incorporating high-energy phosphate groups, is the starting material. Rongine de Fekete and her collaborators (1960) have demonstrated the presence of an enzyme in starch grains from string beans (*Phaseolus vulgaris*) which will incorporate glucose supplied in this form into starch. Sucrose synthesis, the mechanism of which remained unknown for a long time, is known to proceed in a similar way from fructose and uridine diphosphate glucose. The synthesis of both carbohydrates thus depends on the potential chemical energy of a sugar–nucleotide compound which is itself synthesized using energy from ATP. As yet, an enzyme system capable of synthesizing cellulose has not been extracted from plants.

Fat synthesis proceeds in three main stages: synthesis of fatty acids, synthesis of glycerol, and the joining of these two together. It is a striking thing that most naturally occurring fatty acids have an even number of carbon atoms, and this at once suggests that their long chain-like molecules are built up from 2-carbon links. This idea is further supported by experiments with radiocarbon as a tracer, for these show that the 2-carbon substance, acetic acid, or sugars from which this may be produced (Fig. 32) are good starting materials for fatty acid synthesis, whereas 1-carbon (formic) or 3-carbon (propionic) acids are poor. The chief method of breakdown of long-chain fatty acids in bacteria, plants, and animals is by splitting off successive 2-carbon units, a process called β-oxidation. In this, the fatty acid is not oxidized as such, but is first converted to a more reactive form by combination with an activating substance, co-enzyme A. After partial oxidation the molecule is split by combination with a further molecule of co-enzyme A to yield the co-enzyme A derivatives of a fatty acid with two carbon atoms less in its chain and acetyl co-enzyme A. The process is then repeated. Eventually the molecule is dismantled into 2-carbon units, which may be completely oxidized via the organic acid cycle. It seemed that, given a suitable hydrogen-donor, this process should work in reverse, and for a long time it was believed to be the means of fatty acid synthesis. However, when the enzymic components were isolated from a cell-free preparation from pigeon liver that was capable of fatty acid synthesis they were found to be different from those concerned in β-oxidation, and, most surprisingly, required carbon dioxide as a catalyst (Green, 1960). This enzymic complex, which appears to operate in plants also, builds up long-chain fatty acids from acetic acid by the following sequence of reactions:

$$CH_3COOH + \quad CoA \quad \rightarrow \quad CH_3CO \cdot (CoA) \qquad (21\,a)$$
$$\text{acetic acid} \quad \text{co-enzyme A} \quad \text{acetyl co-enzyme A}$$

$$CH_3CO \cdot (CoA) + CO_2 + ATP \rightarrow$$
$$HOOC \cdot CH_2CO \cdot (CoA) + ADP + P_i \qquad (21\,b)$$
$$\text{malonyl co-enzyme A}$$

$$CH_3CO \cdot (CoA) + HOOC \cdot CH_2CO \cdot (CoA) \rightarrow$$
$$CH_3CO \cdot \underset{|}{CH} \cdot CO(CoA) + CoA \qquad (21\ c)$$
$$COOH$$

$$CH_3CO \cdot \underset{|}{CH} \cdot CO \cdot (CoA) + 4[H] \rightarrow$$
$$COOH$$
$$CH_3CH_2CH_2CO \cdot (CoA) + CO_2 + H_2O \qquad (21\ d)$$
butyryl co-enzyme A

ATP supplies the energy which brings the carbon dioxide into combination, and co-enzyme II acts as the hydrogen donor (it may be noted that this may be supplied directly by the photosynthetic mechanism). By repetition of this process, a further 2-carbon unit being added to the butyryl–co-enzyme A from malonyl co-enzyme A and so on, a long-chain fatty acid can be built up.

The source of the other component of fats, glycerol, is the glycolytic process already described on p. 95. An enzyme, lipase, which splits fats into fatty acids and glycerol is generally found in plants and is capable, under appropriate conditions, of catalysing the reverse reaction. However, it seems rather unlikely that fats can be produced by this mechanism under the conditions found in plant cells and more probable that this final stage in the synthesis of fat starts from fatty acid–co-enzyme A compounds and is catalysed by an enzyme other than lipase.

It is a most striking thing that for the examples just considered, sucrose, starch, and fats, and, as we shall see later, for proteins also, the mechanism used by living cells for synthesis is quite different from that used for breakdown. This is in contrast to the reactions of the metabolic pool, from which the building units for these large molecules are drawn, which, according to the exigencies of supply and demand, mostly go with equal facility in either direction. Readily reversible processes are evidently not suitable for the synthesis of the more complex molecules. The greater control obtained by having separate mechanisms is perhaps reinforced by spatial separation. It seems likely, for instance, that the mechanism for β-oxidation of fatty acids is housed in the mitochondria, whereas that for synthesis is confined to smaller protoplasmic structures, the microsomes. This would explain the finding that fat or protein synthesis may take place simultaneously with breakdown of these substances in the same cell.

Carbohydrates and fats contain only the elements carbon, hydrogen, and oxygen. We must now consider the formation of amino-acids, proteins, and other nitrogenous substances.

Although they are surrounded by virtually unlimited supplies of the element nitrogen in the air, flowering plants are by themselves unable to utilize this and must be supplied with nitrogen in a combined form, such as ammonia or nitrate, if they are to grow. On the other hand, bacteria, such as *Azotobacter*, *Clostridium*, and *Rhizobium* species; many blue-green algae; and perhaps some fungi are able to *fix* nitrogen, that is, to assimilate the unreactive molecule of free nitrogen from air. The nature of the mechanism whereby this is accomplished is still almost entirely unknown, but it seems that the product is ammonia, which is then used in the same way as in organisms which are not able to fix nitrogen. Many flowering plants form close associations, *symbioses*, with nitrogen-fixing micro-organisms, for example, members of the Leguminosae (the pea family), which harbour *Rhizobium* in their root nodules. In this symbiosis the flowering plant provides the bacterium with carbohydrates, and the bacterium evidently supplies the plant with nitrogen, which it has 'fixed' from the atmosphere, but the situation is a great deal more complicated than this, because, so far, no one has succeeded in demonstrating that the bacterium is able to fix nitrogen when grown by itself, although it grows readily by itself if it is given combined nitrogen. Because of their importance in agriculture, in building up soil fertility and as fodder plants, the Leguminosae afford the most familiar examples of symbiotic nitrogen fixation, but there are others which are probably of considerable importance in nature. The common alder (*Alnus glutinosa*), the bog-myrtle (*Myrica gale*), and *Casuarina* species, common trees of poor soils in the tropics, are all nitrogen-fixing by virtue of symbiotic micro-organisms. *Gunnera chilensis*, a herbaceous plant with leaves several feet across often seen in European gardens, and various cycads have pockets of blue-green algae in their tissues, and probably benefit to some extent from the nitrogen fixed by these associates.

Nitrogen fixation by these various agencies is of the greatest importance in keeping up the fertility of the earth, but most flowering plants are dependent on nitrogen compounds set free by the decay of organic material. Ammonia is the main nitrogenous product of decay, but this is usually oxidized immediately to nitrate by nitrifying bacteria, which use the energy so liberated for their growth, and nitrate is generally the chief source of nitrogen for plants. However, once it has been absorbed by a plant, the nitrogen of nitrate has to be reduced back again to ammonia or some derivative of this before it can be used and incorporated in amino-acids or other nitrogenous cell components. This reduction requires hydrogen-donors and, perhaps, high-energy phosphates; these can be provided by respiratory processes, for nitrate reduction can take place in the dark and in colourless organs such as roots, but they may also be supplied more or less directly by the photosynthetic mechanism.

Nitrate reduction in green leaves is accelerated in the light, and illuminated *Chlorella* has been found to produce more oxygen in the presence of nitrate than it does in its absence. This suggests that a photochemical reduction of nitrate is taking place, with nitrate substituting for carbon dioxide in photosynthesis. The situation cannot be quite as simple as this, however, because little oxygen is produced by *Chlorella* if it is given nitrate but no carbon dioxide; if nitrate substituted completely for carbon dioxide one would expect oxygen to be produced freely in these circumstances. The reduction of nitrate to ammonia in plants is, in fact, complicated, taking place in several stages the first of which is the reduction of nitrate (NO_3^-) to nitrite (NO_2^-). This first step is catalysed by an enzyme, nitrate reductase, containing molybdenum, which is one reason, probably not the only one, why plants require traces of this element for healthy growth. It has been shown by Evans and Nason (1953) that, in the presence of this enzyme, nitrate can be reduced to nitrite by means of reduced co-enzyme II produced by isolated chloroplasts. Possibly one or more stages in the subsequent reduction of nitrite to ammonia (NH_3) may also use products of the photochemical reaction.

Ammonia itself can be absorbed rapidly from the soil and used directly. For plants such as rice (*Oryza sativa*) ammonia is the best source of nitrogen, but it is often not so favourable as nitrate, since it is absorbed more rapidly than any of the acid radicals with which it is combined in salts, and thus causes the solution to become acid. Ammonium sulphate is a quick-acting fertilizer, but soils to which it is applied need extra liming to counteract the acidity which it develops. The nitrogen of organic manures is largely in the form of complex substances and is not normally absorbed as such but only after conversion to inorganic forms by bacteria. Materials such as horn and dried blood are thus used by gardeners when slow-acting fertilizers are required. Some simple organic compounds of nitrogen can be absorbed directly by plants. Urea is one of these, and is sometimes sprayed directly on the leaves of fruit trees when rapid fertilization with nitrogen is necessary.

In the plant the synthesis of nitrogenous compounds begins with the nitrogen of ammonia being brought into organic combination. This seems to be accomplished mainly in one way – by the formation of glutamic acid. The carbon skeleton for this comes from the metabolic pool in the form of α-ketoglutaric acid (see Fig. 32) and the process requires a hydrogen donor, reduced co-enzyme I:

$$\alpha\text{-ketoglutaric acid} + NH_3 + \text{CoI} \cdot H_2 \rightleftharpoons$$
$$\text{glutamic acid} + \text{CoI} \quad (22)$$

Again we may suppose that these requirements can be provided either by respiration or by photosynthesis. The central position of glutamic acid in nitrogen metabolism is shown by the rapidity with which it becomes labelled with N^{15} when ammonia labelled with this isotope is supplied to plant material. Furthermore, glutamic dehydrogenase, the enzyme catalysing its formation, seems to be of nearly universal occurrence in plants. It often happens that the amount of ammonia available to a plant is in excess of its immediate requirements. This may come about naturally, as in germinating seeds, in which reserve proteins are being broken down, as well as through liberal supply of fertilizers. Ammonia is then accumulated primarily in the form of amides, such as glutamine and asparagine, which are respectively the amino-acids glutamic and aspartic acids with an extra $-NH_2$ group attached on an acidic group:

$$COOH \cdot (CH_2)_2 \cdot CHNH_2 \cdot COOH + NH_3 \rightarrow$$
$$\text{glutamic acid} \qquad + \text{ammonia} \rightarrow$$
$$CO \cdot NH_2 \cdot (CH_2)_2 \cdot CHNH_2 \cdot COOH \qquad (23)$$
$$\text{glutamine}$$

ATP is required for the formation of these amides. Asparagine often accumulates in enormous amounts in germinating seedlings and, as its name indicates, was first discovered in the juice of asparagus shoots. As free ammonia is somewhat poisonous, amide formation may be regarded as a protective mechanism which results in the storage of nitrogen in an innocuous form readily available for synthesis.

Once glutamic acid is available, other amino-acids may be formed by the transfer of its amino-group to other carbon skeletons, a process known as transamination. Thus transfer can take place from glutamic acid to pyruvic acid, another intermediate of the metabolic pool, giving a new amino-acid, alanine, and α-ketoglutaric acid back again:

$$
\begin{array}{llllll}
COOH & CH_3 & & COOH & CH_3 & \\
| & | & & | & | & \\
(CH_2)_2 & + & C{:}O & \rightleftharpoons & (CH_2)_2 & + & CH \cdot NH_2 & (24) \\
| & | & & | & | & \\
CH \cdot NH_2 & COOH & & C{:}O & COOH & \\
| & & & | & & \\
COOH & & & COOH & & \\
\end{array}
$$

glutamic acid + pyruvic acid $\rightleftharpoons$ α-ketoglutaric acid + alanine

It seems likely that the twenty or so amino-acids required for protein synthesis are all formed in this sort of way.

The other group of nitrogen compounds important as building units for large molecules are the nitrogen bases. Not a great deal is known about the way in which they are synthesized, and details need not be considered here, but the starting materials include substances such as the amino-acids, glycine and asparagine, the carbon skeletons of which are supplied from the metabolic pool. Joined to pentose sugar and phosphate, the nitrogen bases form nucleotides, the immediate building units for nucleic acids.

Although other theories have been put forward, it is now generally accepted that proteins are built in the way one would expect – by the joining together of amino-acids, but it is clear that this does not occur by reversal of the action of protein-splitting enzymes. As will be seen from what follows, the energy required for protein synthesis is supplied by ATP in the same general way as in the synthesis of starch, but, whereas starch is composed of identical units, proteins contain as many as twenty different amino-acids. The number of different ways in which these may be arranged is enormously great, and therefore the number of possible proteins is correspondingly large. The important question now is how these units are marshalled into order to form a particular structure with specific chemical and biological properties.

This is a problem which has been tackled along two entirely different lines, genetical and biochemical, which are now beginning to converge. From the statistical laws of heredity, geneticists have concluded that inherited characters are controlled by particles, *genes*, localized in the structures known as *chromosomes* contained in the cell nucleus. In the last analysis this control must be exerted chemically through enzymes, which, as the biochemists have shown, are specific in acting on only one substance or chemical group. Beadle (1946) brought the two lines of investigation together when he put forward a theory, which is now generally accepted, that the synthesis of each enzyme is controlled by one particular gene. The best evidence for this theory has been obtained in experiments with fungi, but flower colour in the poppy (*Papaver* sp.) provides a simple example of the kind of situation that is envisaged. As in many other plants, flower colour in the poppy is due to pigments called anthocyanins and Scott-Moncrieff (1939) has shown that the difference between the pink and salmon-pink varieties is controlled by a single gene which determines the presence of one anthocyanin, derived from cyanidin, rather than another, derived from pelargonidin:

cyanidin (pink)   pelargonidin (salmon-pink)

The difference between the two varieties thus lies in the omission of a single −OH group, a change which we can feel certain is caused by a difference in a single enzyme, although this enzyme has not yet been isolated.

It is generally believed, although there are a few questioning voices (e.g. Pirie, 1960), that genes are very large molecules, *macromolecules*, of a particular kind of nucleic acid, desoxyribose nucleic acid or DNA. It does not seem, however, that DNA itself participates directly in the synthesis of enzyme protein. This is shown in a striking way by experiments with *Acetabularia*, a Mediterranean alga that is unusual in possessing only one large nucleus and in not being subdivided into cells, although it may be two or more centimetres in height, so that, as Hämmerling (1953) first showed, the nucleus may be removed or exchanged easily and with a minimum of damage. If the nucleus of a plant of *Acetabularia mediterranea* is introduced into a non-nucleated piece of the related but distinct species, *Acetabularia crenulata*, the parts which regenerate have the characteristics of *A. mediterranea*. This shows the overriding importance of the nucleus in determining specific characteristics. Yet, if the nucleus of a plant is removed and not replaced with another, growth and protein synthesis continue for some time and the new parts have all the genetical characters of the species to which the alga belongs. Since DNA is not normally found outside the nucleus, it can only be concluded that its control of protein synthesis is indirect and that substances which determine the specific character of proteins are passed from the nucleus to the rest of the protoplasm.

A great deal of evidence points to the other sort of nucleic acid, ribose nucleic acid, or RNA, which is found outside the nucleus, as having this intermediary role. In all kinds of organisms there is a close correlation between the RNA content of a tissue and the rate at which it synthesizes protein, and the protoplasmic particles called *ribosomes*, which contain most of the RNA of the cell, have been found to incorporate amino-acids faster than any other cell fraction. Furthermore, treatments which destroy RNA stop protein synthesis. Brachet (1957), for example, found that if onion root-tip cells are treated with the enzyme, ribonuclease, which breaks down RNA and which penetrates into living cells surprisingly rapidly for such a large molecule, then protein synthesis, and consequently growth and cell division, come to a stop. Protein synthesis is resumed when the ribonuclease-treated cells are supplied with an excess of RNA, RNA obtained from similar onion roots being more effective in doing this than RNA obtained from yeast.

It appears, then, that RNA may carry instructions, derived from the nuclear DNA, for protein synthesis outside the nucleus. 'DNA makes RNA and RNA makes protein' is a useful mnemonic but certainly an oversimplification; there are large gaps in the evidence – it has not yet been proved, for example, that RNA actually passes out from the nucleus into the surrounding protoplasm, as this theory would require – but a plausible biochemical mechanism for the process can now be sketched out. Protein synthesis, like other biological syntheses, begins with the activation of the building units, the amino-acids, by means of ATP:

$$\text{amino-acid} + \text{ATP} \rightarrow \text{AMP-amino-acid} + P_i \qquad (25)$$

AMP stands for adenosine monophosphate, ATP being shorn of two of its phosphate groups in this reaction. The activated amino-acid becomes combined with soluble RNA, and this RNA-amino-acid compound is then incorporated into the RNA of the ribosomes. It seems that it is at this stage that the arrangement of the different amino-acids into the pattern required for a specific protein is brought about. How this is done is still obscure, but the RNA of the ribosomes perhaps acts as a template, that is, it acts as a sort of mould, impressing a complementary pattern among the

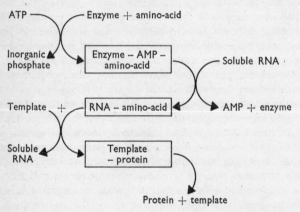

Fig. 33. Simplified scheme for the mechanism of protein synthesis.

molecules which assemble on it. RNA usually consists of only four kinds of nucleotide units, but the various combinations of these are quite sufficient to carry the information required for determining the sequences of amino-acids in all kinds of proteins. Combination of the amino-acids presumably takes place on the template and involves the splitting off of the soluble RNA so that the completed protein chain is freed (Fig. 33).

It can be imagined that the specific pattern of each RNA macro-molecule is acquired during its formation on a DNA template in the nucleus. There remains the problem of how the specific structure of the DNA itself is replicated. Clearly there cannot be an endless series of substances acting as templates. The difficulty is avoided if DNA is supposed to be self-replicating, and how this might occur has been suggested by Watson and Crick (1958). Their theory depends on the DNA molecule consisting of two matching chains of nucleotides lying side by side. This structure could replicate itself by splitting longitudinally to give two complementary, not identical, halves, each of which then acts as a template on which its matching chain is assembled to complete the double-stranded molecule.

We have now seen how the various types of plant substances – sugars, polysaccharides, fats, amino-acids, proteins, and nucleic acids – are put together. The general direction of these synthetic processes ultimately lies with the genes, which, apart from the comparatively rare event of mutation, are reproduced unchanged from generation to generation. Nevertheless, the metabolism of a plant does not follow a rigidly determined pattern, but varies between rather wide limits. A good deal of this variation is, of course, attributable to the shuffling of the genes which occurs during sexual reproduction, a matter which lies outside the province of plant physiology. Nurture, however, has effects as important as those of nature, and much variation in metabolic pattern occurs in response to changes both in the external and internal environments of a plant. These are matters to which we will return later.

Finally, in this chapter something should be said about salt absorption. The complexity and importance of the organic metabolism of plants must not cause us to overlook the inorganic components, which, as we have already seen, are invariably present in plants and, indeed, are essential for their growth. Some of this mineral matter is in life incorporated into organic molecules – many enzyme molecules, e.g. nitrate reductase (p. 136), and chlorophyll itself (Fig. 29) contain one or more atoms of a metal, a fact which explains the essentiality of traces of these metals for growth. However, much of the mineral fraction exists in inorganic form in the living plant, that is to say as ions moving more or less freely within the protoplasm or vacuole rather than as atoms rigidly built into molecular structures.

The concentration of ions in cells often exceeds that in the solution which surrounds them, so that accumulation has taken place *against* the concentration gradient. How this comes about presents a major problem. Certainly salts do not get into plant cells along with water 'by osmosis'; as was explained in Chapter 3, the entry of water into a cell by osmosis depends on the independent diffusion of its molecules and those of substances dissolved in it. Furthermore, cell sap is not simply a concentrate of the solution outside, as a marked selective accumulation of some ions occurs while others are excluded from the cell. For example, the concentration of sodium ions in sea-water is about forty times that of potassium ions, yet in the sap of seaweeds the potassium ion may be as much as six times as concentrated as that of sodium. It is not necessarily the elements which are essential for growth which are thus concentrated. Some plants accumulate elements which are of no apparent use to them – a chickweed, *Holosteum umbellatum*, when growing on soils rich in mercury salts, accumulates these and actually shows droplets of metallic mercury within its cells (Rankama and Sahama, 1950), but it seems highly improbable that this is of any vital importance to the plant. This property of certain plants to accumulate particular elements is made use of in the geobotanical method of prospecting for minerals.

What is clear is that the accumulation of mineral ions is very much bound up with the metabolic processes that we have just been discussing; in particular, it is more rapid the greater the rate of respiration. This is shown very well by the behaviour of the tissue of potato tuber, discs of which are a favourite material for the study of salt uptake. When freshly cut these discs have a low rate of respiration and a low rate of salt intake. However, if they are kept in well-aerated water the starch with which the cells are packed begins to disappear, the respiration rate increases, and at the same time rapid uptake of inorganic ions begins. This rapid

Leaf mosaic: the leaves are arranged with a minimum of overlap and intercept the maximum amount of light. Lower branches of beech (*Fagus sylvatica*).

1

Leaf mosaic: the leaves of *Fatsia japonica.*

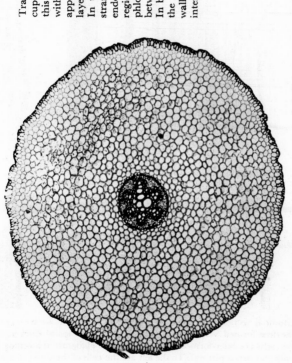

Transverse section of a buttercup (*Ranunculus acris*) root. In this older root the epidermis with its root hairs has disappeared and the outermost layer is the protective exodermis. In the centre is the vascular strand, surrounded by the endodermis; the star-shaped region is the xylem and the phloem occupies the bays in between the points of the star. In between the exodermis and the vascular strand is a thin-walled tissue with abundant intercellular air spaces (× 50).

Longitudinal section through the xylem of *Dahlia* stem. In the centre are the first-formed vessels, with simple annular or spiral thickening. To the right are later-formed vessels with more elaborate thickening of the walls (bordered pitting). To the left are the cells of the pith (× 250).

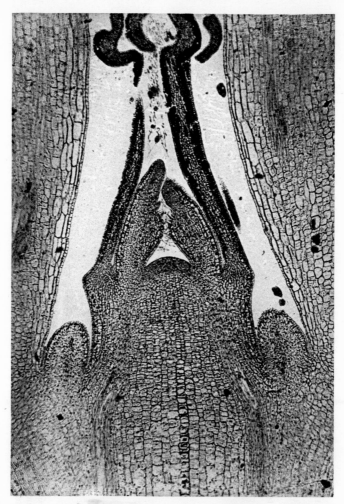

The stem apex of sycamore (*Acer pseudoplatanus*) in median longitudinal section. There are two leaves on each side and in the axils of the lower leaves rudiments of axillary buds are to be seen (× 110).

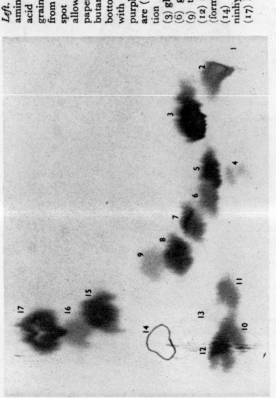

Left. Two-dimensional chromatogram of amino-acids obtained by breakdown with acid of protein (glutenin) from wheat grains. The amino-acids were separated from the mixture, initially placed in a spot in the right-hand bottom corner, by allowing a phenol solution to pass along the paper from right to left followed by a butanol-acetic acid-water mixture from bottom to top, and shown up by spraying with ninhydrin, with which they give a purple colour reaction. The amino-acids are (1) cysteic acid (formed by air oxidation of cyst(e)ine), (2) aspartic acid, (3) glutamic acid, (4) cyst(e)ine, (5) serine, (6) glycine, (7) threonine, (8) alanine, (9) tyrosine, (10) lysine, (11) histidine, (12) arginine, (13) methionine sulphoxide (formed by air oxidation of methionine), (14) proline (gives yellow colour with ninhydrin), (15) valine, (16) phenylalanine, (17) leucine and isoleucine.

Below. Electron micrograph of part of a bean chloroplast, showing lamellate regions (grana) in a stroma with relatively sparse lamellae and three spaces occupied by starch. At the top of the picture a thin layer of protoplasm is present between the chloroplast and a vacuole (× 70,000).

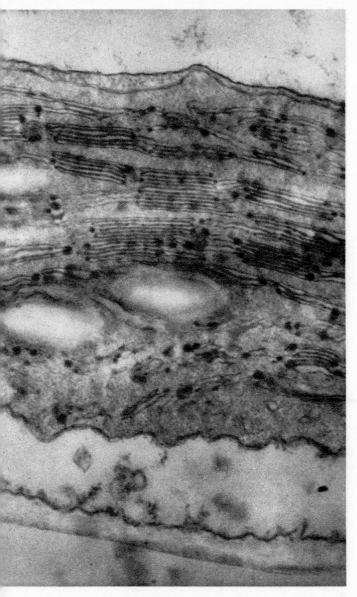

7

Radioautographs of leaves from bean plants (*Phaseolus vulgaris*) which have absorbed phosphate labelled with the radioactive isotope, P³². The leaves were left in contact with photographic film, which became blackened by radiation from the radio-isotope. In these prints the whitest parts are those with most P³². After a short absorption period with labelled phosphate, the radioactivity is fairly uniformly distributed between leaves but concentrated in their veins.

Leaves from the same plant after it had been a further twenty-four hours in a phosphate-free solution; there has been considerable accumulation of radioactivity in the young leaf and bud.

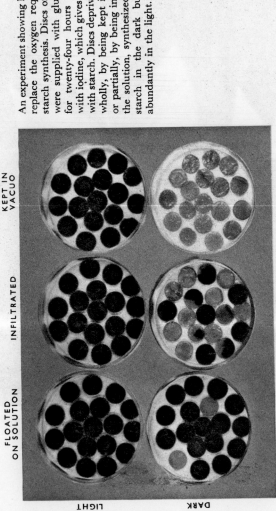

An experiment showing how light can replace the oxygen requirement for starch synthesis. Discs of tobacco leaf were supplied with glucose solution for twenty-four hours then treated with iodine, which gives a blue colour with starch. Discs deprived of oxygen, wholly, by being kept in a vacuum, or partially, by being infiltrated with the solution, synthesized no or little starch in the dark but formed it abundantly in the light.

FLOATED ON SOLUTION   INFILTRATED   KEPT IN VACUO

LIGHT

DARK

Tests made by Went's split pea-stem method of the growth-regulating activities of a series of ω(4-chloro-phenoxy) alkylcarboxylic acids. The two parts of the split stem bend out-wards as a result of the release of tissue tensions but bend inwards again if treated with substances having auxin-activity. Substances having an even number of carbon atoms in the side chain (acetic (A), butyric (B), caproic (C), and octanoic (O)) have given positive reactions in these tests, whereas those with an odd number (propionic (P), valeric (V), and heptanoic (H)) were inactive. x = control plant.

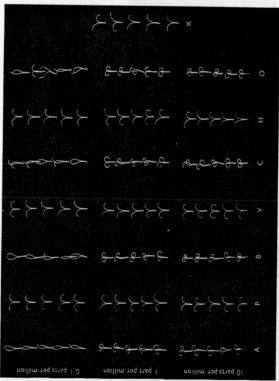

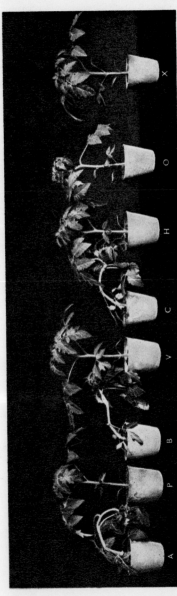

Above. Tomato-leaf epinasty tests on the same series of compounds as in Plate 11. The substances are applied in lanolin paste in the axils of the leaves. Again, those substances having an even number of carbon atoms in the side chain have given a positive reaction, i.e. downward bending of the leaves (epinasty). x = control plant.

Below. Effects of a series of 2-methyl-4-chlorophenoxycarboxylic acids on nettle (*Urtica urens*) two weeks after treatment. The acetic (A), butyric (B), and caproic (C) derivatives have killed the plants, whereas the propionic (P), valeric (V), and heptanoic (H) derivatives, having an odd number of carbon atoms in the side chain, were without effect. x = control plant.

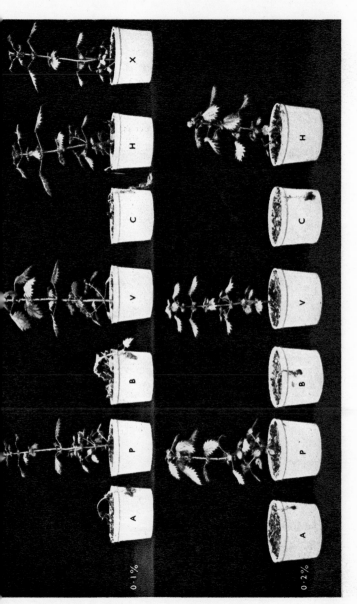

0.1%

0.2%

Effects of gibberellic acid on sweet pea (*Lathyrus odoratus*) var. Cupid; right-hand plants untreated, left-hand plants treated weekly with 1µ-gram of gibberellic acid per plant.

Effects of gibberellic acid on henbane (*Hyoscyamus niger*) biennial strain; left-hand plant untreated, right-hand plant treated.

Left. The effect of gibberellic acid on dwarf bean (*Phaseolus vulgaris*) var. Masterpiece. The plant on the left was untreated, that in the centre was given a small dose of gibberellic acid,'and that on the right a larger dose.

Below. Venus's fly-trap (*Dionaea muscipula*). Some of the traps have been stimulated and are closed.

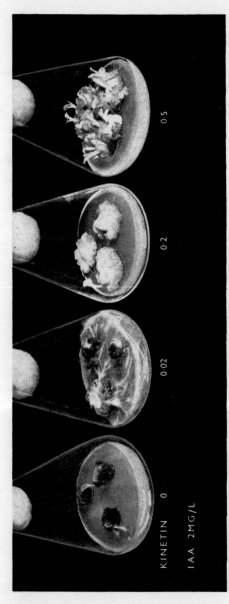

KINETIN   0   0·02   0·2   0·5

IAA 2 MG/L

Above. Effects of kinetin concentration on growth and organ formation in cultures of tobacco callus tissue in the presence of auxin (IAA). Cultures forty-four days old; that second from the left shows vigorous root formation, that on the right is producing shoots.

Below. Interaction of kinetin and auxin effects on growth and organ formation in tobacco callus tissue cultured in a medium supplemented with casein hydrolysate.

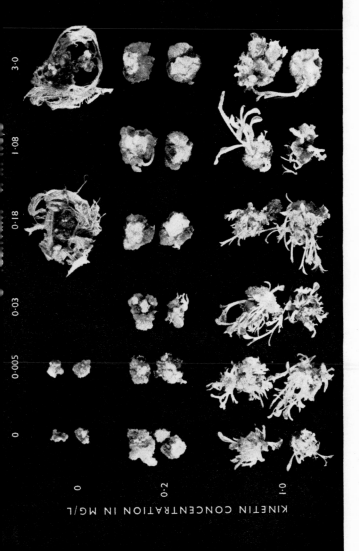

KINETIN CONCENTRATION IN MG/L

0   0·005   0·03   0·18   1·08   3·0

0

0·2

1·0

The sensitive plant, *Mimosa pudica*, unstimulated.

Mimosa pudica stimulated.

Above. A short-day plant, *Chrysanthemum.* Flowering in these out-door plants has been accelerated in the middle clump by covering it for part of each day with a box.

Left. A long-day plant, the orange hawkweed (*Hieracium aurantiacum*). The plant on the right has been given long-day treatment and is flowering; the other, which is of the same age, has been kept under short days and, although healthy, is strikingly modified.

23

Translocation of synthetic auxin and other weed-killers in *Zebrina*. Drops of solution containing the substances labelled with radiocarbon, C^{14}, were applied to leaves as indicated in the lower row of photographs. After four days the plants were freeze-dried and radio-autographs (upper row of photographs) made. The intensity of blackening is a measure of the concentration of the radiocarbon. Translocation which evidently follows the same paths as those for carbohydrates produced by photosynthesis, was least for 2,4-D (left), greater for aminotriazole (centre), and greatest for maleic hydrazide (right).

uptake is dependent on aerobic respiration, and if this is prevented by depriving the tissue of oxygen or by poisoning the uptake ceases. It is possible to inhibit salt uptake without stopping respiration, but impossible to inhibit respiration without stopping salt uptake.

In part, the accumulation of inorganic ions in a cell may be simply the result of the production of organic ions in a structure from which they cannot escape but into which inorganic ions can freely pass. For example, organic acids are produced in respiration as negatively charged ions accompanied by an equal number of positively charged hydrogen ions. The hydrogen ions can escape from the protoplasm provided that electrical neutrality is maintained by the entry of an equal number of similarly charged ions, which need not, however, be chemically the same, but which might be, for example, sodium or potassium ions. In this way, as a result of the production of ionized organic molecules, a cell can accumulate inorganic ions. Proteins are substances having both positive ($-NH_4^+$) and negative ($-COO^-$) ionizing groups, and thus both negative and positive inorganic ions may be collected by them. This type of salt absorption is, in fact, closely linked to protein synthesis, and predominates in actively dividing cells (Steward and Millar, 1954). This cannot be the only mechanism, though, because a tissue may go on taking in inorganic ions even though the amount of protoplasm in it is not increasing.

It should now be made clear that salts are accumulated more in the vacuole of the cell than in the protoplasm itself. The outer membrane of the protoplasm seems to be freely permeable to most inorganic ions, so that exchange between ions in part of the protoplast, the so-called 'free space', and those in the external solution can take place. This exchange does not necessarily involve changes in concentration; if one ion goes in, another with the same electric charge must come out. However, somewhere in the cell there is a barrier to this free coming and going of ions. This barrier is presumably the membrane which surrounds the vacuole. Some mechanism exists by which ions can be pushed through this barrier using energy supplied by respiration. Once the ions are inside the vacuole they cannot get out, and so accumulate as the process goes on. This type of salt accumulation is characteristic of cells which have ceased dividing and which are enlarging and forming vacuoles.

It is still very uncertain what the mechanism is by which salts are moved across the permeability barrier into the vacuole. One possible explanation that may be given as a sample of the several that have been put forward is that entry is brought about by the operation of a carrier substance (James, 1953). Suppose that the salt, AB, being taken up yields ions, A^- and B^+, which can both freely diffuse into the protoplasm, but of which B^+ is unable to penetrate through the vacuole membrane, whereas A^- can. B^+, we further suppose, is able to combine with a carrier substance, X, to form a compound, BX, which can penetrate the vacuole membrane, but which, having done so, immediately breaks down, giving B^+ and X again. X may then be able to return into the protoplasm, leaving the ion, B^+, behind in the vacuole, and, since electrical neutrality must be maintained, A^-, or some other negative ion, must stay with it. To account for the dependence on respiration, it may be supposed that the substance X is produced only during active metabolism – it might very well be, for instance, a respiratory intermediate able to combine with a phosphate ion to form an organic phosphate, or an intermediate in protein synthesis.

PART II

THE GROWTH OF PARTS

. . . the Caterpillar took the hookah out of its mouth and yawned once or twice, and shook itself. Then it got down off the mushroom and crawled away into the grass, merely remarking as it went, 'One side will make you grow taller, and the other side will make you grow shorter.'

LEWIS CARROLL
(*Alice in Wonderland*)

CHAPTER 6

Growth and Differentiation of Cells and Tissues

It is one thing to know how plants increase their substance by synthesis of organic matter and quite another to understand how this stuff is organized during growth into protoplasm, cells, and tissues.

We can be certain that a mixture of all the necessary substances in the right proportions would not sort itself out and become a plant. Nevertheless, many of the structures to be found in plants and animals can be accounted for in terms of simple physical principles, as was shown by D'Arcy Thompson (1917) in his classic work *Growth and Form*, and it is an article of faith with present-day physiologists that all aspects of growth can be explained along similar lines. Given the special physical and chemical environment in which it is placed in a living cell, the behaviour of a particular kind of molecule in building a particular kind of structure can, no doubt, always be accounted for in purely physical terms. The real problems are on a different plane; we need to understand more about the co-ordination and organization that provides the special environments which ensure that newly synthesized material falls into place.

The problem of how the structures found in living organisms are produced begins on the molecular level. For example, the long peptide chains of proteins do not just waggle and drift shapelessly, but are folded in special ways, and if they become unfolded (a process called *denaturation*) their enzymic properties disappear. A detailed study of the shape of haemoglobin and the related protein, myoglobin, by X-ray analysis (Perutz, Kendrew, and others, 1960) has shown that the manner of this folding is characteristic and constant, but it is concluded that it is assumed spontaneously as a result of the attractions and repulsions between different parts of the molecule, depending on the particular amino-acid sequences in the peptide chain. On the next plane, in which molecules are arranged into the sheets, fibres, and granules which can be discerned in protoplasm under the highest powers of the electron microscope (see Plate 7), it seems likely that the patterns arise in a similar way through the mutual attraction and repulsions existing between the individual molecules.

Thus, in a vague way which will call for an enormous amount of refined biophysical research if it is to be given precision, we can see how protoplasmic structures such as chloroplasts, mitochondria, chromosomes, and membranes might be formed by processes not greatly different from those which produce crystallization in a non-living material. Beyond this point we come to the realm of observations, few of which can be fitted into a coherent physico-chemical theory of growth. We saw in Chapter 1 that cell division, cell extension, and cell differentiation are separated to some extent in the plant, so that we may in the first place reasonably consider what is known under these three headings.

Increase in amount of protoplasm normally leads to cell division, an occurrence which may be related to the need for keeping the surface area of the protoplast high in relation to its bulk (see p. 48). If it is to continue to live, a cell must have a set of the necessary parts: nucleus, mitochondria, microsomes, plastids, membranes, and so on. In general, it seems that these parts cannot be produced afresh if they are altogether missing, so that cell division should be preceded by their multiplication or extension and result in the sharing of them between the daughter cells if these are to be replicas of their parent. Normally, the multiplication of cell components is well co-ordinated, but sometimes it is not. If the alga, *Euglena*, is grown at the rather high temperature of 34° C. the cells divide but the chloroplasts are damaged and unable to do so, so that colourless cells result which are incapable of giving rise to green cells again and which can survive only if provided with suitable organic foodstuffs (Pringsheim and Pringsheim, 1952). On the other hand chloroplasts or mitochondria may multiply without causing the cell containing them to divide, and in several different kinds of plant nuclear division has been observed to take place naturally without accompanying division of the whole cell. Nuclear division without cell division can also be induced artificially, for example, in pith tissue from tobacco plants by chemical treatment (Naylor, Sander, and Skoog, 1954). It appears from evidence such as this that there is no one key structure which determines cell division.

It is not an easy matter to find out whether the division of a cell is dependent on any special metabolic processes. It is possible to make certain measurements on single cells, but most biochemical techniques demand a great deal more material than this. If many cells are used, then they are likely to be out of step, so that any measurements which are made on them represent an average for cells in all stages, and it is difficult to distinguish any peculiarities related to the division process itself. There are ways out of this difficulty; one may use a tissue, such as that which gives rise to the pollen in a flower, in which cell divisions take place more or less simultaneously, or one may synchronize cell divisions by some artificial means. Perhaps the most detailed studies have been made by Japanese plant physiologists led by H. Tamiya (1952 onwards), using the alga

Chlorella, in which cell divisions can be brought into step by regulation of light and dark periods.

In contrast to the small cells newly produced by division, which are very active in photosynthesis but which respire at a relatively low rate, the large cells ripe to divide have a high rate of respiration. The rate of photosynthesis of this latter type of cell is low, but nevertheless they show marked activity in photosynthetic phosphorylation. Evidently the demand prior to division is not for carbon compounds but for high-energy phosphates, which, it will be recalled, are equally effectively produced by respiration or photosynthetic phosphorylation. During the growth of a cell to the state in which it is ready to divide, the amounts of protein and RNA increase uniformly, but it is only just prior to division that the DNA increases – the increased demand for high-energy phosphate is perhaps related to this. The increase in DNA is strictly proportional to the number of daughter cells formed – in accord with the idea that there is a constant amount of DNA in each nucleus. As already mentioned above, division of nucleus and cell are not necessarily tied together, and in synchronized cultures of *Chlorella* it has proved possible to separate the two by controlling the supply of sulphur and nitrogen compounds to sulphur-starved cells. It cannot yet be said whether cell division in other plants can be influenced in a similar way, but the general picture of changes in respiration and DNA synthesis probably applies generally. In other organisms it has been noticed that the increase in respiration prior to division is followed by a fall to a low rate during the process of division itself – its energy requirements are anticipated by the processes which go before it.

Various inhibitors, both natural and artificial, specific for various phases of cell division are known. Their use has not yet led to any great insight into the mechanism of the process, but some of them are of practical value, e.g. the efficacy as weed-killers of the class of compounds known as substituted carbamates evidently depends on their ability to dislocate cell division.

In an active meristem all conditions necessary for division are provided, but something, not necessarily a simple lack of food materials, must restrict division in other parts of the plant. The presence of substances which in minute amounts stimulate division may be necessary as well as major nutrients. When pieces of mature tissue are cut from a plant and placed in a solution containing sugar and all the necessary elements, division takes place slowly, if at all, unless certain stimulatory substances are provided as well. For example, the cells of small pieces of tissue from the phloem of carrot root can be stimulated into active division by small quantities of the milk of coconuts (*Cocos nucifera*), as shown by Steward and Caplin (1954). Analysis of this 'milk', the normal function of which is to provide the nutritive material for the growth of the coconut embryo, shows that it contains at least six substances active in promoting cell division. Examination of other plant fluids and extracts also suggests the existence of a whole complex of such growth substances. One of the best characterized of these is kinetin, identified chemically as 6-furfuryl-aminopurine, which has been isolated by Skoog and his collaborators (Jablonski *et al.*, 1954; Miller *et al.*, 1955) as an outcome of their work on the growth of pith cells from tobacco (see Plate 18). It is clear that there is no single substance acting as the key to cell division but, by enabling isolated cells and tissues of flowering plants to be grown in laboratory culture, studies of this sort are undoubtedly helping us to understand more of the complexities of growth. Finally, as a reminder that the distinction between cell division and cell enlargement which has been adopted is an arbitrary one, it may be mentioned that cells from potato tubers are not stimulated to divide by coconut milk unless traces of synthetic auxin, which, as will be described below, is active in promoting cell extension, are supplied as well. One explanation of this is that an inhibitor of the action of the coconut-milk factors, which has been shown to be present in the potato tuber, is neutralized by the auxin (Steward and Caplin, 1954).

In the process of extension, cells commonly undergo a

twenty-fold or so increase in volume. This is sometimes represented as being little more than a distension with water. It is true that actively dividing cells contain little cell sap, whereas those which have increased in size contain conspicuous vacuoles, but there are undoubtedly increases in the solid cell materials as well. The rate of respiration in the region of extension of a root is actually greater than that in the meristem, and it has been shown that active synthesis of proteins and other protoplasmic constituents goes on during expansion. However, cell-wall material is the main product of synthesis at this stage. The wall of a cell newly produced by division is a delicate affair of interwoven micro-fibrils of cellulose. This is passively stretched during extension, new networks of fibrils being deposited where it yields and tears (Frey Wyssling, 1957). Cell extension thus requires conditions suitable for active metabolism and adequate supplies of raw materials. However, study of the process has been dominated by the discovery of substances of which minute amounts have remarkable effects on the growth of plants.

The ground for the discovery of these substances was prepared by Charles Darwin, who carried out experiments on the bending of plant organs towards light and found that the stimulus might be perceived in one region and the response be shown in another. The 'influence' transmitted from the stimulated part to the responding part was found by later investigators to be able to pass a cut in the living tissues, a fact which led Boysen-Jensen (1911) to suggest that the transmission had a chemical basis. The means for the isolation and identification of the substances concerned was provided by F. W. Went in 1926. Went followed previous workers in using the *coleoptile* of seedling oats, *Avena sativa*, as a test object. The coleoptile is the tubular first leaf which sheaths the subsequent ones (Fig. 34), its great advantage for this sort of work being that its growth from 1 centimetre to the final length of 5–7 centimetres, which is reached if it is kept in the dark, is accomplished almost without cell division and entirely by cell extension. This extension is stopped, for a while at least, if the tip of the coleoptile is cut off, and it is renewed when it is replaced. Replacing the tip eccentrically results in more extension on the side immediately under the tip than elsewhere, so that after a few hours the coleoptile becomes bent. Went found that, if the coleoptile tip was allowed to stand on gelatine, this acquired the growth-promoting property and produced similar effects to the tip when put on the coleoptile stump, plain

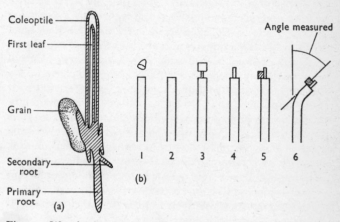

Fig. 34. Went's *Avena* coleoptile method for the assay of auxin. (a) *Avena* seedling in vertical section (diagrammatic, × about 3). (b) the sequence of operations; 1 and 2, decapitation of the coleoptile; 3 and 4, second decapitation, removing any auxin formed after the first decapitation and exposing the first foliage leaf; 5, agar block, containing the auxin to be assayed, placed in position; 6, the curvature produced is measured.

gelatine having no such effect. These effects could be interpreted in terms of a substance produced in the tip which passes longitudinally down the coleoptile and stimulates the extension of the tissues below.

This much was little more than an elegant confirmation of the conclusions of earlier workers; Went's great contribution was to base a method for the measurement of the amount of the growth-promoting substance on these results.

By allowing the substance present in one gelatine block to diffuse into other gelatine blocks he was able to obtain it in various known dilutions and to show that the bending (measured as an angle, see Fig. 34) produced when the block was placed eccentrically on a decapitated coleoptile was proportional to the amount of the substance. This opened the way for the identification of the substance, because this means of measuring its amount by *biological assay* enabled rich sources to be found and techniques for its purification to be worked out. Subsequently other methods have been devised (see Plates 11 and 12 for example), but Went's original technique is still extensively used for the assay of the growth substance.

Using 150 litres of human urine as starting material, Kögl and Haagen-Smit (1931) were able to obtain 40 milligrams of a substance, extremely active in the *Avena* test, which was chemically characterized and given the name of auxin A. Later they found other active substances, auxin B and heteroauxin. Some mystery now shrouds auxins A and B, recent attempts to find them again having proved unsuccessful. Heteroauxin, now usually called auxin, turned out to be a relatively simple substance, β-indolyl-acetic acid (often abbreviated to IAA):

This substance had been known to chemists for many years without having been suspected of possessing biological activity. It is now thought to be the most important of the natural substances active in the *Avena* test, although examination of natural materials by the method of paper chromatography suggests that a plethora of substances having similar effects exists.

As will be seen later, auxins have a variety of different effects on plants, being concerned, among other things, in initiation of root growth, bud inhibition, and leaf fall. For the moment, however, we are concerned with their most characteristic action, that of regulating extension growth. Extremely minute amounts are effective in doing this. As the concentration is increased the rate of extension of coleoptiles and stems increases until a maximum is reached between 1 and 10 parts of auxin per million of the medium applied. Higher concentrations result in lower rates and, if over about 100 parts per million, actually retard extension (Fig. 35). At first it seemed that growth in length of roots was accomplished by a different mechanism, for removal of its tip results in no marked slowing down of the extension of a root, sometimes even stimulating it, and application of auxin or coleoptile tips to a decapitated root inhibits its growth. However, the situation seems to be that auxins, perhaps not identical with those in stems, *are* necessary for the extension of roots, but these are much more sensitive, the whole sequence of reactions being shifted to a range of concentrations about 1/100,000 of those producing corresponding effects on stems (Fig. 35). These concentrations are of auxin applied externally, which are not, of course, necessarily the same as those inside the cells which are affected. It may be imagined that the regulation of the concentration of auxin within the cells is one of the master controls for growth. The concentration of free auxins, even in tissues such as those of the tip of the *Avena* coleoptile, is extremely low, but much larger amounts seem to be bound in the cells and to be extractable only by rather drastic procedures. Perhaps these bound forms are inactive in promoting growth. The auxin produced by the tip of a growing organ is evidently produced there from inactive precursors brought from elsewhere, e.g. the seed in the case of the *Avena* coleoptile.

The regulation of the transformation of precursor into active auxin is obviously of importance for the control of growth within a plant. Another decisive controlling factor is the transport of the auxin from the place where it is produced to that where it exerts its effects. A curious thing is that this transport is one-directional in young actively growing organs such as the coleoptile. This has been demonstrated using pieces of coleoptile with an agar block (agar has now replaced gelatine for making gels for auxin work) containing auxin at one end and a plain block at the other. If the auxin-containing block is applied to what was the tip-end of the piece of coleoptile, auxin is moved from it into the block at the other end at a rate much faster than can be accounted for in terms of simple diffusion. If the experiment

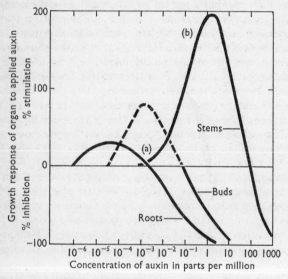

Fig. 35. The relations of the growth responses of roots, buds, and stems to concentration of externally applied auxin. (After Audus, 1959.)

is tried with the auxin in the block applied to the end of the coleoptile originally farthest from the tip no movement of auxin into the other block takes place at all. This one-way transport takes place regardless of which way up the piece of coleoptile is in relation to gravity, and evidently depends on some inherent asymmetry in the protoplasm of the coleoptile itself. The nature of this asymmetry is still a mystery, but it needs energy to maintain, for it disappears if respiration is reduced by lack of oxygen or by poisons. In growing roots auxin seems to move freely in either direction, and in mature tissues it travels, along with food materials, in the phloem (see p. 191). Reactions consuming or destroying auxin must also be important in controlling its effect on growth. An enzyme system inactivating auxin has been found in plant tissues, and may play a part in determining the growth habit of some plants. Thus the tissues of a dwarf variety of maize have a low auxin content relative to that of varieties of normal size, which seems to be the result of a higher capacity for auxin inactivation. There are, however, other causes of dwarfness (see p. 162).

Although auxins have now been known for many years, we still do not know what the basic mechanism is by which their effects are produced. Auxin has been found to bring about a multitude of changes in the cells responding to it, but none of these has been shown to be directly connected with the growth which results. One striking effect is that the cell wall is made more plastic, and a popular theory has been that the cell extension results from the water intake, which as reference back to equation 2 on p. 66 will show, should follow from reduction in turgor pressure if the wall becomes more easily stretched. However, this theory is certainly too simple, and other effects of auxin, as for example in increasing respiration rate and altering nucleic acid metabolism, may be of no less importance (see p. 216). It has even proved difficult to establish what particular characteristics of the auxin molecule are necessary for its action. By examining the activities of a range of substances which the chemist can derive from a biologically active compound by altering parts of its molecule one at a time, it is often possible to establish which of its chemical groups are directly concerned in the reaction by which the biological effects are brought about. However, besides the naturally occurring β-indolylacetic acid, a great number of substances synthesized in the laboratory has been found to have similar effects on plants, and these artificial auxins show such a bewildering variety of structure that the only generalization that can be made is that they are mostly weak acids with molecules containing a ring of carbon atoms, some of which are joined by double bonds.

The mystery which still shrouds the mechanism of auxin action has not prevented these substances becoming one of the most practically useful of the discoveries of plant physiology. As will be seen later, auxins and substances having similar effects can be used to control many different phases of plant growth and development, but while extension growth is being considered, it is perhaps appropriate to say something in particular about the use of these substances as weed-killers.

It is a general feature of auxin action that at concentrations which are still relatively low, growth is inhibited instead of stimulated (Fig. 35). Too much auxin evidently jams the machinery of growth, and the ensuing disorganization of the delicate balance of growth processes, if sufficiently severe and prolonged, results in the death of the plant. Plants treated with excess of auxin take a week or two to die and first become distorted, with twisted leaves and split stems, making an unpleasant sight for anyone who cares for plants. Of course, many chemicals if applied in sufficiently high concentration are poisonous to plants and can be used as weed-killers. The special merits of auxin-like substances as weed-killers are that they are effective in low concentrations, relatively harmless to animals and humans, and noncorrosive, that they may be translocated, and thus reach and kill parts not directly accessible to sprays, and, above all, that some of them are selective and can be used to kill weeds without damage to the crop among which they are growing. Auxin-type weed-killers enable a farmer to eradicate completely a weed such as charlock, *Sinapis arvensis*, without damage to a cereal crop, or a gardener to get rid of daisies, *Bellis perennis*, and plantains, *Plantago* spp., from his lawns without harming the grasses, or to kill bindweed, *Convolvulus arvensis*, without the labour of digging up and destroying its underground rhizome system.

Selective action depends on many things. One is that susceptible plants often have broad leaves, spread horizontally, which retain weed-killer solution sprayed on them, while resistant plants usually have narrow, erect leaves which shed the spray droplets. In addition, the epidermis of some plants is less readily penetrated by toxic materials than is that of others. As a result, sulphuric acid, which is equally damaging to the actual tissues of both kinds of plant, shows a fair degree of selective killing of, for example, charlock in wheat. However, on top of this, there appear to be inherent differences in the susceptibility of the protoplasm of different plants to the poisonous effects of the synthetic auxins and, speaking very generally, that of dicotyledons is affected adversely at concentrations much lower than those needed to poison that of monocotyledons. It is fortunate that many of the more pestilential weeds happen to be dicotyledons and that monocotyledons such as the cereals and grasses make such valuable crop plants. The effects of synthetic auxins on plants varies according to weather conditions, both before and after spraying, soil conditions, fertilizer applications, and the stage of growth, as well as on the species (Fig. 36). Their use may therefore call for a certain amount of scientific supervision.

The synthetic auxins which have proved most useful in weed-control are 2,4-dichlorophenoxyacetic acid (2,4-D), 2-methyl-4-chlorophenoxyacetic acid (MCPA), and 2,4,5-trichlorophenoxyacetic acid (2,4,5-T); auxin itself is relatively ineffective as a weed-killer and has not been used in practice. Certain non-auxin weed-killers, e.g. the substituted carbamates mentioned on p. 150, having a selective action complementary to that of the synthetic auxins, can, to a certain extent, be used for controlling the growth of grasses in broad-leaved crops. It does not seem too sanguine to expect that ultimately substances will be found for eradicating even the toughest weeds among sensitive vegetable crops. Particularly striking investigations to this end have been carried out by Wain and his colleagues (1954 onwards). The substances studied have been the ω-phenoxy-alkylcarboxylic acids, which have a ring nucleus to which is attached a fatty acid side chain. This side chain is broken down in the plant by β-oxidation (p. 133) and, if it contains

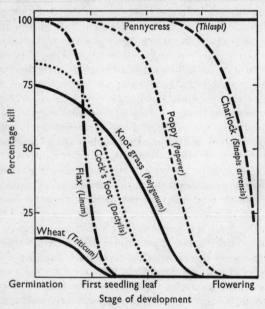

Fig. 36. The relation of sensitivity to the weedkiller 2-methyl-4-chlorophenoxyacetic acid (MCPA), applied as a 0·2 per cent spray, to stage of development for a number of crop plants and weeds. (After Blackman, Holly, and Roberts, 1949.)

an odd number of carbons, will be removed entirely, leaving a residue which has no auxin activity:

If, however, the side chain has an even number of carbon atoms, the residue will be a phenoxyacetic acid which is active as an auxin:

$$O \cdot CH_2 \cdot CH_2 \cdot CH_2 \cdot COOH \qquad O \cdot CH_2 \cdot COOH$$

$$\rightarrow$$

Cl   Cl

If β-oxidation takes place, plants treated with a series of these compounds will consequently show growth reactions to those with even numbers of carbons in the side chain and be unaffected by the others (Plates 11, 12, and 13). The ability of a particular species to carry out β-oxidation of these compounds depends on the nature of the ring system, so that if a ring system is chosen which prevents β-oxidation in a particular crop species but not in the weeds which grow with it, these can be killed without damage to the crop if the side chain has an even number of carbons in it. In this way it is possible to kill annual nettle (*Urtica urens*, Plate 13) and creeping thistle (*Cirsium arvense*) growing in celery (*Apium dulce*) crops by spraying with ω-(2,4-dichlorophenoxy)-butyric acid, having a 4-carbon chain, because this compound, which has no appreciable auxin activity itself, is not changed to the toxic acetic derivative by the celery plant.

Apart from the natural and synthetic auxins, there are other substances, the gibberellins, which also stimulate cell extension but which seem rather different in certain respects from auxins. The discovery of these arose from studies made by the Japanese worker Kurosawa (1926) of a disease of rice caused by the fungus *Gibberella fujikuroi* (now known as *Fusarium moniliforme*). The characteristic symptom of this disease is that the plants become tall and thin, overgrowing their healthy neighbours, hence the name 'bakanae', which means 'foolish seedling', given to it. Specific substances having a considerable accelerating effect on the growth of seedling stems were eventually isolated from the fungus (Yabuta and Sumiki, 1938). These, and substances obtained from other sources but having similar effects, have been called gibberellins. They accelerate extension growth in organs such as shoots and coleoptiles when applied in concentrations of the order of 1 part per million, but differ from auxins in not stimulating the growth of roots, in not being translocated in a polar fashion, and in lacking other growth-regulating properties of auxins which will be described later. Gibberellin-like substances are now known to be widely distributed in flowering plants, and thus appear to be important in controlling growth in normal healthy plants.

The following structure has been proposed for gibberellin A_3:

Other gibberellins have structures closely related to this. It will be noticed that, like auxins, they are weak acids and have a ring system containing double bonds. Again, we do not yet know on what particular chemical interaction their activity depends, but their effect seems to be bound up with that of auxin. Thus, while the growth of stems in intact dwarf peas is greatly accelerated by application of gibberellic acid, pieces of stem cut from these plants show no response to gibberellic acid unless auxin is supplied as well (Brian and Hemming, 1957, 1958). Other evidence points to the same conclusion.

It seems that plants normally produce sufficient gibberellin-like substances to ensure maximum growth and that most dwarf varieties are dwarf because they are short of these substances (the dwarfness in maize depending on low auxin content mentioned on p. 157 is perhaps exceptional). A spectacular demonstration of this is the changing of the dwarf bean (*Phaseolus vulgaris* variety) into a climbing bean by application of gibberellic acid (Bukovac *et al.*, 1956; see

Plates 14, 15, and 16). Plants such as cabbage (*Brassica oleracea*), lettuce (*Lactuca sativa*), and henbane (*Hyoscyamus niger*), which have first a rosette of leaves carried on a very short stem, are evidently limited at this stage by lack of gibberellins, since application of these substances results in premature 'bolting' so that the plants have long stems on which the leaves are borne at intervals (Plate 15).

The possibility of using gibberellins as stimulants for the growth of crop plants is obviously an attractive one, but it must be realized that they only affect the form of growth and do not directly increase the total yield of plant material. A cabbage 10 feet high with leaves at 6-inch intervals has entertainment value of a sort, but does not have any more leaves or weigh much more than a normal cabbage, and is of distinctly less value as food. More useful effects of gibberellin treatment may be to produce increase in stem length in hemp (*Cannabis sativa*), which may be of economic value, since fibre production increases correspondingly. Increase in length of the edible leaf-stalks of celery which can be produced by gibberellin treatment is likewise of potential economic value.

Most cells finally become to a greater or lesser extent differentiated and specialized for performing particular functions. This involves, among other things, the attainment of a particular size and shape, and thus necessarily overlaps the extension phase (Fig. 37). The cells which form the pith of the stem, for example, expand to more or less the same extent in all directions, whereas those of the conducting issues elongate in the direction of the axis of the stem or root, but do not increase much in diameter. It is known that during expansion the relative activities of the different enzymes in cells change, and we may guess that these changes are different in different cells, so that during this phase there is also preparation on the chemical level for the visible differentiation that is to come. Differentiation finally affects the general character of the protoplast and the wall which contains it. The protoplasts of cells of photosynthetic tissue come to contain numerous chloroplasts, whereas the protoplasts of the tracheids and vessels of the xylem disintegrate and disappear. The walls of mature cells nearly always become thickened to some extent, but in these xylem cells thickening is extensive and often laid down in an elaborate pattern (see Plate 4). In places the walls may be dissolved away so that a series of vessel segments comes to form a long continuous tube through which water can flow without obstruction. The wall may retain its cellulose-pectin composition almost unaltered when thickened, but

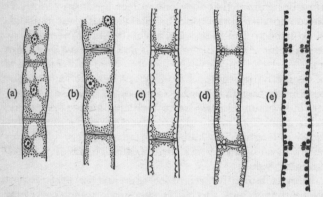

Fig. 37. Stages in the development of a xylem vessel in celery. (a) enlarged cambial cell; (b) young vessel segment with thickenings on end walls; (c) spiral thickenings forming on side walls; (d) protoplasm disintegrating, spiral thickening on thin portions of end walls; (e) mature vessel in which the end walls have disappeared. (After Esau, 1936.)

often becomes impregnated with additional substances – lignin, a complex substance formed by condensation of carbon ring systems, for example, makes up about 25 per cent of the wall material in the xylem and confers on wood its strength and resistance, while the waterproof nature of the epidermis is due to the cutin and waxes deposited in and on its outer walls.

We must suppose that differentiation has a chemical basis, but little definite is known about this. Kinetin and similar substances, it is true, have remarkable effects in causing undifferentiated tissues to become differentiated (see p. 211), but their action does not seem to be very specific. Certainly no substance has yet been found, for example, which will cause undifferentiated cells to turn into xylem – indeed, for all we know it may be lack of a particular substance which causes cells to differentiate in this way. It is clear, however, that the chemical differences, whatever they are, are not intrinsic to particular kinds of cell, for, as already mentioned (p. 35), a differentiated cell can sometimes be got to revert to the meristematic condition and after division give rise to a complete range of cell types. It seems to be the relation of a cell to its neighbours which is all-important. Plant cells grown in artificial culture in a nutrient solution do not differentiate so long as they remain separate or in small groups, but as soon as a mass is formed by cells remaining stuck together after division, differentiation can begin, and a complete plant with its entire range of cell types may eventually be produced from it (Steward *et al.*, 1958). The critical stage in differentiation in such cultures seems to be the formation of a complete sheath of dividing cells cutting off the central ones from direct access to the nutrient solution. This suggests that differentiation depends on the diffusion pattern of nutrients and growth-controlling substances which is set up when some cells in a tissue are more active than others. Study of the development of all sorts of tissues has shown that it is a general rule that groups of dividing cells suppress division in their vicinity so that new centres of division arise in positions as far as possible from those already there. The complex and delicately balanced diffusion pattern which arises as a result is eventually made manifest in a pattern of differentiated cells which not only shows astonishing accuracy in having the right kind of cells just where they are needed but which is often so highly characteristic that the plant anatomist can identify the species of plant from it alone.

PART III

THE ORGANIZATION OF THE WHOLE

The hundred parts of the body are all complete in their places. Which should one prefer? Do you like them all equally? Are they all servants? Are they unable to control one another and need a ruler? Or do they become rulers and servants in turn? Is there any true ruler other than themselves?

CHUANG TZU
(*Translated by Fêng Yu-lan*)

CHAPTER 7

Some Interrelations between Processes

Now that something has been said of the ways in which the various life processes are carried out it must be emphasized that these processes do not go on independently but are inextricably interrelated and correlated in a way which is the very essence of the living plant. Photosynthesis and cell division can now be studied separately in test-tubes, but in a growing plant no process is independent of the others; cell division is dependent on photosynthesis, and photosynthesis and the capacity of the plant for photosynthesis in the future are dependent on cell division. In this chapter some examples of these interrelations between physiological processes will be considered, the first being that between water economy and photosynthesis.

As was seen in Chapter 3, the arrangements which enable a terrestrial plant to photosynthesize efficiently inevitably make it equally efficient in evaporating water. In situations where the atmosphere is permanently humid or the water supply unlimited, as in tropical rain-forest or swamps, this does not matter, but in most situations plants have to strike a balance between economizing water, and consequently limiting their photosynthesis by shortage of carbon dioxide, and becoming water deficient, which reduces photosynthesis and if allowed to continue results in permanent damage. The stomata, the tiny pores through which most of the carbon dioxide entering a leaf passes (p. 51) and which are sited just where they can most effectively control the escape of water vapour from the leaf (p. 81), might be expected to play a major part in attaining this balance. They do, in fact, open and close in response to changes in conditions affecting photosynthesis as well as in response to changes in the water relations of the leaf, and the complicated behaviour which they show as a result does seem generally to be such as to make the best of the prevailing conditions.

Opening and closing of a stoma results from changes in the water content of the cells adjacent to the pore. The mechanics of this are slightly different in different kinds of plant, but a common type is illustrated in Fig. 14. The thickening in the walls of the guard cells is not uniform but concentrated in ridges along the edges of the pore. These thickened parts are inextensible, whereas the thinner parts can stretch, so that when it becomes turgid each guard cell bends and the pore between them becomes wider. Conversely, when the guard cells are flaccid they straighten out and the pore is closed. If stomata are cut out of the epidermis they open if floated on water and close if floated on a sugar solution of high osmotic pressure. In the intact epidermis their behaviour may not be so straightforward as this because of the pressure of the surrounding cells; here it is the difference in turgor between the guard cells and those adjacent which determines the opening and closing. For example, if a leaf is rapidly wilted the stomata open more widely at first because the epidermal cells lose water more rapidly than the guard cells. However, under more normal conditions the guard cells remain in osmotic equilibrium with other cells and behave in the way we should expect them to, closing as the leaf begins to wilt, thus reducing the rate at which water vapour escapes, and opening again when the water supply is restored and the tissues regain their turgor.

This much is generally accepted, but there is still argument about the mechanism which produces the responses which stomata show to light and carbon dioxide. Provided that other factors are not operating to make them close, stomata generally open in the light and close in the dark. An early theory to account for the opening in the light was that photosynthesis takes place in the guard cells, producing sugar which raises their osmotic pressure so that water enters and the stoma opens in the usual way. The objection to this is that the photosynthetic capacity of the guard cells is low and the opening takes place too rapidly to be accounted for on the basis of the sugar produced. A generally accepted, but still not conclusively proven, theory is that light causes starch, which is osmotically nearly inactive, to be converted to sugar. Guard cells do indeed usually contain starch, and this is normally greatest in amount at night, decreasing rapidly during the day and increasing again towards evening, but it has yet to be conclusively demonstrated that illumination is the direct cause of the starch disappearing. It is supposed that light acts by causing carbon dioxide in the leaf tissue generally to be used up in photosynthesis so that conditions become less acid, which favours the breakdown of starch to sugar by the enzyme phosphorylase. Conversely, accumulation of carbon dioxide produced by respiration in the dark would render the cell contents more acid and shift the balance in favour of starch synthesis. Stomata are sensitive to the same wavelengths of light as are effective in photosynthesis, and illumination does produce the expected changes in acidity of the sap of the guard cells. Furthermore, as already mentioned in Chapter 3, artificial removal of carbon dioxide by putting the leaf in carbon-dioxide-free air produces the opening which would be expected on this hypothesis. Only changes in carbon dioxide concentration between 0·03 per cent – the normal concentration in air – and zero are effective in producing stomatal response (Heath, 1948). Although many facts are thus explained and alternative explanations of the light effect on stomata are all rather unsatisfactory, there are serious objections to this hypothesis, as, for example, that the guard cells of onion never contain starch and yet its stomata respond to illumination by opening in the usual way (Heath, 1952).

Whatever the underlying mechanism, the effects of light and carbon dioxide on stomata are not in dispute, so that it is clear that they respond to factors affecting photosynthesis as well as to the water balance of the leaf. The interaction of these factors and others, such as temperature, which have less marked effects, is complicated, and in addition the stomata of some plants have an inherent daily rhythm of opening and closing which they show even when kept under constant environmental conditions. All this results in patterns of behaviour of stomata under natural conditions which sometimes give the impression of being entirely capricious. With ample water supply the stomata of many plants, including potato and onion, remain open all the time, but commonly under dry conditions stomata close at midday and remain closed for much of the night. Cereal stomata have been reported never to open at night and, even in favourable circumstances, may be open for only an hour or two during the day. In certain plants, notably those with fleshy leaves, the stomata are usually open at night.

Weather conditions, of course, are important, so that stomata may be found wide open at noon on sunny, humid days, whereas at the same time on a sunny dry day they will be shut. This behaviour clearly should result in the plant conserving water; closure throughout the day will reduce transpiration greatly, midday closure will cut down transpiration when the evaporating power of the air is reaching its maximum, and closure at night will cut out what little transpiration there is then without restricting photosynthesis at all. At the same time we should expect closure during the day to impose severe restrictions on photosynthesis. Closure of the stomata stops carbon dioxide getting into a leaf as effectively as it stops water vapour getting out, and Maskell (1928) found in experiments with cherry-laurel (*Prunus laurocerasus*) leaves that the rate of photosynthesis was controlled by stomata when the concentration of carbon dioxide was low and the light intensity relatively high, as they usually are for plants growing in dry situations. It appears then that plants put water economy well before photosynthesis, and it is not surprising to find that water is usually the limiting factor in crop production (see p. 61).

Nevertheless, in the light of what we now know about photosynthesis it appears that the light energy received by the plant when carbon dioxide is nearly unavailable because of shut stomata may not necessarily be wasted. As Arnon, Whatley, and Allen (1958) have suggested, and Maclachlan and Porter (1959) have shown to be possible, the assimilatory power may be directed to other ends than the reduction of carbon dioxide (e.g. the synthesis of organic phosphates) at such times and the potential chemical energy thus stored may be used in syntheses not requiring carbon dioxide.

The problem of surviving in a situation which is normally dry may be solved by plants in various ways. *Ephemerals*, the plants of sand-dunes and deserts which appear after rain and complete their life cycle within a few weeks, surviving as seed until the next rainy season, are drought escaping rather than drought enduring and do not have any special water-conserving structures. The more long-lived species of dry places, on the other hand, have certain characteristic features of general form and internal structure which one might expect to have the effect of reducing transpiration. Such plants are called *xerophytes* in contrast to thin-leaved *mesophytes*, which are characteristic of moist conditions. Direct evidence that *xeromorphic* features are actually of appreciable use in conserving water is not always easy to obtain; sometimes they may be merely the effects of water shortage rather than adaptations of positive biological advantage. However, the thick epidermis and cuticle which is always possessed by xerophytes are certainly effective in that they prevent practically all transpiration when water is in short supply and the stomata are closed. Reduction in the surface/volume ratio of the plant, as by reduction in leaf area, is also a general feature of xerophytes which may reasonably be expected to reduce the transpiration from a given bulk of plant tissue. Plants such as broom, *Sarothamnus scoparius*, which grow in moderately dry places, have relatively small leaves, and some, such as *Kleinia articulata*, sometimes grown as a house plant, produce quite mesophytic leaves during the cooler and damper season and lose them when the dry period begins. Desert plants often lack green leaves altogether. In these plants the stem remains green and to a greater or lesser extent takes over the function of photosynthesis. Another device which we must suppose to be quite effective in conserving water is for the stomata to be confined to the inside surface of a leaf which rolls up when conditions are dry. Most grasses show this to some extent, but marram grass, *Ammophila arenaria*, common on sand dunes, is a particularly good example. Rolling is produced by the shrinkage through loss of turgor of large thin-walled *motor cells* in the upper epidermis. When these cells regain their turgor as water becomes plentiful again the leaf is unrolled and the stomata are exposed to the outside air.

It has been shown repeatedly that when the supply is ample and their stomata wide open, xerophytes are prodigal with water, transpiring quite as much, or even more, on an area-for-area basis as do mesophytes. It is only when water is in short supply that xeromorphic features are of value in conserving water. Stocker (1954) has found with plants of the Sahara that the curve for transpiration levels off or declines early in the day (see also Fig. 22), well before the evaporating power of the air reaches its maximum. When its stomata are tightly closed a xerophyte loses scarcely any water.

In addition to devices which reduce water loss, many plants of dry places have large amounts of tissue with large, colourless, thin-walled cells in which water may be stored.

These plants are called *succulents* and are well exemplified by the cacti. A typical cactus shows extreme xeromorphic characters. The leaves are reduced to spines, and it is the stem which is green and photosynthetic. The plant is swollen to a barrel shape with water-storage tissue and has ridges or protuberances so that when this tissue shrinks during dry weather contraction can take place without damage (Fig. 38). Otherwise a perfect sphere would have the lowest surface/volume ratio and thus be best from the point of view of reducing transpiration to a minimum. The epidermis is thick and waxy with few stomata, and these are sunk in grooves or protected by hairs so that they are not directly exposed to moving air. It seems that the tissues of succulents do not have any intrinsic resistance to the harmful effects of drought; survival of the plant depends on its outer defences and its storage capacity. In this, succulents contrast with non-succulent xerophytes, e.g. the creosote bush, *Larrea* sp., and mesquite, *Prosopis* sp., of wild westerns, in which the tissues have an intrinsic drought resistance and can stand considerable reduction in water content without damage. A similar property is possessed by many lichens and algae, which can survive for many years in an air-dry condition – eighty-seven years appears to be the record – and yet quickly

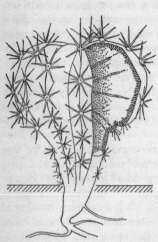

Fig. 38. *Echinocactus*, a desert succulent. A young plant with a segment cut away on the right-hand side. The dark shading represents the green photosynthetic tissue. The centre is occupied by colourless water-storing tissue, penetrated by vascular bundles running towards the groups of spines on the ridges. (After James, 1936.)

resume active growth when supplied with water again. The nature of this capacity of the cells of some species to endure desiccation is still somewhat obscure.

The sparse and slow-growing nature of the vegetation of dry situations suggests that photosynthesis is greatly restricted in these plants. This is not because of anything intrinsic to the photosynthetic tissues of the plants – under favourable conditions of water-supply xerophytes usually have a higher rate of photosynthesis per unit area of leaf or stem than do mesophytes. But anything which reduces transpiration is bound to restrict carbon dioxide intake to a similar extent. In the extreme case, a cactus with its stomata closed all day – a normal state of affairs – is losing scarcely any water, but at the same time it would appear to be cut off almost entirely from supplies of carbon dioxide for photosynthesis. In addition, green tissues function efficiently only when turgid, and their photosynthetic efficiency falls off rapidly if they become water deficient. As a result, the photosynthesis of plants under dry conditions is usually confined to the early morning and late evening (Stocker, 1960), and the amount of carbon dioxide assimilated for a given volume of water transpired may be as little as an eighth of the corresponding amount for mesophytes.

With the cactus in mind, with its stomata closed all day, one may be surprised that plants of this sort are able to photosynthesize at all. However, it seems that in succulents, at least, there is a metabolic adaptation, usually referred to as *crassulacean acid metabolism*, which permits carbon dioxide to be stored as well as water.

The sour taste which is possessed by the tissues of many plants is due to the presence in them of high concentrations of organic acids. In rhubarb, *Rheum officinale*, oxalic acid accumulates as the plant grows, sometimes reaching concentrations in the leaves high enough to be poisonous, and does not appear to be involved actively in metabolism, evidently being of the nature of a by-product. In succulents, which are characteristically acid-forming plants, the situation is different, for the acids are actively concerned in metabolism. This is evident first of all from the fact that in these plants the acidity shows a daily variation. This was recorded as long ago as 1815 by Benjamin Heyne, who found that the leaves of *Bryophyllum calycinum*, now often grown as a house plant, '. . . are in the morning as acid as sorrel, if not more so; as the day advances, they lose their acidity, and are tasteless about noon and become bitterish towards evening'. This can easily be confirmed in more objective terms, for other succulents as well as *Bryophyllum*, either by titration of the acids or by measurement of pH (an index of hydrogen-ion concentration). Increases during the night of as much as 1,260 per cent in amount of acid in *Bryophyllum* have been recorded, but amounts may be much smaller or zero in seasons unfavourable to photosynthesis.

Various organic acids are present in succulents, but the fluctuations in total acidity are generally due largely to production or consumption of malic acid. This is one of the acids involved in the Krebs cycle (p. 102), and it has been shown beyond reasonable doubt that it is formed from carbohydrate via the respiratory mechanism. Malic acid has four carbon atoms, so its formation from the 3-carbon pyruvic acid, which is the substrate supplied to the Krebs cycle by carbohydrate breakdown, involves the addition of another carbon (see Fig. 26). This is provided by uptake of carbon dioxide. As was mentioned on p. 119, all organisms are capable of fixing carbon dioxide by 'dark' reactions, but this normally takes place only to a slight extent. Unlike other plants, which, of course, evolve carbon dioxide while respiring in the dark, succulents may absorb considerable quantities of this gas, as well as oxygen, from the atmosphere in the dark. This was reported in 1804 by de Saussure, but it was left to Thomas (1947) to show that it is associated with acidification. If the concentration of carbon dioxide in the air is increased, say to 0·1 per cent, the synthesis of acid is intensified. Conclusive evidence that the carbon dioxide is incorporated in malic acid was obtained by Thurlow and Bonner (1948) by feeding succulents with carbon dioxide labelled with radiocarbon. The process, which may be summarized as:

$$C_6H_{12}O_6 + 2CO_2 \rightarrow 2C_4H_6O_5 \qquad (26)$$

glucose $+$ carbon dioxide $\rightarrow$ malic acid

probably depends on the reduction of oxaloacetic acid formed from pyruvic acid according to equation 18.

In the light, photosynthesis competes with this process of dark fixation into malic acid for the available carbon dioxide. The reactions by which malic acid is formed are reversible, so that when carbon dioxide is consumed in photosynthesis they go backwards, yielding, besides carbon dioxide, a 3-carbon fragment. This may be oxidized via the Krebs cycle to give more carbon dioxide, or built back directly by the usual pathway into carbohydrate. Whatever the details of the mechanism, it is firmly established by C^{14}-labelling experiments that carbohydrate is synthesized from the carbon of malic acid in the light and that usually there is no loss of malic acid carbon as carbon dioxide into the air. Succulents therefore possess a metabolic mechanism whereby they are able to fix massive quantities of carbon dioxide in the dark and subsequently reduce this to carbohydrate in the light. The biological advantage of this to plants which as a result of chronic water deficiency normally have their stomata closed during the hours of daylight scarcely needs emphasizing.

Photosynthesis and growth are obviously closely connected. The growth of a green plant depends on photosynthesis and, equally, its capacity for photosynthesis depends on growth. This much is obvious, but the relationships between the two functions are far from simple. The study of these relationships is of some practical importance, since a basic problem of agriculture is how to increase the total annual photosynthesis per unit area of ground to produce the maximum amount of growth from which the farmer can harvest his crop.

The amount of photosynthesis carried out by a plant depends on two things: (1) the area of leaf or other photosynthetic organs which it possesses; and (2) the photosynthetic activity per unit area of this tissue. The former may be measured as *leaf area index*, which is the area of leaf blades above unit area of ground, or *leaf area ratio*, leaf area per unit dry weight of plant. A measure of photosynthetic

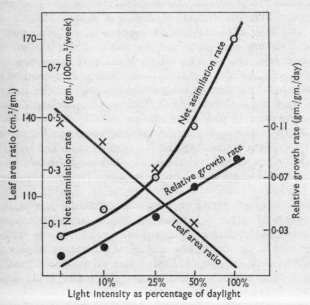

Fig. 39. The relation of net assimilation rate, leaf area ratio, and relative growth rate of young sunflower plants to light intensity. (After Blackman and Black, 1959.)

activity is given by the *net assimilation rate*, the rate of increase in dry weight per unit leaf area, which can be obtained from determinations of the dry weight and leaf area of successive samples of plants.

These two things can vary independently, as is clearly shown by some results obtained by Blackman and Black (1959). They determined leaf area ratio and net assimilation rate for sunflower (*Helianthus annuus*) plants, initially all at the same stage of development, subjected to different degrees of shading. As shown in Fig. 39, leaf area ratio decreased as light intensity increased, so that the relative growth rate did not increase proportionately with the net assimilation rate.

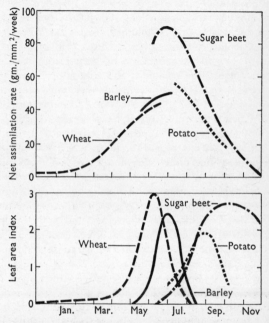

Fig. 40. Changes with time in the net assimilation rate and leaf area index of some common crop plants grown at Rothamsted. (After Watson, 1956.)

The characteristic seasonal trend in leaf area and net assimilation rate for common crop plants is shown in Fig. 40, due to Watson (1956). Although net assimilation rate varies through a wide range, this is mostly dependent on seasonal climatic changes, something which will be discussed more fully later (p. 247); fertilizers have little effect on it, and there is some tendency for the net assimilation rates of different species to be of about the same magnitude when the plants are under similar environmental conditions and at equivalent stages of growth. This perhaps we should expect, since the machinery of photosynthesis appears to be basically the same in all plants. The differences in yield of dry matter between species seem to lie mostly in when and for how long they attain their maximum leaf area. The dry weight yield of a crop is more closely proportional to the integral of leaf area over time than to anything else. From zero at time of germination, leaf area index increases slowly at first, and then more rapidly to a maximum, which is held for only a short time before it falls off at the end of the growing season. This pattern of leaf production is wasteful of the light available. At the beginning of the growing season most of the light falling on arable land falls on bare earth, and its energy is lost as far as photosynthesis is concerned. Only for a week or two in the summer are the two or three thicknesses of leaf, which are necessary to intercept most of the sunlight, present above the whole of the ground area occupied by the crop. Furthermore, as the curves for sugar beet show particularly clearly, the maximum leaf coverage does not necessarily occur at the time when the leaves are functioning most efficiently. In fact, net assimilation rate tends to decrease as leaf area index increases simply because as more leaves are produced the lower ones become shaded.

To obtain the highest possible yields in terms of dry weights from annual crops, therefore, one should use large-seeded species, which are able to produce leaves quickly following germination, and sow them at such a time as to ensure that the maximum leaf area is produced at the time of the year most favourable to photosynthesis. In practice, of course, this would not always lead to the best results from the farmer's point of view, since he is not necessarily interested in total production of dry matter, but rather in some fraction of it, such as the grain of cereals, which is not necessarily a constant proportion of the whole. Furthermore, it is an oversimplification to take only leaf area into account –

the dry matter that swells the grain of barley, *Hordeum vulgare*, for example, is produced almost entirely by the photosynthesis of the ear itself, and the leaves present before its emergence make no direct contribution to grain yield (Porter, 1950).

The general dependence of dry matter production on the area and duration of leaves holds good for other plants besides annual crops. The leaf-area index of natural vegetation is about the same as for crop plants. Thus the value of this index for oak and beech woods, deduced from the average weight of dead tree-leaves per unit area in a wood in autumn, is of the order of 2 or 3. Deciduous woodland produces about the same total amount of dry matter per year per acre, 4,000–5,000 pounds, as a crop of wheat, in spite of the fertilizer and labour lavished on the latter. This is evidently because forest trees produce their full complement of leaves at the beginning of the growing season. Evergreen coniferous forest produces about twice the amount of dry matter per year as does deciduous forest in a comparable situation, presumably because the leaves are there all the year round and ready to function whenever weather conditions are suitable (Pearsall, 1954). The highest annual rate of production so far recorded is 70,000 pounds dry matter per acre for sugar cane (*Saccharum officinarum*) growing in Hawaii. The leaf-area index for this plant can exceed 5, and conditions in Hawaii are favourable for photosynthesis for most of the year.

Not only the quantity but also the quality of the products of photosynthesis may vary. The pattern of the metabolism of a plant changes continuously as it develops, so that the nature of the products formed is dependent on growth. In an actively growing plant cell the potential for synthesis is mainly devoted to producing more of the substances actively concerned in synthesis: nucleic acids, enzyme protein, and co-enzymes, and a minimum of material is used for structural purposes or laid down in forms such as starch which are inert as far as growth is concerned. The meristem of a flowering plant obtains its raw materials, in the form of amino-acids, sugars, and other organic substances, from other parts of the plant, and they are transformed by way of the respiratory mechanism. For actively growing green cells, as in a still expanding leaf or a rapidly growing unicellular alga, the raw materials are carbon dioxide, water, and mineral salts, and these are built directly into proteins and other protoplasmic constituents by the photosynthetic mechanism.

For a long time it was thought that carbohydrate is the product of photosynthesis in the sense that the carbon fixed appears exclusively in this form before being incorporated into any other type of compound. The evidence for this is that starch, a carbohydrate, frequently appears quickly upon illumination of starch-free leaves, and in mature green tissues the gains in dry matter occurring during photosynthesis can be almost entirely accounted for as carbohydrate. Moreover, determinations of the *photosynthetic quotient*, the ratio of the volume of oxygen evolved to that of the carbon dioxide absorbed, have nearly always yielded a value close to unity, and this value denotes photosynthetic products corresponding in average composition to carbohydrate (see equation 1, p. 44). However, for the sake of convenience plant physiologists have nearly always used non-growing plant material in experiments on photosynthesis, and quite a different state of affairs appears to exist in actively growing photosynthetic tissues. In these, carbon from carbon dioxide labelled with radiocarbon appears within a few seconds in amino-acids and the protein fraction, and the photosynthetic quotient has a value of around 1·1, corresponding to the production of a high proportion of protein. From what is known of the biochemical mechanisms involved, there is certainly no necessity for protein synthesis to proceed via storage carbohydrates. The sugar phosphate cycle, on the other hand, is probably essential for photosynthetic carbon fixation, but nevertheless its function can be purely catalytic, and a little consideration of Fig. 30 will show that a third of the carbon fixed in the form of phosphoglyceric acid need not pass through it. Carbon fixed in phosphoglyceric acid can be incorporated directly into carbon skeletons needed for protein synthesis (Fig. 32).

This pattern is altered and the flow of materials diverted along other paths when growth is retarded. Exactly what happens depends on the kind of organism and tissue and what it is that is stopping growth. With a unicellular alga it is often exhaustion of the nitrogen supply that brings growth to a standstill. Protein synthesis must then cease because an element necessary for it is no longer available. Shortage of nitrogen, however, does not immediately impair the photosynthetic mechanism, and carbon fixation continues, but its products are now perforce directed along another path. What this path is will depend on what enzyme systems are available to cope. Perhaps in most plants the path of carbohydrate synthesis normally has the largest capacity, so that storage products, such as sucrose or starch, accumulate immediately following exhaustion of the nitrogen supply. During continued nitrogen starvation differential breakdown of proteins and other nitrogenous substances may take place. The rate of photosynthesis becomes reduced as a result of this, but the balance of enzymes may be altered too so that the carbon fixed follows a different path from that which it took at first. In many algae the fat-synthesizing enzymes are favoured by prolonged nitrogen starvation, and large amounts of fat may be accumulated in the cells. If carbon dioxide labelled with radiocarbon is supplied to such cells the tracer appears rapidly in the fat fraction. Again, there is no reason to suppose that carbohydrate is a necessary intermediate and fat synthesis evidently takes place directly from phosphoglyceric acid (Fig. 32). In flowering plants the effects of shortage of an element such as nitrogen are not so clear cut as in unicellular algae, because growing regions may be maintained at the expense of tissues which have ceased to grow (see p. 195). However, similar general effects are observed. Nitrogen-deficient tobacco plants, for example, accumulate especially large amounts of starch in their leaves.

Substances such as starch and fats which are accumulated

when growth is slowed down are usually referred to as 'reserve' or 'storage' products. Often they are accumulated in quantity in special tissues or organs. For example, fat is stored in the seed of the castor oil plant (*Ricinus communis*), and starch in the tuber of the potato. These substances usually do provide carbon and energy sources for fresh growth when conditions become favourable again, but it is unscientific to think of a plant as purposefully accumulating reserves for the future. A plant which is able to store material, which cannot be used immediately for growth, in a form which can be mobilized at a later date, obviously has a distinct biological advantage, but not all products of metabolism which accumulate in plants are necessarily useful to them. Although some plant products, such as rubber and alkaloids, are extremely useful to us, there is no evidence that they are of any use to the species which produce them – in the wild, at any rate; the production of a latex-yielding rubber has, of course, led, through man's intervention, to *Hevea brasiliensis* becoming a highly successful species. Many plant products seem to be little more than the inevitable by-products of a particular pattern of metabolism. Successful competition with other species does not necessarily imply 100 per cent efficiency in utilization of material and, if not actually detrimental, a biologically unnecessary reaction need not inevitably be eliminated.

However nicely regulated the metabolism of a plant may be during active growth, it inevitably becomes disorganized with age. Some enzymes are more easily destroyed than others, some substrates are more easily attacked, and protoplasmic organization which controlled enzyme action begins to break down. The study and control of the changes in metabolic pattern which ensue are sometimes of economic importance, for example in the case of ripening fruit. The sweetening which occurs during ripening is a result of the breakdown of starch. Respiration rate in fruit shows characteristic changes, falling from a high rate in the young fruit to a minimum at maturity. A secondary rise in respiration rate, which occurs at about the time of picking, seems to be due to a partial breakdown of protoplasmic organization so that substrates such as starch become more accessible to enzymes.

The autumn colours of leaves:

> Lemon, amber,
> Umber, bronze and brass, oxblood, damson,
> Crimson, scalding scarlet, black cedar,
> And the willow's yellow fall to grace* . . .

provide striking evidence of change in metabolic patterns with age. As a leaf gets older its rate of synthesis falls off and breakdown processes are accelerated, much of the soluble material being moved to other parts of the plant, where it is converted back into storage materials. The chlorophylls break down before the carotenoids so that the yellow colour of the latter is unmasked. In some species, such as the English oaks (*Quercus* spp.), no other pigments are produced, and the autumn change is from green to yellow and eventually to brown as the tissues die and post-mortem oxidations occur. Red colours, as found in dogwood (*Cornus sanguinea*) and sumac (*Rhus* spp.), are due to anthocyanins similar to those found in flowers (p.140). These pigments generally exist in solution in the cell sap as sugar derivatives and are particularly associated with the presence of large amounts of sugar in the tissues. Their appearance in autumn leaves can thus be related to the increase in sugars produced by a breakdown of starch which occurs in ageing leaves and which is especially promoted by temperatures near freezing point. Autumn colorations can be induced out of season in some species by treatments which cause sugar to accumulate in the leaves, e.g. bending back a stem so as to constrict the conducting tissues and prevent sugar transport from the leaves (Pearsall, 1949).

* Christopher Fry (*Venus Observed*)

CHAPTER 8

Transport of Materials

IF a plant has parts specialized for different functions, transport, or *translocation*, as it is usually called by plant physiologists, of materials from one part to another becomes a necessity. Over microscopically small distances simple diffusion along the concentration gradient, set up when a substance is produced in one place and consumed in another, may suffice, but this process is too slow to account for the movements, which undoubtedly occur in plants, of materials over distances which may sometimes be 100 feet or more. Mineral salts absorbed by the roots are moved into leaves; organic substances manufactured in the leaves are moved to the growing regions of shoot and root; growth-regulating substances produced in the shoot apex affect growth elsewhere. That such movements are very much involved in the correlation of the activities of a plant scarcely needs emphasizing, and before we consider these correlations further something must be said of the general features of the translocatory processes.

The account of the transpiration stream, the flow of water through the xylem of a plant induced by evaporation from the leaves, was concluded with a statement that it plays an important part in the movement of materials. Since the xylem is essentially a system of water-filled tubes and is continuous throughout the plant, it is well suited for this function. The simple experiment of putting the cut end of a shoot into a solution of the dye eosin shows that water-soluble substances may be carried quickly into the finest ramifications of the xylem system, and analysis demonstrates that substances in variety are normally there to be carried, dissolved in the water in the xylem of intact plants. The problem, then, is not whether such translocation takes place but how important a part it plays.

In 'ringed' plants, in which a girdle of bark (containing the phloem) is cut away from the stem (Fig. 41), mineral salts continue to accumulate in the shoot above the ring, showing that sufficient mineral nutrients may be carried up through the wood (containing the xylem) to suffice for growth. Results pointing to the same conclusion are obtained in more refined experiments in which radioisotopic tracers are used to follow the path of translocated salts, as, for example, in the experiments which Stout and Hoagland (1939) carried out on the movement of potassium, sodium, phosphate, and bromide ions in cotton (*Gossypium* sp.), geranium (*Pelargonium zonale*), and willow (*Salix* sp.) plants growing in sand culture. In one of these experiments, with a geranium plant, a slit nine inches long was made in the bark to allow the insertion of a strip of oiled paper to separate the bark from the wood. A solution of potassium phosphate labelled with radioactive phosphorus was supplied to the roots, and after six hours, during which conditions were kept favourable for transpiration, the radioactivity of various parts of the plant was determined. In intact plants the radioisotope seemed to move upwards equally rapidly in wood and bark, whereas in the plant which had been operated on the wood was found to be highly radioactive above, below, and along the incision, but the bark showed high radioactivity only where it was in contact with the wood, showing that the main movement of the radioactive ions had taken place in the wood.

The translocation of mineral salts in the xylem thus seems a fairly straightforward matter. The problem of how mineral salts get into the xylem in the first place is quite otherwise. The concentration of salts in the cells of the root and, usually, in the xylem sap itself, is considerably higher than that in the soil solution, and therefore any simple diffusion processes would result in movement of salts out of the root, not into it. The absorption of salts by roots, like the absorption of salts by excised tissues (p. 144), is dependent on respiration and can be stopped by depriving them of oxygen or by applying a repsiratory poison. We suppose therefore that salt intake

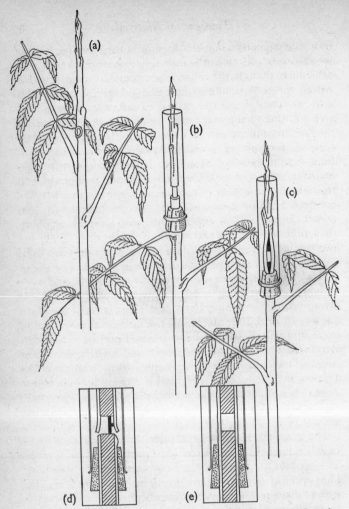

Fig. 41. Methods of cutting xylem and phloem in translocation studies. (a) control shoot with leaves removed from upper part; (b) ringed shoot; (c) shoot with xylem cut. The tubes open at the top are filled with water to prevent drying out of the exposed tissues; (d) shoot with both xylem and phloem cut; (e) longitudinal section of (c) showing cut xylem. (After Curtis, 1935.)

by a root depends on metabolic mechanisms similar to those which operate in discs of potato or carrot tissue. There is the difference, though, that in excised tissue the ions accumulate within the cell vacuoles, whereas in a root they are passed into the water in the dead xylem of the vascular strands. It seems as though somewhere in the root there is a barrier to the free movement of ions which by active metabolic processes is instrumental in maintaining concentrations higher than those in the external solution in the vascular tissue. The endodermis (p. 72) looks very much as though it might have this function, but how the one-way passage of ions across it is effected we do not know. Outside the barrier ions may travel through the protoplasm of the cells which, because they are joined by protoplasmic connexions through the cell walls, form a continuous system. Or they may diffuse freely from the soil in the water held in the cell walls.

The expectation that a plant will absorb more salts the more rapidly it transpires has a superficial reasonableness of which plant physiologists have been highly suspicious. The principal mechanisms of water and salt uptake are, of course, different, and many experiments have shown no consistent relationship between the amounts of water which a plant transpires and of the salts which it accumulates. However, recent work. e.g. that of Russell and Shorrocks (1959), has shown that the rate of transpiration does have a marked effect on salt uptake when the concentration of ions supplied to the roots is high. It is only when this concentration is low and the plant itself poor in salts that wide variations in transpiration rate are without effect on salt uptake. The transfer of ions into the xylem is evidently reduced if high concentrations accumulate there because of sluggishness of the transpiration stream.

At the other end, in the leaves and growing points of the stem, salts may be carried from the xylem in the water which moves through the cell walls. This is suggested by experiments with certain dyes which because of their fluorescence can be detected in low concentrations in tissues and which can be seen under the microscope to move most rapidly in the cell walls (Rouschal and Strugger, 1940). We can thus envisage each cell as being bathed in a dilute salt solution from which it can absorb ions. Unabsorbed salts may eventually be carried to the surface of the leaf, mainly by the process of guttation (p. 72), where they are deposited as a crust. Species of *Saxifraga* are particularly notable as accumulating deposits of calcium carbonate in this way.

Since the xylem sap contains dissolved organic substances, these will also be carried with the transpiration stream. Deciduous trees store large quantities of starch in the living cells of their wood during the winter, and it is possible that some of the sugar produced by breakdown of this is transported upwards in the transpiration stream and provides for the developing shoots in the spring. Certainly the xylem sap of many trees – especially the sugar maple (*Acer saccharum*) – contains a high concentration of sugar in late winter and little or none after the leaves have expanded. However, that the xylem is the main route of transport of the carbohydrate seems rather unlikely, since it has been found that the sugar disappears from the sap before the flow of the transpiration stream becomes appreciable. Practical use is made of the ability of the transpiration stream to carry organic substances in the application of certain growth substances, antibiotics, and insecticides. For example, the swollen shoot virus of cacao, *Theobroma cacao*, is transmitted by mealybugs which cannot be killed by direct spraying of insecticides because of tents which are built over their colonies by ants. Control of the disease is possible if a suitable insecticide is applied through a bore-hole in the trunk, from whence it is carried upwards in the transpiration stream so that the whole tree becomes toxic to the mealy-bugs, which live by sucking its sap (Hanna, Judenko, and Heatherington, 1955).

However, since the direction of the transpiration stream is normally upwards, whereas the movement of organic substances during the summer is downwards from the leaves, it is unlikely that this mode of translocation is the main one for organic substances, as Dixon (1924) at one time maintained. Although reversals of the transpiration stream un-doubtedly occur, they do not happen sufficiently regularly to provide the means for transport of large quantities of organic material downwards.

The structure of phloem strongly suggests that it is also a tissue concerned in conduction. Like the xylem, it forms a continuous system through-out the plant. Its cells are elongated, and some of them, the *sieve tube elements*, are arranged end to end and communicate via con-spicuous perforations in their end walls (Fig. 42).

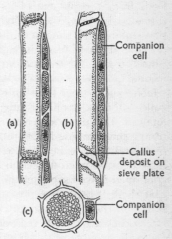

Fig. 42. Sieve tubes of marrow (*Cucurbita pepo*). (a) longitudinal section of sieve tube in functional condition; (b) after closure of the sieve-plate pores by callus de-posit; (c) transverse section show-ing a sieve-plate in face view (×200). (After Troll, 1954.)

Ringing and various other surgical operations on plants produce effects which point to the phloem as the major transport system for organic substances. Com-plete ringing to remove the bark, which contains the phloem, below the leafy part of a shoot causes car-bohydrates and organic nitrogen compounds to ac-cumulate above the ring, especially in the bark im-mediately above it, whereas the tissues below the ring become depleted of these substances. In a famous series of experiments on cotton plants, Mason and Maskell (1928–34) showed that in intact plants variations in sugar and organic nitrogen concentra-tions in the leaves were followed after a lag by similar variations in the bark, whereas in the wood the concentra-tions of these substances remained nearly constant. This again points to the phloem as the main channel for

conduction of organic substances, and the matter seems
settled by recent experiments using more refined techniques.

One of these techniques, suggested by Kennedy and
Mittler (1953), makes use of aphids. These insects have
mouth-parts modified to form extremely fine needles or
stylets, which together make a tube through which the aphid
feeds from the phloem of its host plant. The stylets are
threaded between the overlying cells and inserted into a
sieve-tube, and if the rest of the feeding insect is cut off they
provide an inert tube through which sieve-tube sap continues to flow for twenty-four hours or so. A large aphid
feeding on willow is particularly suitable, and the liquid
which exudes from the stump of its severed stylets can be
collected in a capillary tube in quantities sufficient for
analysis. This provides a means of obtaining a sample of sap
from a single series of sieve-tube elements under nearly normal conditions, which makes the performance of even the
most delicate microdissection apparatus seem clumsy. The
continued flow of sap after the aphid has been cut off shows
that there is a positive pressure within the sieve-tube and
shows up these insects in an even poorer light than that in
which they are usually regarded – they appear not even to
go to the trouble of sucking, but have their food pumped
into them. Weatherley and his collaborators (1959) found
that the exuded sap from willow contained sucrose in a concentration of between 5 and 15 per cent, scarcely any other
carbohydrate, and about 0·5 per cent of amino-acids. Other
investigators using the same method with other species of
plants have also found sucrose to be the principal sugar,
glucose and other hexoses being absent from sieve-tube sap.

Another method of approach is to use organic substances
labelled with radiocarbon to trace the channels of translocation. This may be done by applying preformed labelled
substances to a leaf or by supplying labelled carbon dioxide
and allowing the leaf to make its own labelled organic substances. The labelled substances are found to move rapidly
both upwards and downwards in the stem from the point of
attachment of the treated leaf but to stop at a killed section

of stem. Since xylem transport can still take place through a killed section, this shows that the labelled organic substances are being moved in the phloem. The results of many such studies with radiocarbon show that carbohydrate is translocated almost exclusively in the form of sucrose. It is interesting therefore that comparisons of the photosynthetic carbon fixation cycle of flowering plants with that in simple algae, in which translocation to non-photosynthetic tissue does not have to take place, show that the former produce sucrose much more readily (Norris, Norris, and Calvin, 1955). The metabolism of flowering plants seems specialized to handle sucrose as the principal carbohydrate currency. The translocation of auxin-like weed-killers has also been studied using radiocarbon-labelled substances. 2,4-D, for example, has been found by Crafts (1956) to be translocated in the phloem and to move with the main stream of translocated carbohydrate, not against it (Plate 24). Since 2,4-D is translocated in this way, if it is sprayed on leaves it will be carried down into the underground parts, in which starch is stored or which use sucrose in their growth, and kill them too. This is a property of great value in coping with weeds such as bindweed which can regenerate from even the smallest piece of rhizome.

The experiments with various radioactive mineral ions, which showed that the main upward translocation of these takes place in the xylem (p. 185), showed only slight upward translocation of these ions in the phloem. The downward translocation of certain mineral ions, on the other hand, takes place almost entirely in the phloem. Mason and Maskell (1928–34) obtained evidence that this is so for potassium and phosphorus by ordinary chemical analysis, and confirmation has more recently been obtained using radioactive tracers. The calcium ion, however, is not translocated in the phloem, and, having once been absorbed by a leaf, it stays in it.

Simple calculations show that materials are conducted through phloem at surprisingly high rates. Thus a pumpkin fruit would need to be supplied with 10 per cent sucrose solution flowing through the sieve tubes in its stalk at a rate of about 110 centimetres per hour in order to maintain an average rate of increase in dry matter of 0·6 gram per day. This is assuming that the entire space inside the sieve-tubes is available for transport, which is unlikely, and movement may well be confined to the thin layer of protoplasm lining the walls, so that actual rates may be much higher. Observed rates of movement are of the same order as the calculated ones. Deduced from the rate of exudation from aphid stylets, the rate in willow has been found to be about 100 centimetres per hour.

These rates are some 40,000 times greater than could be achieved by simple physical diffusion, but phloem transport resembles diffusion in that it always results in movement of molecules from a region of high concentration to one of low concentration, that is to say, materials such as carbohydrates are transported from the parts where they are produced to parts where they are consumed or stored up in insoluble form. Transport is not polar like that of auxin in the young stem. Unlike diffusion and like auxin transport, however, phloem transport is dependent on metabolism and ceases if the phloem tissue is deprived of oxygen or poisoned.

No really satisfactory theory to account for phloem translocation has yet been put forward, but the *mass flow* hypothesis of Münch (1930) has much to be said for it. In this hypothesis the sieve tubes are visualized as forming a continuous osmotic system extending throughout the plant. In leaves and other regions of synthesis, substances are supposed to be 'loaded' into it by active metabolic processes, dependent on respiration as the source of the necessary energy, and in regions of consumption these substances are removed from it. There will thus be an increase in osmotic pressure, with a corresponding intake of water in the loading regions and lowering of osmotic pressure and a loss of water in the unloading regions, which will result in a mass flow of water through the system which will carry dissolved substances with it. Since the phloem is everywhere in close association with the xylem, this latter tissue will provide for the necessary movement of water in the opposite direction and a circulatory system will be set up (Fig. 43). Obviously, if this hypothesis is correct different kinds of substances should be carried in the same direction and we should have to reject it if proof were obtained that different substances can travel in opposite directions in the same sieve-tube. So far, movement in opposite directions in the same channel at one particular time has not been convincingly demonstrated. Movement in opposite directions in adjacent sieve-tubes, which has been observed using fluorescent dyes, does not, of course, provide evidence against the theory. The most serious objection to it at present appears to be that the pores in the sieve plates – the end walls of the sieve tube elements – are usually found to be plugged with dense protoplasm when examined microscopically, which would seem to be a barrier that would effectively prevent any mass flow. Since exudation of sap from cut phloem ceases rather quickly, this plugging may be a reaction to injury and not a

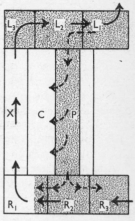

Fig. 43. Diagram to illustrate the mass-flow hypothesis of translocation. L_1, L_2, L_3 are leaf cells; R_1, R_2, R_3 are root cells; X represents the xylem, C, the cambium, and P, the phloem. Dotted arrows represent the movement of dissolved organic substances, solid arrows, the transpiration stream. (After Crafts, 1931.)

normal thing in the intact plant, but this has yet to be conclusively proved.

Throughout its life, a continuous movement of substances from one part to another takes place within a plant. The pattern of this translocation changes as the plant develops and its centres of growth and sources of food materials shift.

In the young seedling food materials are obtained from reserves in the seed – starch, protein, or fat – which are usually insoluble and so have to be broken down to give simpler, soluble, products before being translocated. Thus enzyme activity during germination is high; to take a familiar example, germinating barley – malt – is a rich source of the starch-splitting enzyme amylase (p. 93). The main translocated carbon compound again seems to be sucrose, and nitrogen is moved in the form of various amino-acids, but especially as asparagine, $COOH \cdot CH(NH_2) \cdot CH_2 \cdot CONH_2$, which accumulates in high concentrations in seedlings from proteinaceous seeds such as those of lupin, *Lupinus luteus*. These substances are translocated upwards and downwards to the growing points in shoot and root.

The young leaves on becoming photosynthetic probably do little more than contribute towards their own growth. Jones, Martin, and Porter (1959) found that after supplying a single young leaf on a tobacco plant with radiocarbon-labelled carbon dioxide there was little movement of labelled materials out of it except to the stem immediately below its point of attachment. As leaves mature they begin to export material to other parts of the plant. During active photosynthesis carbohydrates are made faster than they can be exported and the surplus is accumulated as starch. In the dark this is converted to sucrose and moved out of the leaf. Jones and his collaborators found that after it had assimilated labelled carbon dioxide for two or three hours about 50 per cent of the radioactive products were translocated from a mature tobacco leaf within six hours and another 20 per cent after four days, the remaining radiocarbon being irreversibly incorporated in the leaf material. Most of the exported material went to the stem below the leaf in question and to the roots. Rather surprisingly, less than 3 per cent of the total carbon fixed by a mature tobacco leaf appeared in the leaves above it and in the apical bud. However, when the number of leaves and the relatively small bulk of the growing tissues are considered, this amount appears adequate enough. Translocation from a given leaf may be both upwards and downwards, but the pattern of distribution is largely determined by the vascular system. There is little lateral transport, that is to say, movement from one strand to another, as can be prettily demonstrated for the xylem by allowing a shoot to take up a dye solution through a cut leaf stalk, when some leaves become differently coloured while others remain their original green in a pattern which can be predicted exactly from a knowledge of the way in which the vascular strands are connected up (Roach, 1939). This poor lateral transport has the result that if the vascular tissue is damaged or a branch or root cut off, those parts in direct longitudinal connexion with it are affected particularly.

As the germinating plant becomes photosynthetic its roots begin to absorb mineral salts which are carried upwards in the plant by the transpiration stream. Some ions, especially those containing nitrogen, phosphorus, and sulphur, are mostly converted into organic derivatives before they pass upwards. This explains an old horticultural observation that a ringed tree may acquire an appearance of nitrogen deficiency; ringing stops the supply of carbohydrate reaching the roots from the leaves which is necessary for the synthesis of the organic substances in the form of which the nitrogen is translocated upwards. Tracer experiments show that the main carbohydrate translocated into the roots is sucrose, and this fits with the finding that sucrose is the best sugar for growing excised roots in artificial culture (Dormer and Street, 1949).

The mineral nutrients translocated upwards are accumulated mainly in young leaves and other growing parts (Plate 8). Some elements, however, do not stay put in the parts to which they are first translocated, but are re-exported to other parts of the plant, usually those which are more actively growing. Nitrogen, phosphorus, potassium, and magnesium are mobile in this way, so that when plants are deficient in one of these elements the deficiency symptoms appear first in the older leaves, which have yielded up their stock to the younger parts. On the other hand, symptoms of calcium and sulphur deficiencies appear first in the younger parts, since these elements are not re-exported once they have been absorbed from the transpiration stream.

With the ageing of a plant and the production of fruit the pattern of translocation changes again. Old leaves export more of the products of their photosynthesis, and as they become senescent begin to lose other material as well to other parts of the plant. Proteins in old leaves begin to break down, and as a result the concentration of nitrogenous substances dissolved in the phloem sap rises severalfold. At the time when fruits or storage organs, such as tubers, are developing, there is a general movement towards them of organic materials from all parts of the plant.

CHAPTER 9

Correlations of Growth and Formation of Roots, Leaves, and Flowers

THE growth of any one part of a plant is not independent, but is nicely coordinated with that of other parts. Furthermore, although there are many centres in a plant which are potentially capable of growth, growth at any one time is restricted to a few of them. For example, it is a matter of common observation that the terminal bud is usually the most active, whereas those immediately below it remain dormant, so that a shoot extends into the light and air instead of becoming a dense bunch of competing branches as it would if all buds developed equally. Where growth does occur the activities of the various meristems are correlated, so that as a shoot increases in length it also increases in thickness and the root system extends proportionately. No one centre of growth in, say, a tree develops disproportionately so that a branch becomes long and thin and unable to support its own weight or goes on increasing in girth when extension has ceased. We must now consider how these harmonious relations are achieved.

As indicated at the end of the last chapter, the correlation which exists between the growth and development of the various parts of a plant can be explained, in part at least, in terms of supply and demand and the manner in which materials for growth are translocated. A growing part, by consuming food materials, lowers their concentration in the adjacent supply channels, and the concentration gradient thus set up seems automatically to bring about movement of further supplies from organs which are taking in or manufacturing the materials or simply yielding them up in old age. The more actively a part is growing, the more of the available material will be diverted to it and the more growth elsewhere will be restricted.

This sort of relationship exists between vegetative and reproductive growth. Rapidly growing fruits may so monopolize the resources of the plant as to deprive completely the vegetative parts. If the flowers or newly set fruit of tomato plants, for example, are removed, vegetative growth continues, whereas in similar plants in which the fruits are allowed to enlarge it gradually slows down. This checking of vegetative growth may result from the enlarging fruits taking all the available nitrogenous substances in the plant, for, in some experiments at least, carbohydrate continued to accumulate in vegetative parts as well as in the fruits and the application of more nitrogenous fertilizer to the soil resulted in more fruits developing before checking became apparent. A similar relationship exists between fruiting and flowering. As all gardeners know, old flowers must be picked from plants such as the sweet pea, *Lathyrus odoratus*, if there is to be continuous production of blossom. If this is not done the fruits take the available materials for growth and new flowers are unable to develop.

Where two parts of a plant are mutually dependent for materials, as are the shoot and the root, we should expect to find a close relationship between their respective rates of growth. Roots are completely dependent on the shoot for the carbohydrates necessary for their growth and possibly for vitamins or other growth substances as well. On the other hand, absorption of water and minerals depends on the metabolism and growth of the roots, so that restriction in carbohydrate supply results in reduction in the absorption of the materials required for shoot growth. This is seen in the checking of shoot growth when a plant becomes 'pot-bound'. The dependence of the yield of a crop on root growth was demonstrated for Egyptian cotton by Balls (1953), who showed that restriction of root growth, whether laterally by too close planting or in depth by a deoxygenated water table carrying poisonous hydrogen sulphide, resulted in diminution of yield. The converse is equally true:

clipping the shoots of a plant, for example, immediately stops root growth. A practical aspect of this is that too frequent cutting of hay crops, or mowings of a lawn, or overgrazing, reduce root growth and consequently result in greater injury to the grass should there be a drought.

As a result of this mutual dependence, the ratio of shoot to root for any particular species tends to be constant under any given set of conditions. The ratio changes, however, with developmental stage and environmental conditions. The level of fertilization with nitrate, for example, has been found to have a distinct effect with many different kinds of plants. For barley the shoot/root ratio, obtained by dividing the dry weight of shoot by the dry weight of root at the end of a given period of growth, has been found to be 5·3 for plants grown with low nitrate and 9·1 for plants grown with high nitrate supply. That is to say, a liberal supply of nitrate almost doubled the amount of shoot which a given amount of root could provide for. The explanation of this seems to be that with a low nitrate supply the roots use most of what is available for their own growth and little is left over for the shoot. When plenty of nitrate is available, proportionately more is translocated to the shoot, the growth of which is correspondingly increased so that less carbohydrate is left over to be translocated to the roots, and the growth of these is consequently held back.

In a similar way anything which reduces the amount of carbohydrate available in the shoot tends to increase the shoot/root ratio. Shade plants, in which, of course, photosynthesis is reduced, thus may have shoot/root ratios about twice those of plants of the same species grown in a sunny position. Shoot/root ratios also increase as the soil water content becomes higher, but the explanation of this is not so clear. Increased transpiration may increase salt uptake, and thus encourage relatively greater development of the shoot, whereas in soil of high-water content poor aeration may adversely affect the growth of the roots. On the other hand, restriction of photosynthesis under conditions of water shortage might be expected to work the other way.

Something more than these simple interrelations is involved in other growth correlations. The terminal bud of a shoot, for example, is usually the most active in growth, although, in point of distance, it is least favourably situated in relation to the supply of the substances which it needs for growth. This *dominance* of the terminal bud, although general in both herbaceous and woody plants, varies a good deal in degree. In some species it extends a long way down the shoot, while in others the dominance is weak, and not far below the tip of the shoot lateral buds begin to grow out so that a bushy plant results. In many woody species some of the lateral buds grow out to form branches in the growing season following that in which they were formed. The inhibiting effect of the terminal bud on buds below it is abolished if it is injured or cut away; one or more lateral buds lower on the stem then grow out and in their turn exert an inhibitory effect on the buds below them. This, of course, is what enables the horticulturalist to shape a tree by pruning.

The dominance of the terminal bud was shown by Thimann and Skoog (1934) to depend on its production of auxin. If the bud is cut off and replaced with an agar block containing auxin the lateral buds below remain dormant and continue to be so indefinitely if the agar block is replaced by fresh ones so that the auxin supply is maintained. Agar which does not contain auxin has no such effect. Further evidence that auxin is the inhibitory substance is supplied by experiments with ethylene chlorhydrin, a substance which destroys auxin. If this is applied to potato tubers, on which only the terminal buds normally sprout, rapid growth of lateral sprouts as well as the terminal ones results.

In so far as auxin is produced in the growing point from inactive precursors and then translocated only downwards, it would seem to provide an excellent means of ensuring that lateral buds are subordinated to the terminal one, but the way in which it inhibits the growth of buds is not certain. It may be that the concentrations in the stem below an active growing point are too high, so that a direct inhibition like that of root growth (Fig. 35) is occurring, but this seems unlikely, because the concentration of free auxin in a bud actually increases as its dormancy ends and, of course, the apical bud itself has a particularly high auxin content, but nevertheless shows vigorous growth. Another possibility is that auxin is converted into a growth inhibitor during its passage down the stem. Growth-inhibiting substances have, in fact, been demonstrated in dormant buds by Hemberg (1949). However, nutrient materials are also involved: in flax (*Linum usitatissimum*), although lateral growth is entirely suppressed by the terminal bud under deficiency conditions, its dominance almost disappears at high levels of nitrogen nutrition, and in these latter circumstances auxin applied to decapitated plants has a negligible effect on the growth of lateral buds. Gregory and Veale (1957), who made these observations, also found that high-auxin concentrations limit or prevent the development of lateral vascular strands and suggest that the auxin-induced dormancy of lateral buds is thus simply due to them being deprived of nutrients.

Although the mechanism of this auxin effect is debatable, there is again no doubt about its practical usefulness. Synthetic auxins have been used to delay the opening of flower buds on fruit trees so as to avoid the devastating effects of late frosts; to retard shoot growth in nursery trees and bushes during storage or transport; and to inhibit the sprouting of potato tubers and other vegetables during storage.

Besides inducing dormancy, auxins play a seemingly opposite role in growth correlation in stimulating cell division. The opening of the buds of a tree in spring is followed several days later by the cambium (p. 33) in the older stems becoming active. Division of the cambium and the differentiation of new xylem and phloem from the cells produced begins near the tips of the twigs, and from there spreads in a wave into the branches, trunk, and roots. Some evidence points to auxin, produced in the opening buds and travelling down the stem, as being responsible for this awakening. Certainly auxin has some stimulatory effect on the division of cells in plant-tissue culture (p. 151), but so do other quite different substances, and it is probable that the stimulation of cambial activity is more than a simple auxin effect.

The cambium, besides being the means of increase in girth, also has an important role in wound-healing. If a branch is sawn from a tree the cambium will usually produce a thick ring of tissue at its cut edge, which, if the wound is not too large, may spread over the exposed wood. This *wound callus* has an obvious protective function and plays an important part in grafting, in that it joins the scion and stock. The readiness with which callus is produced runs parallel with the activity of the cambium in normal division, and is therefore presumably related to auxin concentration. Again, however, another growth substance beside auxin seems to be involved. This is traumatic acid, a substance generated in wounded tissue, which on diffusion into neighbouring unwounded cells stimulates them to divide. Traumatic acid is chemically unrelated to auxin and has no auxin activity.

The cambium is not the only tissue which is stimulated to divide by auxin. The growth of fruits is also auxin-controlled. A fruit is formed from the ovary, the female organ of the flower, and, in some cases, from the neighbouring tissue of the flower stalk, and normally contains the seeds, the fertilized ovules, in each of which is the embryo of a new plant. The tissues which go to make a fruit grow only slowly until the flower is pollinated, when some stimulus is released which causes active cell division to begin in them. This stimulation seems to depend on the arrival of pollen on the stigma of the flower, rather than on fertilization, that is, the fusion of the sexual nuclei, which follows pollination in the ordinary course of events, because dead pollen or even pollen of a quite alien species may sometimes bring about fruit development, as, for example, *Azalea* pollen will in tobacco (*Nicotiana* sp.). A water extract of pollen may even suffice, and it was by following up this observation that

Laibach (1932) was able to show that the stimulatory substance was probably auxin. This has been confirmed by the finding that artificial application of auxin or any of a wide variety of synthetic auxins can bring about fruit development from the unpollinated flowers of all sorts of different plants. The amount of auxin in pollen is very small and quite insufficient to provide for the extensive growth of the fruit tissues which actually takes place. It seems that the auxin from the pollen does no more than trigger off growth, and it is the developing seeds which provide the main supply of auxin. This perhaps explains why the size of a grape is usually proportional to the number of pips it contains and why apples and similar fruits are sometimes misshapen – if an ovule is not fertilized the adjacent part of the fruit may not receive its proper supply of auxin and consequently does not develop fully.

This role of auxins in fruit development is another discovery of great practical importance. The presence of fertilized seeds in most fruits is unnecessary, if not a positive nuisance, from the consumer's point of view. Some varieties of fruit, of the banana (*Musa paradisiaca*), for instance, may be naturally seedless; evidently the ovules themselves, whether fertilized or not, produce a sufficient amount of auxin to stimulate the development of the fruit tissues. In species which do not do this, seedless fruits may be obtained by spraying the flowers with a dilute solution of a synthetic auxin. Apart from eliminating the pips, this method of inducing fruit development is useful when natural pollination is inefficient or impossible. Under greenhouse conditions in northern Europe, for example, failure of pollination in tomato is common, so that few of the flowers give rise to fruit unless something is done about it. Spraying with synthetic auxin solution gives complete setting of fruit; although these are largely seedless, size and flavour are not necessarily impaired. This treatment is not, however, effective with all kinds of fruit. Stone fruits, in particular, have not been induced to set with auxin. Several different kinds of auxin having different functions have been detected in some fruits, so that it is possible that different substances are required at different stages for proper development.

Besides being concerned in the development of the fruit, auxins also inhibit the formation in the fruit stalk of the separation layer, about which more will be said in a moment. It is the formation of this layer which causes unpollinated flowers to be shed.

Sometimes the regulation of growth in a plant breaks down, and uncoordinated, abnormal tissue growth takes place, giving rise to a tumour. Tumours may be induced by application of high concentrations of auxins and, indeed, this is one of the ways in which these substances bring about the death of plants when used as weed-killers. Crown gall, a natural tumour, which because of its resemblance to an animal cancer has been widely studied, is produced in a variety of plant species by infection with the crown gall bacterium, *Agrobacterium tumefaciens*. This bacterium produces auxin when grown in culture by itself, but the simple explanation that it is this which induces the tumour has not stood up to examination. Tumours, free from the bacterium, have been transplanted from red beet to sugar beet and also grown in isolation in pure culture, thus showing that the infecting organism has induced a heritable change in the cells of the host plant so that they continue to proliferate as tumour tissue in the absence of the bacterium. The tumour in pure culture does not require a supply of auxin, but produces this substance itself in relatively high concentrations. Some important change in metabolism seems to have been induced, but exactly what this is is not known. A tumour-inducing material, which may be DNA, has been obtained from the bacterium. We saw in Chapter 4 how DNA appears to be the substance ultimately controlling the pattern of metabolism in the cell; evidently this foreign DNA is able to replicate itself in the cells of the host plant, and thus bring about a permanent distortion of metabolism.

At the end of the growing season auxin has another part to play, in leaf fall. The shedding of a leaf in the autumn is the result of the differentiation of a *separation layer* at the

base of the leaf stalk. This is a thin plate of small cells, produced by renewed division, the walls of which become soft
and gelatinous so that eventually the slightest air movement
is sufficient to break the stalk at this point. Similar separation layers may be formed in the stalks of flowers and fruit.
Artificial application of auxins delays or prevents the formation of the separation layer, and under natural conditions
its formation is associated with a fall in the concentration of
auxins in the leaf or fruit. A young leaf has a high auxin
content, whereas the stem to which it is attached has a low
one. As the leaf matures its auxin content declines, and it is
when it reaches the level in the stem that the separation
layer is formed. The mechanism of this effect is unknown.
It may be noted that traces of the gas, ethylene, have a remarkable power of inducing leaf fall in some species – as
many people who have attempted to cultivate exotic house-
plants in rooms in which coal gas, which contains a small
proportion of ethylene, is burnt have found to their dismay –
but it is not known whether this is tied up with the auxin
effect.

One of the most difficult and basic questions which the
botanist must try to answer is what it is that determines the
form of a plant. We have now seen something of the way in
which growth in different parts of a plant is correlated, but
this takes us only a little way towards an answer. Obviously,
the greater part of the problem remains if we cannot say
how growth comes to be located in particular centres and
how such different structures as branches, leaves, and roots
arise from cells which are essentially similar at the beginning.

As mentioned in Chapter 1, a step of prime importance in
establishing the form of the mature plant is taken very early
on, in the single cell from which it develops. The first division of this cell determines the *polarity* of the plant, that is,
determines its axis and which end of it is to be the shoot. One
of the cells formed by this first division continues to divide
and forms the embryo, whereas the other, which marks the
end where the root is to be, enlarges but does not divide,
and eventually disintegrates. As cell division goes on,

polarity becomes further manifest in a gradient of cell size and function; those cells at the end which is to be the shoot being smallest and most active in division, whereas those at the other end are larger and evidently take up food materials, which are then moved up towards the apex of the embryo, from the surrounding tissues of the seed. Polarity shows in many other ways besides these, but its fundamental nature is still a matter for speculation. It is evidently not necessarily inherent in the original fertilized egg cell, for, in some plants at least, this can be freed from the ovule and then proliferates to form a disorderly mass of cells with no polarity and no differentiation of organs.

Polarity can be established in the egg-cells of the seaweed, *Fucus,* which in the normal course of events are not retained in the parent plant but liberated, by such things as unilateral illumination and gradients of temperature or of concentration of various substances. In the developing seed, however, cell division in the early embryo takes place in an orderly fashion, and polarity is established apparently because of the regulatory effect of the surrounding tissues. Once established, polarity cannot be upset by centrifuging, which results in the displacement of the nucleus and other bodies in the protoplasm, and thus cannot depend on the more obvious features of cell structure. Polarity is probably established by subtle patterns of diffusion of chemical substances, and depends on the active maintenance of orientation of molecules or protoplasmic structures not visible under the ordinary microscope. So far, however, no such structural basis for polarity has been discovered.

Once the shoot apex, the seed leaves, and the primary root are formed, the polarity of the new plant becomes self-maintaining. This may happen even before the embryo becomes completely self-sufficient for growth factors. Mature embryos of some species may be grown in a medium containing nothing more than sucrose and mineral salts, but very small embryos of thorn-apple, *Datura stramonium,* dissected out of the ovules, grow only in a culture medium supplemented with auxin and unidentified growth factors present in coconut milk; yet even these embryos maintain their polarity when removed from the seed.

Because it establishes the dominance of the apical growing point and determines the way in which nutrient substances and auxins are distributed, polarity plays an important part in shaping a plant throughout its life. As Vöchting demonstrated as long ago as 1878, polarity is still present even in small pieces cut from a plant; the end of the piece that was towards the apical growing point producing buds under suitable conditions and the other end producing roots. This polarity of plant material must always be borne in mind when considering the effect of different conditions on the development of plant organs.

Various experimental approaches to the problem of organ formation in plants are possible. One is to isolate parts of whole plants by surgical operations and observe the effects. If the apical meristem is partially isolated from the surrounding tissues by cuts it continues to develop normally and to differentiate conducting tissues below, and if it is cut out completely, a whole plant can be regenerated from it under favourable conditions. Away from the stem apex this capacity for growth and development becomes progressively less, and the behaviour of each part becomes more dependent on its relations to other parts. Below the apical meristem local groups of cells continue to divide and give rise to lateral outgrowths, which later become leaves (Plate 5). These leaf initials are formed in a definite pattern, the rule being that each successive new one is formed in the largest gap which exists between those previously formed. Leaves are laterals of limited growth, that is, they do not grow indefinitely, as a branch may, but stop when they have reached a certain size. The apical growing point has a distinct antagonism towards meristems like itself, and no lateral structures of potentially unlimited growth, in other words, branches, are formed in its immediate vicinity. However, if a leaf initial is isolated from the influence of the apical meristem by incisions it may develop into a shoot (Wardlaw, 1952) – a good example of the behaviour of a part being determined by its relationship to other parts. Normally, branches are only initiated some way below the apex, and then always in a definite relationship to a leaf. Flower formation takes place at the apex of a shoot, which, after producing laterals of limited growth destined to become the sepals, petals, stamens, and ovaries, ceases to be meristematic.

The meristem of a root tip has more limited potentialities than that of a shoot. As White (1934) was the first to show, it is capable of potentially unlimited growth, with differentiation of conducting tissues and branch roots, if cut off and placed under suitable conditions. He did this with tips from tomato roots, culturing them aseptically in a carefully balanced nutrient solution, containing sugar, mineral salts, and vitamins, which was regularly and frequently renewed. Roots grown in this way, however, have never yet given rise to a complete plant. Branching is usually rather irregular, and nothing resembling leaves or flowers is produced.

These patterns of organ formation undoubtedly have a chemical basis. Sachs, a famous German plant physiologist active in the last quarter of the nineteenth century, was the first to suggest that organ formation is brought about by specific chemical substances and postulated root-forming, flower-forming, and other organ-forming substances moving in different directions through the plant. While this idea had an important influence on subsequent investigations in this field and contains a great deal of truth, it is, in fact, unlikely that specific organ-forming substances actually exist, and it is more likely that organs are initiated as the result of the interaction of several chemical factors. This present picture has emerged as the result of experiments with cuttings and with tissues and organ fragments grown in culture.

The horticultural practice of taking cuttings scarcely needs any detailed description here. Suffice it to say that most plants can be propagated from pieces, usually of young stem but sometimes of mature twigs, leaves, or roots, which, placed under favourable conditions, will root and grow up into a new plant. The ease with which this can be done varies enormously; cuttings from plants such as willow will strike if left with their ends in water, while those from some other plants will do so only rarely, even under what seem to be the most favourable conditions. A great deal of empirical knowledge about conditions and treatments favouring rooting has accumulated, but understanding of what is involved started with the observation by van der Lek (1925) that roots are formed on cuttings of plants such as currant (*Ribes* spp.) and willow only if there are developing buds or leaves on them. Cuttings taken in mid-winter, with only dormant buds, do not root even under the most favourable conditions. Ringing the cutting immediately below developing buds prevents rooting. This suggested to van der Lek that a root-producing hormone was involved, and tests with extracts of leaves showed that something stimulating rooting was indeed present in them. Meanwhile auxins had been isolated and found to stimulate rooting, and it was soon shown by Thimann and his collaborators that the root-forming substance and auxin were identical. Application of auxin to a cutting promotes the formation of roots, within limits, in proportion to the amount of auxin. The effect of auxin is here to increase the rate of formation and final number of root initials, something quite different from its effect on the rate of elongation of already established roots. The polar transport of auxin is very evident in cuttings, for the roots appear on the end originally farthest removed from the terminal bud, even if the auxin is applied only to the other end or even if the cutting is kept upside-down. Heavy applications of auxin may, however, sometimes result in roots being produced at the 'wrong' end of the cutting.

Synthetic auxins have similar root-forming properties to those of natural auxin and are used extensively in nursery practice in propagating plants by cuttings. This is not quite such an innovation as it may appear, for the old way of getting better rooting by inserting a germinating wheat grain in a slit made in the cutting probably depends on auxin production by the grain.

Again it has to be said that the mechanism by which

auxin promotes the formation of roots is not yet known, and again it is clear that auxin is only one of several factors involved. This is evident because auxin treatment will not bring about rooting of cuttings which never root naturally, and its effect shows seasonal variation, being only an enhancement of the natural capacity to form roots. Furthermore, developing buds on a cutting increase its rooting capacity even when the most favourable amount of auxin is applied to them. The buds appear to be providing substances, other than auxin, necessary for rooting. Among these are certainly carbohydrates and other nutrient materials, for the capacity of a cutting to root depends on the amount of reserve material it contains and, if this is low, can be increased by supplying sugar or allowing photosynthesis to go on. In addition, vitamins B_1 and B_6 have been reported to promote rooting in certain species. Whether or not a specific root-forming substance, 'rhizocaline', exists is not certain. An indication of the existence of some such substance came from experiments carried out by Cooper (1935-8) in which cuttings were treated with auxin, then, after roots had formed, the parts bearing them were cut away and the stumps again treated with auxin. In spite of ample food reserves being still available, few roots were produced this second time. This is explained by the upholders of the rhizocaline theory, among whom Bouillenne has been the most prominent in recent years, by supposing that rhizocaline accumulated in the root-producing zone and was removed when this was cut away, leaving insufficient for any further root formation. However, in similar experiments with some other species a good second crop of roots can be obtained, and rhizocaline has still to be isolated and chemically characterized.

In recent years great strides have been made in the practice of growing pieces of plant tissue aseptically in artificial culture in solutions containing mineral salts, sugar, and various vitamins and growth substances. By periodically transferring fragments of the tissue to fresh solutions, growth of many tissues can be maintained indefinitely. Two of the principal workers in this field have been White in America and Gautheret in France. In some of these tissue cultures it has proved possible to control organ formation chemically. Auxin is essential for root formation by pieces of stem in culture just as it is for cuttings under more natural conditions. Bud formation, on the other hand, has been found by Skoog (1944–54) to be promoted by adenine, a nitrogenous base which is a component of nucleic acids and adenosine triphosphate. With pieces of stem of tobacco and horse-radish (*Armoracia rusticana*) it has been shown that, within limits, the number of buds per piece increases with the concentration of adenine supplied. Certain other nitrogenous bases and their derivatives are inactive or even inhibitory, but some have an effect similar to that of adenine, notably kinetin, the cell-division factor which is a derivative of the nitrogenous base, purine (see p. 151). There is thus no single specific bud-forming substance in the sense that Sachs had in mind. This point is emphasized by the finding that the effect of adenine or kinetin is dependent on the level of other factors, notably auxin concentration. Both auxin and the kinetin type of factor appear to be essential for growth and organ formation, and the end result obtained depends on their relative amounts. Skoog (1951) has shown that a high level of auxin with a low level of kinetin favours root formation, whereas a low level of auxin and a high level of kinetin favours bud formation (Plates 18 and 19). A cutting dipped in a solution of kinetin will thus behave in an opposite fashion to one treated with auxin and produce many buds, but few, if any, roots. The inhibitory action of auxin on buds can be completely overcome by supplying kinetin in high concentration. How kinetin is transported in the plant is not known, but these different ratios of the two factors are perhaps automatically brought about in a piece of stem by polar transport in opposite directions. We can as yet only guess at the nature of the master-reaction which is influenced by these two substances, but the facts that nitrogenous bases are components of nucleic acids and that auxin alters nucleic acid metabolism (see pp. 90 and 216) seem to point to a direct effect on the machinery for protein synthesis.

Leaves are produced only at the apex of a shoot and never directly on mature stem tissue or root. This is a point of difference from buds and roots, which under suitable conditions can arise anywhere on the plant. There is also the peculiarity already noted that, unlike the groups of cells which develop into buds and which are also produced at the shoot apex, the groups of cells which give rise to leaves have only a limited potentiality for growth. What special chemical conditions are responsible for this different behaviour we do not know.

In the development of leaves different factors seem to control the growth of the veins and the intervein areas, the mesophyll. Experiments show that auxins stimulate or inhibit the growth of veins, according to concentration, but have no effect on the mesophyll. The mesophyll, on the other hand, requires one or more specific factors, other than food materials, manufactured only in the light. Pea seedlings grown in complete darkness have vestigial leaves with scarcely any blade, even though they are amply provided with sugar. Expansion of the leaf blade depends on illumination, and it can be shown that this is not simply due to photosynthesis. Attempts have been made to identify the growth factor for mesophyll, using cultures of small discs, punched from the intervein areas of leaves, floating on nutrient solutions. No very conclusive results have yet been obtained; under these conditions adenine and kinetin have some stimulatory effect, but neither seems to be a master-factor in leaf growth. Variations in the relative amounts of the vein growth factor and of the mesophyll growth factor may be the cause of the striking variation in leaf shape which occurs during the development of many plants. Usually the older leaves are simplest in outline, while those produced later have more pronounced toothing and lobing, although, when in the reproductive stage, some plants, the ivy (*Hedera helix*), for example, revert to a simpler shape again. Modification of leaf form due to environmental conditions is best seen in water plants having submerged and aerial leaves, the contrast between the two often being extremely pronounced, as in the arrow-head, *Sagittaria sagittifolia* (Fig. 10). Artificially applied auxin can produce considerable change in leaf shape, but a detailed explanation of these various natural variations in shape on a chemical basis seems a long way off at present.

Normally a plant sooner or later produces reproductive structures, the flowers. The initiation of flowering is primarily under genetic control, and may be elicited by different sets of environmental conditions in different species. A great deal is now known about environmental conditions necessary for flowering, but this is a matter for discussion later. For the moment we are concerned with the internal conditions which are involved, a matter about which we are still pretty much in the dark.

It is fairly obvious that nutritional factors have some effect on reproduction. Lack of light, for instance, tends to reduce flowering – all gardeners know the difficulty of finding plants that will flower in deep shade. Also, it is common practice to provide extra nitrogenous fertilizers to plants such as cabbage and asparagus, which are valued not for their flowers or fruit but for their leaves or young shoots, but to go easy on the nitrogen and give extra potassium or phosphate, which are especially concerned in carbohydrate metabolism, when flowers or fruit are wanted. Out of such observations there came the idea that the crucial factor in flowering is the ratio of carbohydrates and nitrogenous substances present in the plant. One of the best known set of results pointing to this conclusion was obtained by Kraus and Kraybill (1918). They found that a good supply of nitrate and favourable conditions for photosynthesis, that is, for carbohydrate production, led to lush vegetative growth in tomato plants but little production of fruit. A moderate supply of nitrate under similar conditions gave less vegetative growth and maximum fruit production, while a poor supply of nitrate led to both vegetative growth and fruit production being small.

Fruiting thus seems to be associated with a particular range of values of carbohydrate/nitrogen ratios, outside of which vegetative growth predominates. With few exceptions, similar behaviour is found in other species, and it is plausible to suggest that a carbohydrate/nitrogen ratio suitable for fruit production is automatically attained in the course of growth as the nitrate supply in the soil is used up and as conditions become more favourable for photosynthesis with the advance of the season. However, difficulties arise if one attempts to give the carbohydrate/nitrogen idea greater precision. It is unlikely that all the multifarious kinds of carbohydrate and nitrogen compounds to be found in a plant are effective in determining the type of growth, yet it seems impossible to pin down any particular substances as the active ones. Furthermore, as we shall see later, the amount of light which suffices to bring about flowering is too small to have any appreciable effect on the carbohydrate content of the plant and, in any case, the effect of the carbohydrate/nitrogen ratio seems to be on fruitfulness rather than on the formation of flowers, that is, its effect is a straightforward nutritional one. Carbohydrate/nitrogen ratios give a good general guide to the behaviour of plants, but have not led to any great understanding of the problems of the initiation of the reproductive phase in plants.

As perhaps the reader may have been expecting, auxins have effects on flower formation. These effects are, however, somewhat unpredictable; flowering of pineapple (*Ananas sativus*) is promoted by spraying with a dilute solution of the synthetic auxin, 2,4-D, and this is used by growers to obtain a steady succession of fruit. Similar treatment of cocklebur (*Xanthium* sp.), by contrast, results in inhibition of flowering, and in this species flowering can be induced by substances having anti-auxin activity. The effect of auxin depends considerably on environmental conditions and is usually negligible unless the plant is on the verge of forming flower initials anyway. Some analyses have indicated that the change from vegetative to reproductive growth is accompanied by a fall in auxin content of the plant, but investigations using the most modern techniques have yielded conflicting results on this point.

There is also some suggestion that auxin level may be concerned in sex determination in plants. This comes chiefly from observations on species in which the male and female organs, stamens and ovaries, are borne on the same plant but in separate flowers. Laibach and Kribben (1950) found that treatment of cucumber (*Cucumis sativus*), a species of this type, with auxin, decisively accelerated the transition from production of male flowers, which normally appear first, to production of female flowers, and also increased the total number of female flowers. Heslop-Harrison (1956) has succeeded in causing genetically male plants of hemp (*Cannabis sativa*), in which species male and female flowers are normally borne on separate plants, to bear female flowers by treatment with a synthetic auxin. It thus appears that the auxin concentrations necessary for the development of female organs are distinctly higher than those for male-organ development. However, the mechanism of this effect, like that of the effect of auxin on the initiation of flowering, is still unknown.

Various other substances, including the gibberellins, have been found to have effects on the formation of the reproductive organs of plants, but their action appears to be indirect. As we shall see later, there are indications that specific flower-initiating substances exist, but so far these have not been extracted from plants nor identified chemically. It may be that the flower-forming substance is a will-o'-the-wisp diverting attention from lines of investigation that might prove more rewarding. As Heslop-Harrison (1960) has pointed out, it is worth looking at what happens in the apex itself as it undergoes the transition from the vegetative to the flowering condition. Profound changes are obvious even on casual examination under the microscope; the general shape alters from a dome to a cone, and the balance and arrangement of leaf and bud initials is changed. This is accompanied by equally striking changes at the biochemical level – for example, a marked increase in RNA concentration in the flowering apex has been detected. The potentiality of flowering is, after all, carried in the genes, and the formation of flowers is primarily a matter of activation of these genes by suitable conditions which one would not necessarily expect to depend on the presence of a single substance, and which might even require the absence of specific substances. In other words, the flower-forming substance may really be there all the time, but can only operate under a particular combination of many conditions, which one cannot, of course, hope to get separate from the tissues simply by making a water extract of them. Presumably flowering involves synthesis of special enzymes, so that it is interesting that RNA, which, as we have seen, appears to be the intermediary between the DNA in the genes and protein, should be prominent during the formation of the flower initials.

In concluding this chapter perhaps a general comment should be made about auxins. As we have seen, these substances are concerned in a bewildering variety of roles in cell growth, growth correlation, and organ formation. Some of this diversity can be accounted for in terms of the differing sensitivities of cells to auxin, as seen between elongating cells in shoot and root, but, even allowing for this, there is great multiplicity of effect. In no case is the mechanism by which auxins exert their action known for certain and, always, they are not the only factors operating. Plant physiologists who are not auxin enthusiasts have been heard to express the opinion that these substances 'do too much', and certainly it is inconceivable that one molecular type can be sufficiently versatile to be directly concerned in so many different processes. There are fashions in science almost as much as in dress, and perhaps the importance of auxins is currently exaggerated. Nevertheless, the evidence is beginning to suggest that these substances are concerned in some master-reaction. An effect of auxins on nucleotide metabolism, for which there is a little evidence, might occupy such a key position in the control of growth and development. If it is correct that protein synthesis is regulated by the nucleic acids, then an effect of auxin on nucleotide metabolism could produce through the nucleic acids changes in the synthesis of enzymes, and thus result in alterations in the metabolic processes on which growth and differentiation depend. With this sequence of effects the possibilities for different end results according to the initial composition and metabolic activity of the cell would be considerable.

PART IV

PLANTS AND THEIR ENVIRONMENTS

*And the trees, when the weather is waking, quicken without
Question, their leaves assemble in a perfect faith
Of Summer . . .*

CHRISTOPHER FRY
(*Venus Observed*)

CHAPTER 10

Adjustment to Environment

MUCH has been said in the foregoing pages about the effects
of external conditions on the activities of plants, yet a great
deal more remains. Knowledge of the way in which individual processes respond to particular environmental factors,
as, for instance, photosynthesis to light intensity or cell
elongation to temperature, is surprisingly inadequate as a
basis for predicting what a plant will do under natural conditions – which perhaps explains why many plant physiologists are but poor gardeners. Even when we take into
account the interaction and correlation between processes
which occur in a whole living plant, the picture is still in-
complete. Plants not only respond to changes in their surroundings with a subtlety which has not yet been sufficiently
emphasized in this book but also by their own activities they
modify the environment and alter the conditions affecting
themselves. To take an obvious example, by producing new
leaves a plant changes the conditions of intensity and colour
of light, temperature, and humidity, affecting its own lower
leaves. For this and other reasons it is difficult to draw a
hard-and-fast line between a plant and its environment. It is
obviously impossible to say at what point a carbon dioxide
molecule diffusing into a leaf ceases to be part of the

environment and becomes part of the leaf. Furthermore, if, as sometimes happens, a plant exudes from its roots organic substances which may react with and change the properties of the inorganic constituents of the soil or encourage the growth of certain micro-organisms, it cannot be said that the surface of the root definitely marks the boundary between plant and not-plant. In the words of J. C. Smuts (1931), 'there is an overflow of organic wholes beyond their apparent spatial limits', and it is unrealistic to think of a plant as in a vacuum without reference to its past and present environment.

As was mentioned in Chapter 1, rapport between a plant and its environment is achieved by *response to stimulus*. A great many phenomena in plants can be regarded as responses to stimulus. An increase in respiration rate brought about by a rise in temperature or a change in leaf shape brought about by increase in light intensity might, for instance, be classified under this head. However, for the moment, attention will be confined to the more obvious responses, those which take the form of movements. In the simplest kind of plant the whole organism may move in response to stimulus; *Chlamydomonas*, a unicellular plant which is able to swim about, for example, will respond, if illuminated from one side with light of moderate intensity, by swimming towards the light source. Such bodily movement is impossible with flowering plants and, in these, movement usually results in a change in the orientation of a part in relation to the rest of the plant. Movement of the guard cells bringing about opening and closing of the stomata is a response of this kind that we have already discussed, but the more conspicuous plant movements are of whole organs. These movements may be brought about by unequal distribution of growth, as, for example, when a root or shoot bends as a result of one side growing faster than the other. Or movement may be brought about by changes in turgor pressure, as in the spectacular response of the sensitive plant *Mimosa pudica* to contact (Plates 20 and 21). The direction of some of these plant movements may be related to that of the application of the stimulus, in which case they are called *tropisms*, in contradistinction to *nastic movements*, the direction of which is dependent on the plant alone.

Growth of a root downwards is an example of *geotropism*, the growth of a root towards wetter soil an example of *hydrotropism*, and the twining of a tendril about a support of *haptotropism*. The growth of a shoot towards a light source, with which everyone must be familiar, is an example of *phototropism*. Since the bending is towards the light source, it is *positive* phototropism. The magnitude of the response depends on the amount of light received, and the same effect can be produced by a low intensity of light given over a long time as by a high intensity given in a short flash. At very high light intensities, however, the phototropic reaction of a shoot may alter and become negative, i.e. bending away from the light source takes place. Leaves also may be phototropic and usually come to lie at right angles to the light rays striking them, in a position to intercept the maximum amount of light. This response is largely accomplished by bending of the leaf stalk, as with *Fatsia japonica* (Plate 2), in which it results in a leaf mosaic with a minimum of overlapping. A more familiar example of the same thing is provided by the common 'nasturtium' (*Tropaeolum majus*). Roots, generally speaking, are indifferent to light, and in only a few species, one of which is white mustard (*Sinapis alba*), do they show the reaction one might expect, namely negative phototropism.

Phototropic response is usually accomplished by differential growth, although in those plants the leaves of which show daily movement related to the course of the sun (p. 56) it is brought about by turgor changes in the tissues at the base of the leaf stalk. The growth mechanism has been investigated in most detail. Charles Darwin and his son Francis made the first important advance by showing that whereas the response of a shoot to unilateral illumination takes place some way below the tip, it is the tip itself which is most sensitive to the stimulus. *Avena* coleoptiles, of which the tips are covered by opaque caps of tin-foil, do not bend towards the light. Darwin concluded 'that when seedlings are freely exposed to a lateral light, some influence is transmitted from the upper to the lower part, causing the latter to bend'. We have already touched on this as the beginning of a train of investigations which eventually led to the discovery of auxin (p. 152), and a long story can be cut short by saying that Darwin's phototropic 'influence' eventually turned out to be auxin itself. The positive phototropic curvature of the *Avena* coleoptile is brought about by a greater elongation of the cells on the shaded side as compared with that of the cells on the illuminated side.

Cell elongation is dependent on auxin produced in the tip, and elongation at different rates on the two sides of the coleoptile takes place because auxin is present in greater concentration on the shaded side than on the illuminated side. This unequal distribution of auxin was demonstrated by Went (1928) by placing a coleoptile tip on a razor blade and catching the auxin coming from the illuminated and shaded sides in separate agar blocks (Fig. 44), which were then assayed for auxin in the manner already described. On the basis of this and other observations, Cholodny put forward in 1929 a general theory of plant tropisms, usually known as the Cholodny–Went theory, which states that the growth curvatures involved are due to unequal distribution of auxin between the two sides of the curving organ. This is now generally accepted, and the chief problem is to explain how the unequal distribution of auxin is brought about.

Light

Fig. 44. Coleoptile tip mounted on razor-blade for demonstration of effect of unilateral light on distribution of auxin.

This might arise in several ways: there might be destruction of auxin on the illuminated side of the organ, or increased synthesis of it on the shaded side, or it might be moved laterally from one side to the other. Went showed that the total amount of auxin in a coleoptile tip is scarcely altered by phototropic stimulation, a fact which other workers have repeatedly confirmed and which seems to point fairly conclusively to lateral transport. Since auxin is an acid, it will migrate in an electrical field, and it has been established that electrical charges which might cause movement in the required direction are actually set up when a coleoptile is illuminated laterally. Quite a lot of evidence points to light-induced electrical charges as being responsible for lateral movement of auxin in coleoptiles, so it is extremely puzzling that experiments using auxin labelled with radiocarbon have shown that movement of auxin from one side to the other of a stimulated coleoptile does not occur to any appreciable extent.

Another approach has been to investigate the pigments which are concerned. It is axiomatic that in order to produce a chemical effect light must be absorbed, i.e. there must be a pigment. We can obtain information about the pigment or pigments responsible for an effect in a living organism by determining the *action spectrum*, that is, by determining the efficiencies of light of different wavelengths in eliciting the response. When this is done for the phototropic response it is found that blue light is most effective, whereas red light is ineffective (Fig. 45). Galston (1949) found that riboflavin, a yellow substance and therefore an effective absorber of blue light, sensitizes auxin so that it is destroyed in the light but not in the dark. Riboflavin, which is the vitamin B_2 of animal nutritionalists, occurs naturally in coleoptiles, and indeed in plants generally, so that it is attractive to suppose that the unequal distribution of auxin arises as a result of its greater destruction, under the influence of riboflavin, on the illuminated side. This does not fit with the fact that the total amount of auxin remains unchanged in a stimulated coleoptile; there might be a simultaneous stimulation of synthesis of auxin on the shaded side, but there does not seem to be any good evidence for this as yet.

There are other complications. Although riboflavin has its greatest absorption at the blue end of the spectrum, its absorption spectrum does not quite match with the action spectrum of phototropism, as we should expect it to do if it were the only pigment involved. Besides riboflavin, plant organs showing phototropic responses usually contain appreciable amounts of other yellow pigments, carotenoids. It was once supposed that carotenoids are directly concerned in phototropic response – they are, after all, the principal pigments concerned in light detection in the eye – but the demonstration that seedlings of mutant strains of

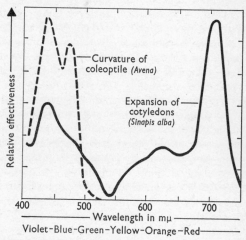

Fig. 45. Action spectra for phototropic curvature of *Avena* coleoptile (after Johnston, 1934), and expansion of white mustard cotyledons (after Mohr and Lunenschloss, 1958).

barley lacking these pigments altogether still respond to light has disposed of this idea. The role of carotenoids in the phototropic response of *Avena* coleoptiles and similar organs seems to be to serve as inactive screening pigments. The tissues of the coleoptile are almost translucent and colourless, so that there is, in fact, little difference in light intensity between its illuminated and 'shaded' sides. The distribution of riboflavin along the length of the coleoptile is nearly uniform, but towards the tip the concentration of carotenoids becomes much greater, with the result that an appreciable amount of light is absorbed and there is sufficient difference in light intensity between opposite sides to produce different rates of riboflavin-sensitized destruction of auxin.

The theory that carotenoids are important because of their screening effect thus neatly explains the high phototropic sensitivity of the coleoptile tip as compared with the lower parts. The importance of the light conditions *inside* the responding organ is even more evident in the case of the stalks of the spore-bearing structures of certain fungi and other lower plants, which are positively phototropic. These stalks are sufficiently transparent to act as cylindrical lenses, so that the light is concentrated on the opposite side to that on which it falls. This produces increased growth on the 'shaded' side by some means not involving auxin, which evidently is not important in fungi. Confirmation that this is what is happening is given by an experiment in which the stalk is subjected to unilateral illumination while immersed in paraffin, which abolishes the lens effect, with the result that the stalk now shows negative phototropism.

Geotropism, the response of plants to the gravitational field, is another conspicuous plant response, and no one will need to be reminded that roots grow downwards and shoots upwards. The stimulus is exerted in one direction only, from the centre of the earth. Since they grow directly towards the stimulus, primary roots are said to be positively geotropic in contradistinction to main shoots, which are negatively geotropic (Fig. 46). The behaviour of lateral roots and branches is not so straightforward. They too show a definite orientation in the gravitational field but at an angle, not parallel, to its direction of action. Leaves of dicotyledons usually respond by lying at right angles to this direction. The biological advantages of these differences in behaviour, in enabling the roots to tap a greater volume of soil and the shoot to intercept a greater amount of light, seem obvious enough. If the primary root or leading shoot is damaged a lateral then comes to grow straight downwards or straight upwards as the case may be. The kind of response may also

change as an organ matures. For example, the buds of poppy
are positively geotropic and hang on their stems, whereas
the fruits to which they give rise are negatively geotropic
and stand erect. Again there seems to be some advantage in

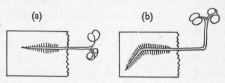

Fig. 46. Geotropic curvature in a mustard seedling. (a) seedling
just placed in horizontal position, and (b) the same a day later.
(After Meyer, Anderson, and Böhning, 1959.)

this, for the drooping of the buds probably renders them
less liable to mechanical damage, while the dispersal of seeds
from the fruits is better effected if they are held up aloft.

In the experimental investigation of geotropism it is desirable to eliminate the effects of gravity. Fortunately, to do
this it is not necessary for the plant physiologist to escape
from the earth's gravitational attraction by going into outer
space; the simple device of rotating a potted plant or seedling slowly about a horizontal axis will ensure that no part
remains long enough in any one position for geotropic response to occur. A plant can thus be exposed to gravitational
stimulus for a given time then placed on the wheel, or *klino-
stat* as it is called, for the response to develop. If the wheel is
rotated sufficiently rapidly, centrifugal force becomes appreciable, and the plant responds to this in a similar way as to
gravity, the roots reacting positively and growing in the
direction of the force, i.e. outwards from the hub, while the
shoot reacts negatively and grows towards the hub. This
device was first used by Knight in 1806. The centrifugal
force can be varied by varying the speed of rotation, and so
it is possible to subject plants to different intensities of geotropic stimulus. In this way it has been found that the time
taken for a given response to develop is inversely proportional to the intensity of the stimulus.

Geotropic curvature, like phototropic curvature, depends on growth. The downward bending of roots does not result merely from their own weight, for in doing it they will penetrate mercury, a liquid on which, of course, roots float.

The geotropic response of an organ takes place in its most rapidly elongating region, which can readily be demonstrated by marking the root of a bean seedling with equally spaced spots of Indian ink then leaving it in a horizontal position, when bending occurs in that part in which the marks become most widely separated. A root from which the tip has been cut does not respond to geotropic stimulus, which suggests that it is the tip which perceives the stimulus, so that, as with phototropism, the seats of perception and response are spatially separated. However, this is a crude experiment, and the lack of response might well be due to an unfavourable reaction of the elongating part to the wound inflicted. A more elegant method of demonstrating that it is the tip which is most sensitive to the stimulus was devised by Piccard (1904), using the centrifugal wheel. If a seedling is placed with its root lying across the axis of rotation the root will be subjected to stimulus in one direction towards its tip and in the opposite direction towards its base. By shifting the root about, Piccard found that with seedlings of broad bean (*Vicia faba*), runner bean, and lupin, if the tip projected more than 1·5–2 millimetres beyond the axis of rotation, then the whole root responded as if only the tip were perceptive, whereas if only 1 millimetre of the tip projected the root curved in the direction to be expected if only the part of the root behind the tip were sensitive to stimulus. This shows that although other parts of the root have some sensitivity, the tip is much the most perceptive part.

Again there is good evidence that geotropic growth curvatures are brought about by unequal distribution of auxin. We need not consider this evidence in detail, but one of the more striking observations supporting the idea may be mentioned. Pineapples, as we have seen (p. 214), can be induced to flower by treatment with dilute solutions of synthetic auxin. Plants of one pineapple variety can also be induced to flower simply by putting them in a horizontal position for three days, similar plants kept in a vertical position remaining vegetative. Evidently in accumulating on the lower side of the shoot auxin reaches locally a sufficiently high concentration to trigger off the formation of flowers. It will be recalled that concentrations of auxin which stimulate the elongation of shoots slow down the elongation of roots (Fig. 35). This gives a ready explanation of the opposite geotropic reactions of shoots and roots. It has been found that, in both, auxin accumulates on the lower side during geotropic stimulation, so that we might expect the elongation of a shoot to be accelerated on the lower side, with the result that it bends upwards, whereas we might expect the elongation of a root to be retarded on the lower side, with the result that it bends downwards. Unfortunately, this explanation is altogether too neat and leaves certain awkward facts out of account.

One of these facts is the behaviour of underground rhizomes which are *diageotropic*, that is, which grow horizontally. Bennet-Clark and Ball (1951) found that if rhizomes of ground elder (*Aegopodium podagraria*), a particularly pestilential garden weed, are turned so that they still lie horizontally but with what was previously the under surface on top, they bend sharply upwards after a while then equally sharply in the opposite direction, finally becoming horizontal again after a decreasing series of bendings up and down. This behaviour cannot be explained simply in terms of redistribution of auxin, and it seems necessary to invoke a hypothetical inhibitor which neutralizes the action of auxin but which, like auxin, becomes concentrated on the lower side of the organ. If it is supposed to move through the tissues more slowly than auxin, then the agitated bendings of the inverted rhizome before it settles down to grow horzontally again become explicable. The apparently simple behaviour of main roots seems actually to involve something similar. Audus and Brownbridge (1957) found that supplying low concentrations of auxin increased the growth rate of *both* sides of a pea-seedling root during response to geotropic stimulus. On the simple Went–Cholodny theory the auxin concentration on the lower side of the stimulated root is supposed to be already at the inhibitory level, and further auxin should certainly not result in an increase in rate of elongation on this side. Again the anomaly can be explained away if it is supposed that an inhibitor is produced or accumulated on the lower side of the organ as well as auxin. Direct evidence of the existence of inhibitors of this sort has been obtained, but the substances have not yet been identified chemically.

The problem of how the redistribution of auxin and other substances occurs during geotropic response is a formidable one, for it is scarcely conceivable that gravity can have a direct chemical effect. Bodies such as oil droplets and starch grains may shift position within the cells under the influence of gravity, and it is possible that these may be the means by which the stimulus is perceived. Most plant organs capable of geotropic response do, in fact, contain cells, called *statocytes*, in which are conspicuous movable starch grains. It has been supposed that when the orientation of the organ is changed, these grains fall against another part of the protoplasm, which is thereby stimulated. How such stimulation might lead to a redistribution of auxin is not known, and the *statolith theory* has not so far led to a greater understanding of the mechanism of geotropism. As in phototropism, the electrical charges which are set up in a stimulated organ may have something to do with the lateral movement of auxin, but, again, this has not been demonstrated conclusively.

Nastic responses are of a kind in which the direction of movement is dependent entirely on the plant and bears no relation to the direction in which the stimulus is applied. The opening and closing of flowers during the course of the day, for example, is of this type. A petal unfolds because one side of it grows faster than the other in response to a temperature change. Before the flower opens, both sides of each petal elongate at the same rate. Opening occurs because the inner sides develop a remarkable sensitivity to rise in temperature, so that the rate of elongation, instead of increasing the usual 2- to 5-fold for an increase of 10° C., increases 20- to 30-fold. The result is that the flower opens as the sun warms it. Closure is brought about by the rate of elongation of the inner sides of the petals decreasing relatively more than that on the outer sides when the temperature falls. Wood (1953) found that the temperature sensitivity depends on the accumulation of carbon dioxide in the intercellular spaces of the petal tissue. So far, surprisingly enough, auxin does not appear to have been implicated in this response.

A few plants show more or less dramatic nastic movements in response to contact with a solid body. The tentacles on a leaf of sundew (*Drosera* spp.) show a growth curvature towards the centre when the leaf is stimulated by a fly alighting on it or by some other contact. When an insect in settling on a leaf of the Venus's fly-trap (*Dionaea muscipula*, see Plate 17) touches one of the bristles, the halves of the blade fold together, the formidable-looking spines along the margins interlocking to imprison the victim. The stamens of barberry (*Berberis* spp.) spring inwards when touched, so that an insect visiting the flower is well dusted with pollen. Pride of place, however, here belongs to the sensitive plant *Mimosa pudica*, which on being stimulated by contact, electrical shock, or injury, immediately flops as if it had wilted (Plates 20 and 21). The base of the leaf stalk of this plant is swollen and contains especially thin-walled cells in its lower part. When the plant is stimulated water escapes from these cells into the capacious intercellular spaces between them, so that there is a loss of turgor in the lower part of the base, and the leaf stalk consequently drops. A similar mechanism at the base of each leaflet causes these to fold against the stalk. Gentle stimulation of a leaf produces a reaction in only that leaf, but more violent shock may affect the whole plant. There is obvious transmission of the stimulus from one part of the plant to another. The rate of transmission may be as much as 30 millimetres per second, a rather slow speed compared with the 100,000 millimetres per second at which stimuli may be transmitted in the nerves of a man, but fast for a plant. Rapid response, however, depends on the plant being well supplied with water and kept at a temperature of 25–30° C. At 10° C. or below the plant remains rigid, but, although no reaction takes place, a stimulus can be perceived at this low temperature, because if the plant is subsequently transferred to a warmer environment the response takes place. It seems firmly established that the stimulus can be transmitted in killed sections of stem and across watery gaps, so that we may suspect that it is of a chemical nature. However, the substance concerned has not yet been identified, and there are electrical phenomena associated with the reaction which may play a part in the transmission.

While we may see some value in the nastic movements of insectivorous plants, in that they may benefit from nutrients obtained from the bodies of the insects caught, it is difficult to imagine that the sensitive plant derives much advantage from its sensitivity. Sachs (1887), it is true, observed that sensitive plants escaped injury in a hail-storm in which other plants were seriously damaged because, being stimulated by the first few hail-stones, their leaves hung limp and pendent. Nevertheless, species with far more delicate foliage manage to do well without any such protective mechanism, and it is perhaps best to regard the exaggerated sensitivity to shock of *Mimosa* as a gratuitous result of evolution which is of no particular biological advantage or disadvantage.

Tropisms obviously play a large part in shaping a plant, and although nastic responses can hardly be said to be important in the same way, it is convenient to consider them together with tropisms. In addition, there is a variety of responses which, while not involving anything so definite as a movement, are similar in general nature to those which we have just been discussing and which also have a role in determining the form of a plant. Some further effects of light may be considered to exemplify this.

The most striking effect of light upon plant form is to be

seen in certain seedlings, such as those of the broad bean. If grown in total darkness these have greatly elongated stems with the tip bent into a characteristic hook, and undeveloped leaves, presenting an appearance greatly differing from that of similar seedlings which have been exposed to the light. This condition is commonly called *etiolation*, but this term, strictly speaking, only denotes the absence of chlorophyll resulting from the lack of light, a phenomenon which accompanies but which is not directly related to the peculiarities of form just mentioned. It is quite clear that the latter are not the result of shortage of food materials due to prevention of photosynthesis; they occur even when ample amounts of food reserves are available in the seed, and a brief exposure to light, insufficient to have any appreciable effect on photosynthesis, causes the plant to assume a more normal appearance. Thus Priestley (1925) found that a two-minute exposure to weak light per day was sufficient to straighten out the stem tip of pea seedlings, whereas illumination for an hour per day with the same light source was needed to induce chlorophyll formation. The drawn-out form of seedlings grown in complete darkness results chiefly from greater cell elongation, but perhaps partly also from increased cell division. The inhibitory effect of light on elongation depends on something more than destruction of auxin in the light (p. 222) for dark-grown pea stems are more sensitive to auxin than similar ones grown in red light (Galston and Baker, 1953). On the other hand, light promotes cell differentiation and increases the amount of woody and other mechanical tissues in the plant (Williams, Preston, and Ripley, 1955).

Red light, of around 660 mμ wavelength, is most effective in producing these changes in form of seedlings. The action spectra for the various different effects – inhibition of stem elongation, straightening of stem tip, and leaf expansion – seem to be similar, indicating that they depend on the same pigment system, which, however, is quite different from that of phototropism, as Fig. 45 shows. Another common feature of the various effects of red light is that they are reversed by exposure to light in the far red of wavelength about 735 mμ (see, for example, Liverman and Bonner, 1953). This seems to be identical with a red–far-red reversible effect on the germination of seeds, to be described in Chapter 11, which had been discovered previously.

Some of the effects of light on the form of older plants growing under more natural conditions are also to be classed as responses to stimulus, since their magnitude is out of all proportion to that of the variations in light which induce them. Experiments in which whole mature plants or portions of them are put in darkness have yielded varied results; usually the apex ceases growth, but leaves may expand although not to full size, and the extreme effects seen in seedlings grown from the start in darkness are not normally shown. It thus seems that light has some irreversible effect, so that once a growing shoot has had a little light it cannot again revert to the kind of growth characteristic of complete darkness. Experiments to determine the responses of growth to light quality on plants are difficult to carry out. The only practical method with flowering plants is to use filters of coloured glass or cellophane interposed in front of the light source, but these not only alter the intensity to different extents but also transmit a wide range of wavelengths, so that the light reaching the plant is not spectrally pure. However, Wassink and his collaborators (1952–6) have been able partly to overcome these difficulties and have found that most plants show short growth in white, blue, or violet light, but in green, and still more in yellow and red, show marked stem elongation. Such effects are not, of course, likely to be of any importance under natural conditions. The duration of the daily light period also has effects on the form of plant growth. This is especially evident in relation to flowering, a phenomenon, known as *photoperiodism*, to be discussed in Chapter 11. Such effects do not depend simply on alterations in amount of photosynthesis, and are true responses to stimulus. Photoperiodic effects on purely vegetative growth, although probably simpler in nature than those on flowering, have not been studied so extensively. However, it is known that tuber formation in potatoes and bulbing in onions are dependent on day length. Thus, bulb formation in most varieties of onion can begin only in response to the stimulus of long days, i.e. more than twelve to sixteen hours of light, according to variety and temperature conditions, per day (Heath and Holdsworth, 1948).

CHAPTER II

Climate and Amount of Growth

THE amount of growth which a particular kind of plant makes is obviously very variable, whether it fends for itself in the wild or is protected and encouraged in field or garden. Sometimes an outstandingly good or bad crop can be reasonably related to some particular event such as a dressing of fertilizer, an unusually sunny summer, a drought, or the ravages of a pest. More often it is far from obvious what factors have been important. From what has already been said about growth it can be realized that the situation may well be of almost intractable complexity. Growth depends on various processes – uptake of water and salts, photosynthesis, increase in protoplasm, cell division, cell differentiation, and inception of organs – all of which are interrelated but which respond differently to environmental factors. The optimum temperatures for different growth processes in the tomato, for example, have been found by Went (1944) to be widely different; growth in dry weight of the whole plant is best at 18° C., whereas the optimum for isolated root tips of the same species is above 30° C., and evidence of various kinds shows that translocation of the materials for growth is most rapid at temperatures below 10° C. (Fig. 47). Most flowering plants have shoot and root in quite different environments, but, as we have already seen, effects of the environment on the shoot have their repercussions in the root system, and vice versa. Few of the environmental factors have simple or direct effects; rain, for example, influences not only soil water content but also soil aeration and the humidity of the air. Furthermore, complicated interrelations exist between the environmental factors themselves and between them and the activities of plants, as, for instance, between air temperature and the humidity of the air, and between the latter and the rate of transpiration.

A general principle which is of considerable help in making sense of the situation is one that we have already met with when considering the effect of different conditions on plant processes in the laboratory. In academic plant physiology this first appeared in the form of Blackman's 'principle of limiting factors' (see p. 47), but to agricultural scientists the idea was already familiar before Blackman's time as the 'law of the minimum' put forward by Liebig in 1843. This

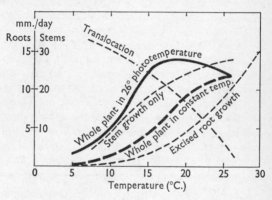

Fig. 47. Growth rates and physiological processes in the tomato plant as functions of temperature. (After Went, 1957.)

stated in effect that the yield of a crop is determined by the factor which is relatively the minimum. Both Liebig's and Blackman's ideas are over-simplifications, because they imply that there is a sharp transition, as the level of a particular factor is increased, from strict proportionality of yield to the level, to a state where any further increase is completely without effect. Actually, as we saw for photosynthesis (p. 45), the change is gradual and there is always a level at which a factor is still limiting but at which variation of other factors has effects also. Mitscherlich came nearer the mark when in 1909 he put forward a 'law of diminishing returns' which recognized that several factors may limit the yield of a crop and that the increase in yield obtained by successive increments in any one factor progressively diminishes as the optimum level is approached. This accords well with what is actually found in experiments.

The growth rate of a plant shows daily variations as the different factors affecting it become limiting in turn. In experiments carried out by Thut and Loomis (1944) in Iowa, for example, the rate of elongation of maize plants

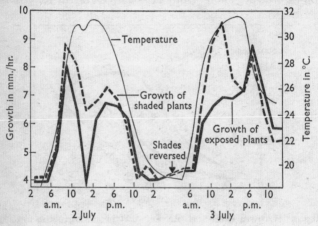

Fig. 48. The growth of maize plants in sun and shade in relation to temperature. (After Thut and Loomis, 1944.)

was most closely correlated with temperature, so that there was a general tendency for it to increase during the day and to drop to a low level at night. Even full summer sunlight had no direct adverse effect on elongation, but falls in rate of elongation usually occurred around midday as a result of water deficiency, so that two peaks of maximum growth, one in the morning and the other in the evening, were commonly observed (Fig. 48). Other species and maize plants growing in other situations may show different daily cycles of growth.

Two main lines of attack on the problem of the effect of environmental factors on plant growth are open to the investigator. The classical method is to endeavour to regulate all the environmental factors which may affect growth and to determine the effects of alterations made in the level of individual factors while the other conditions are held constant. The proponents of this approach point out that, whereas it is axiomatic in chemistry and physics that experiments should be carried out under exactly controlled conditions, biologists often too readily accept the variability of the material with which they have to work and too often carry out experiments under insufficiently defined conditions, with the result that experiments in plant physiology are frequently, one might almost say notoriously, not reproducible. Certainly there is room for experiments with all factors controlled as rigidly as possible. On the other hand, it must be remembered that it is, in fact, normally impossible to alter only one factor at a time in experiments with plants. An alteration in light intensity, for example, will produce changes in stomatal opening and thereby alter carbon dioxide supply and the water relations of the plant as well. Furthermore, the farmer or horticulturist, who must perforce grow plants under continually fluctuating conditions, naturally sets more store by the results of experiments the conditions of which correspond most closely with practical reality. Agricultural research stations therefore favour another method, which is to grow plants in the more or less natural environment of field or greenhouse and to make up for the lack of experimental control by statistical analysis.

Those who have favoured the classical experimental approach have found their way beset with difficulties, as anyone who has slaved to maintain conditions in a greenhouse even tolerable for plants, let alone constant, will readily appreciate. For experimental purposes it is often desirable to extend or curtail the period of illumination, and illumination, whether natural or artificial, is generally accompanied by heat, which must be dissipated somehow.

Temperature, of course, must be regulated and, while this is fairly easily achieved by thermostated heaters so long as the outside temperature is low, air-conditioning is essential for it in warm weather. In addition, not only do different species have different optimum temperatures, but plants of the same species have different optimum temperatures at different stages of development, and for maximum growth or full development may require different temperatures for shoots and roots, and at day and night. The atmosphere must be kept humid for satisfactory growth of most plants, but ventilation is necessary to provide sufficient carbon dioxide for photosynthesis. For a long time, because of the cost of all the arrangements needed for these various ends, controlled conditions for plant growth could be achieved only in small rooms or cabinets, and experiments were consequently limited. Only comparatively recently have facilities for growing large numbers of plants in a variety of controlled environments become available. The first and most famous of these enormously expensive suites of greenhouses is that which was directed by F. W. Went, of auxin fame, at the California Institute of Technology. This is described (Went, 1957) as being equipped with twenty separate air-conditioners which provide air of different temperatures and humidities to fifty-four separate chambers, comprising greenhouses, artificial light rooms, dark rooms, and a wind tunnel. The plants are grown on trolleys which can be moved between the fifty-four chambers, so that an enormous number of permutations and combinations of temperature, light, humidity, rain, and wind treatments are possible. The rooting medium is gravel or vermiculite watered with a nutrient solution so that nutritional conditions are uniform. Rigid precautions are observed to keep the greenhouses insect- and disease-free, all air and materials entering the building being sterilized as far as possible, the workers themselves following a routine of changing clothes and washing to decontaminate themselves. All the equipment is regulated from a central control room, the complexity of which rivals that of a cyclotron or other large piece of apparatus for nuclear physics, hence the name 'phyto-tron' by which such set-ups are now generally known.

By such means an extremely high degree of repro-ducibility can be achieved in experiments with plants. Nevertheless, a comment made by the Greek botanist Theophrastus (born 370 B.C.) – 'In fact your plant is a thing various and manifold, and so it is difficult to describe in general terms' – appears to be only too true in the light of the extensive results obtained by means of the phytotron. Each species appears to be a law unto itself as far as re-sponse to environmental conditions is concerned. Since the tomato is both a good plant for experiments and economi-cally important, some of the information obtained about its growth may be summarized here as a sample. For a more detailed account of the results for this and other species the book by Went (*The Experimental Control of Plant Growth*, 1957) should be consulted.

The growth rate of tomatoes, measured in terms of stem elongation, under any set of constant conditions gradually increased until a constant rate was attained. Plants grown at constant temperature in artificial light given for 8 hours daily did almost equally well whatever the temperature be-tween 20° and 26° C., but grew scarcely at all at 10° C. and were spindly with thin stems and small leaves at 30° C. However, better growth was obtained when the tempera-tures during the light period and during the dark period were different. The night or dark temperature is of more importance for growth than the light or day temperature. In terms both of height and dry weight tomato plants of the variety Essex Wonder given artificial light for 8 hours daily did best at a day temperature of 20° C. and a night tem-perature of 10° C. Some growth was possible with a night temperature as low as 2° C., but when the temperature difference was too great the plants eventually died without producing fruit, although they looked healthy and sturdy. The favourable effect of a low night temperature is perhaps related to the inhibition of respiration, which, of course, uses up the products of photosynthesis, and to the more rapid translocation which is possible at low temperatures (Fig. 47). It is striking that the relative amount of root growth, which is largely dependent on rate of translocation, is very sensitive to variation in night temperature. At a constant night temperature of 30° C. a change from 5·1 to 5·2 was found in the shoot/root ratio when day temperature was varied from 4° to 30° C., whereas at a constant day temperature of 20° C. the shoot/root ratio varied from 1·6 to 5·4 over the range from 4° to 30° C. night temperature. The optimum temperatures for growth shifted downwards somewhat as the plants aged.

Growth of tomatoes in natural light was slightly, but only slightly, better than in artificial light (mixed, from fluorescent and incandescent lamps). The saturating intensity for growth was about 1,250 foot-candles, that is, about $\frac{1}{8}$ of the intensity of direct summer sunshine (a figure rather lower than that reported by other workers). The lower the light intensity, the lower were the optimum temperatures for growth until at 250 foot-candles the compensation point (see p. 45) was reached and no growth could be sustained. The period of illumination, the *photoperiod*, had an important effect on the amount of vegetative growth. If the photoperiod was less than 8 hours, growth decreased sharply. The tomato plant cannot utilize light efficiently for more than about 16 hours daily and growth is less in continuous light than with a 16-hour photoperiod of saturating intensity. If plants are given cycles of light and dark of other than 24 hours periodicity, growth rates decrease and there may be actual injury to the leaves. There appears to be a basic adjustment to the 24-hour cycle, a matter which will be taken up again in the next chapter.

As the plants in Went's experiments grew the lower leaves died, either because of lack of nutrients or insufficient light intensity, or, in plants with neither of these factors limiting, because of the drain on the materials in the leaves by the developing fruits. Flowering is a matter to be dealt with in the next chapter, but it may be noted here that in the tomato it occurs regardless of environmental conditions.

Fruit growth, on the other hand, which is physiologically similar to vegetative growth, was found to be strongly dependent on temperature and light intensity, the range being narrower than for vegetative growth. Decreased fruit production at low night temperatures was in the first place due to failure of fertilization, the pollen produced below 13° C. being abnormal. For this reason, spraying with synthetic auxins to induce fruit-set is particularly valuable early in the season when the nights are cold. Fruit that was set at low night temperatures grew well, evidently because of the rapid translocation of the necessary sugars which takes place under these conditions. The poor fruit growth at night temperatures above 26° C., on the other hand, could be ascribed to the reduced sugar supply brought about by the slowing down of translocation. In the tomato plant there is competition between vegetative and fruit growth, so fruit growth at high temperatures can be improved by nipping out actively growing shoots. Different tomato varieties, although showing the same general responses, were found to require somewhat different day and night temperatures for maximum fruit production. In no variety was the photoperiod found to be of great importance for fruit growth. Fig. 49 shows how these various factors interact to affect fruit set.

Growth of the tomato plant thus responds predominantly to night temperature. Other factors may be of most importance for other plants; peas, for example, are most affected by day temperature, *Xanthium*, the cocklebur, by photoperiod, and *Veratrum*, a member of the lily family, by seasonal variations in temperature. Some plants are dependent on several factors, thus for strawberries, *Fragaria virginiana* × *F. chiloensis* var. Marshall, both temperature and photoperiod are important, although seasonal variation in temperature has little effect. In each case we must suppose that the particular environmental factor which is of most importance controls the process which is limiting development.

On the whole, closely related plants respond most strongly to the same factors. Thus the tomato, potato, chilli pepper (*Capsicum annuum*), and tobacco all belong to the same family, the Solanaceae, and are all most strongly affected by night temperature, whereas for the pea and other members of the Papillionaceae, day temperatures are most important. Related species and races of the same species usually differ only in respect of the level of a particular factor to which they respond. Thus there are races of *Achillea*, milfoil, in California, whose habitats range from

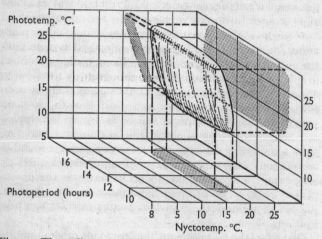

Fig. 49. Three-dimensional diagram showing the effects of night temperature (nyctotemperature), day temperature (phototemperature), and photoperiod on fruit set (shaded areas) in the tomato. (After Went, 1957.)

sea-level to 9,000 feet in the mountains and whose response to environmental conditions differ mainly in respect to night temperature; those plants found highest up requiring, as we might expect, the lowest night temperatures for satisfactory growth (Clausen, Keck, and Hiesey, 1948). On the whole, in fact, it is found that the conditions required for best growth of a particular species do correspond closely with those which are found in its natural habitat. This means either that during the evolution of a plant species there is a considerable degree of adaptation of its physiological processes to the prevailing conditions, or that species migrate into regions in which the climate most nearly meets their requirements. Probably both occur, to differing extents according to species. Only occasionally does there seem to be a lack of fit; the African violet (*Saintpaulia*) needs a higher temperature (23–26° C.) at night than during the day (14–17° C.) for best growth, a requirement that does not seem to have arisen by adaptation, for there is no such climate on earth.

It is scarcely necessary to emphasize the importance of a knowledge of the controlling environmental factors when the cultivation of a plant of economic importance in a new area is being considered. An example of this is afforded by *Veratrum viride*, which is of potential economic importance because it produces an alkaloid of value in lowering blood pressure. This plant had never been grown in cultivation, and field tests completely failed to give any indication of the factor controlling its growth. Phytotron tests, however, established its climatic requirements, the principal one being storage for several months at 2–4° C. to break the deep dormancy of its corms. On this basis it was possible to suggest locations where it might be grown, and when tried out in these places it grew as predicted (Went, 1957).

Field trials to find out how plants do in new situations or with different fertilizers must be almost as old as agriculture itself, and have gradually developed into an elaborate and precise means of experimentation. One of the most famous and long-continued of field experiments was begun in 1843 by Lawes and Gilbert on the Broadbalk wheat field at what is now the Rothamsted Experimental Station, Hertfordshire, England. The original aim of the experiments was to test Liebig's hypothesis that plants obtain all their carbon, hydrogen, oxygen, and nitrogen from the air, obtaining only their mineral constituents from the soil. Plots were treated with different mineral fertilizers or organic manures and their yields of grain and straw recorded. The results established the inadequacy of the atmosphere as a source of nitrogen for wheat, the yield being closely related to the amount of this element supplied in the fertilizer or manure. After nine years the programme was rearranged and stabilized with the object of studying the exhaustion of nutrients from the soil over a prolonged period and the effects of weather on yield. From 1852 onwards most of the plots have, in fact, remained under the same treatment each year to the present day.

In the absence of adequate methods for the examination of highly variable data such as are obtained in experiments of this kind, the conclusions which Lawes and Gilbert drew were perforce largely intuitive assessments. Their conclusions were shrewd and have stood up to the test of application in practical agriculture, but, while intuition has a most valuable part to play behind the scenes in science, so capricious a human faculty cannot be allowed any public role in scientific argument. To enable impartial assessment of data in which random variation is high, various statistical techniques have been devised both for the examination of the data themselves and for the design of the experiments by which they are obtained. These techniques have now reached a high degree of sophistication; they are widely used and not confined to agricultural experimentation, but it is worth noting that a statistician working at Rothamsted, R. A. Fisher, played a notable part in their development. This is not the place to go into details, but the essence is that the total variation found among a number of measurements of a particular quantity, such as the yields of a crop, can be regarded as being made up of smaller variations, each correlated, directly or inversely, with variations in one of the factors the effects of which are being studied, and a residuum of variations due to other, unrecorded, factors or error. If the variation ascribed to a particular factor is large in comparison with the variation due to unknown causes, then it will probably not have arisen by chance, and it can be said that there is a significant positive or negative correlation between the quantity being measured and the level of that particular factor. It always has to be borne in mind that a statistical correlation does not imply the existence of any particular mechanism connecting the two things under consideration. This will be exemplified presently when the effects of rainfall on yield of wheat are described.

Statistical analysis of the Broadbalk data, summarized by Russell and Watson (1940), shows that there is surprisingly little falling off in yield if wheat is grown continuously on the same land, provided that adequate amounts of fertilizer are supplied to the soil. Over the period 1852–1918 the annual diminution of yield from plots receiving farm-yard manure was 0·1 per cent of the mean yield and not statistically significant. That from plots dressed with complete artificial fertilizer was 0·26 per cent and only just statistically significant. This agrees well with the idea that soil provides only mineral and not organic constituents for the plants, the slight superiority of farmyard manure over artificial, that is, mineral, fertilizer being attributable to secondary effects resulting in improvement of the physical condition of the soil. Among climatic factors, rainfall appears to be of most importance. The average rainfall at Rothamsted, 29 inches per annum, is too high for optimum wheat yields, and better results are obtained in dry than in wet seasons. The most favourable rainfall is probably near 21 inches a year; below this level the effect is reversed and yield becomes positively correlated with rainfall. The effect of rain varies with the season, winter rain being more harmful than that in the summer (Fig. 50). The bad effect of winter rainfall is partly attributable to washing out of nitrates from the soil – the diminution of yield from the maximum attainable under a particular treatment is greatest on the plots most heavily manured with nitrogen, i.e. those that have most nitrate to wash out – partly to the growth of weeds, and partly to deterioration in the physical condition of the soil. The negative correlation of yield with rainfall thus depends on several different mechanisms. Since more rain means less sunshine, we might suspect that lack of light might also be at least partly responsible for the negative correlation of yield with rainfall, but this effect can be eliminated by appropriate statistical procedures and, as Fig. 50 shows, is actually quite small.

In the majority of field experiments the final yield – all that the farmer is interested in – has been the only recorded measure of plant growth, whereas the plant physiologist would prefer much more extensive sets of data which would enable him to determine the effects of environmental factors

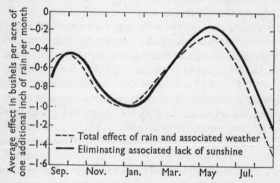

Fig. 50. Effect of rainfall at different seasons on the yield of wheat from a plot treated with farmyard manure in the Broadbalk experiment, Rothamsted, before and after elimination of the effect of associated lack of sunshine. (After Russell and Watson, 1940.)

throughout the course of growth. One such set of data, that for maize already referred to in Chapter 1, was obtained by Kreusler and analysed by Briggs, Kidd, and West (1920–1). Their analysis gave an indication that the responses of the plants to changes in environmental factors varied during development. If the environmental factors and the responses of the plants to them vary simultaneously through the growing season, then data obtained with plants all sown at the same time will be difficult to interpret. If the relationships between growth and seasonal changes in factors such as light intensity and temperature are to be determined, then it is desirable to make measurements on plants which are sown at intervals so as to be at a comparable state of development at the beginning of each successive set of observations.

An experiment of this sort has been carried out by G. E. Blackman, Black, and Kemp (1955) with sunflower (*Helianthus annuus*). A continuous supply of young plants growing in pots out of doors was maintained throughout the season and, each week, batches of plants which had reached a standard state of development were selected for the experiment. At the beginning and end of each week half of each batch was harvested and measurements made of leaf area and dry weights of stem, leaves, and root. Temperature and light intensity were recorded. Statistical analysis of the data obtained showed that the relative growth rate of the plants was positively correlated with both temperature and light intensity and that the variations which it showed could be interpreted in terms of the effects of these two factors on the rate of photosynthesis (measured as net assimilation rate, see p. 176) and the area and weight of leaf. In this instance the temperature range between day and night seemed of little importance, the changes observed showing most relation to the average temperature. The rate of assimilation per unit area of leaf was strongly correlated with light intensity but independent of temperature. The ratio of leaf area to leaf weight and the ratio of weight of stem to weight of the whole plant both decreased as light intensity increased, thus confirming in quantitative terms the general observation that 'sun' plants are stockier and have smaller leaves than 'shade' plants (a later series of experiments (Blackman and Black, 1959) in which the sunflower plants were shaded artificially showed similar effects of light intensity on leaf area ratio and net assimilation rate even more clearly, see Fig. 39). The positive correlation of relative growth rate with temperature was accounted for by an increase in the ratio of leaf area to weight correlated with rise of temperature, that is, the intrinsic capacity for photosynthesis was not increased, but a rise in temperature resulted in relatively more photosynthetic surface being formed so that a greater rate of synthesis of dry matter was possible. Root growth was scarcely affected by light intensity, but was positively correlated with temperature.

The results of experiments like this, with plants under more or less natural conditions, point to the same general conclusion as those obtained using controlled environments, namely that the pattern of environmental factors required for best growth is different for each species. A study by Black (1955) of subterranean clover (*Trifolium subterraneum*) by similar methods to those used for the sunflower, showed that it has quite different responses to temperature, there being a positive correlation of net assimilation rate with temperature, as well as with light intensity, and a negative correlation with minimum night temperature. The investigation of the underlying causes of these differences will certainly call for controlled environmental conditions – a point which emphasizes that the two contrasting methods of investigation of the relation of plant growth to environmental conditions are complementary and that neither can be considered sufficient by itself.

From the results of experiments such as those which have been described in this chapter certain general conclusions can be drawn about the prospects of increasing crop yields. Certain environmental factors, such as amount of mineral nutrients, irrigation, and, to a certain extent, soil condition, can be controlled fairly easily. If all that could be done in this direction were done, then, given good farming practice all round, it is likely that the average yields for such crops as wheat and potatoes in Britain could be increased by perhaps 50 per cent. Increases above this are dependent on weather, and if this is exceptionally favourable may result in yields double the average of those obtained by the best farmers. Clearly it is only worth attempting to control the climate, that is, to grow the plants in specially equipped greenhouses, for crops which command particularly high prices. However, the beneficial effect of a climatic factor may depend on its effect on the form of the plant; in the sunflower experiment, for example, the growth rate increased with temperature because of an increase in the leaf area/weight ratio. As Hudson (1961) has pointed out, the form of a plant is controllable by growth substances, and it is conceivable that some of the effects of special climatic conditions could equally well be achieved by application of the right growth substance to the crop at the right time. Needless to say, this would call for a great deal more detailed knowledge of the behaviour and effects of these substances than we possess at present, and would have to be carried out most judiciously. Finally, given the most favourable environmental conditions, the limit on yield is presumably imposed by genetic factors, a matter which is outside the province of this book.

CHAPTER 12

Rhythms of Plant Growth

PLANT growth never proceeds steadily even for a few hours, but undergoes fluctuations which often occur at more or less regular intervals in a daily or seasonal rhythm. Some of these fluctuations, obviously related to daily or seasonal variations in environmental factors, have already been discussed, but others, which form the subject for this chapter, seem to have no direct relation with the prevailing conditions, but to depend more on internal circumstances.

We must first take notice of the fact that environmental conditions which favour growth in active plants are not necessarily sufficient to elicit growth in dormant plants. Seeds which remain unresponsive under seemingly ideal conditions may give exasperating proof that they are capable of germination months after they have been thrown out as dead. The English oak produces its buds in the early summer, but, although a few may grow out into 'Lammas shoots' at the beginning of August, the rest normally remain inactive until the following spring; a mild sunny spell in early winter will not cause them to open, nor will they do so if twigs are taken into a warm greenhouse. Such inability to grow under apparently favourable conditions is called *dormancy*.

The seeds of all plants require water, a suitable temperature, and oxygen for germination. Some require a less obviously necessary condition and fail to germinate unless exposed to light. This is not, of course, because they require light for photosynthesis at this stage, but must be because some other photochemical process is necessary to remove an inhibitor or to provide a growth factor. The seeds of the mistletoe (*Viscum album*) and of certain varieties of lettuce (*Lactuca sativa*) are of this kind. On the other hand, the germination of the seeds of some plants, the onion, for example, is retarded or even entirely prevented by exposure to light. Lettuce seeds of a variety not requiring light for germination can be made light-requiring by treatment with the germination-inhibiting substance coumarin, and many kinds of seeds are known to germinate in darkness at one temperature but to become light-requiring as the temperature is increased towards the maximum at which germination is possible. This seems to suggest that light-requiring and dark-requiring seeds are not fundamentally different but that some rather delicate balance of opposing processes must be struck if germination is to occur. The same impression is given by the results of detailed investigation into the light requirement. For lettuce and similar seeds a short exposure to red light of a wavelength of about 660 mμ. is sufficient to induce germination, but if this treatment is followed immediately by exposure to red light of longer wavelength, about 735 mμ, the effect is counteracted and the seeds do not germinate (Borthwick *et al.*, 1952). This switching on and off of the capacity to germinate can be done a number of times. The nature of the reactions are not yet known, but they are evidently of general importance in plants, for, as already mentioned (p. 231) and as we shall see again later on (pp. 259 and 266), red and far-red light have similar effects on other plant processes.

However, we are considering dormancy, which is taken to mean an inability to grow when all environmental conditions are suitable, that is, dependence on conditions in the seed itself. The causes of dormancy in seeds are various. It may be simply that the seed coat is so tough that the embryo is confined in a strait jacket and physically prevented from expanding. This is so in mustard (*Brássica* spp.). Or the impermeability of the seed coat may prevent entry of the necessary water, as in the 'hard' seeds of many members of the pea family including the sweet pea, or, more rarely, oxygen, as sometimes in *Xanthium*. The coats of seeds such as these usually become weaker and more permeable on storage under fluctuating conditions or as the result of bacterial and fungal attack in the soil, so that germination can eventually occur naturally. Dormancy of this sort can be broken artificially by treatments which damage the seed coat. For many members of the pea family the damage sustained during machine threshing is sufficient, while better germination of precious sweet pea seeds may be obtained by nicking them individually with a file. Treatment with strong sulphuric acid is an effective way of breaking the dormancy of some seeds. It goes without saying that treatments of this sort should not be drastic enough to injure the embryo.

Often, however, dormancy of seeds is due to more obscure causes. Many species of plants, including orchids and the ash (*Fraxinus excelsior*), produce seeds in which the embryo has scarcely developed even though on other counts the seed is fully ripe. The germination of such seeds must necessarily be delayed until the embryo is fully developed. With the cow-parsnip (*Heracleum sphondylium*) Stokes (1953) found that in seeds kept moist at 2° C. the embryos developed at the expense of food reserves and germination started, even at the same low temperature, whereas in seeds kept moist at 15° C. or above, development started only to stop again. This seemed to depend on the production by protein breakdown at low temperatures of amino-acids, glycine and arginine having a stimulatory effect on embryo development which the predominant amino-acid alanine, produced at higher temperatures, did not possess. In other species, although the seed contains a fully developed embryo, this is in a physiological condition such that it will not grow until a period of 'after-ripening' has taken place. This is a common condition in the rose family, Rosaceae. Usually, seeds of this kind will not germinate in the autumn in which they are produced, but do so the following spring.

In some species the after-ripening takes place over a much longer period, so that only a proportion of the seeds becomes capable of germinating each year. After-ripening is affected by external conditions. The seeds of many plants of temperate regions, for example, require a long period under moist conditions at low temperatures for germination.

Apple seeds must be kept moist at a temperature of around 4° C. for about two months before complete germination is possible. Luckwill (1952) found that growth-promoting substances appeared in the embryos of seeds which had completed their after-ripening but were absent in seeds kept in dry storage. On the other hand, after-ripening may be a matter of an inhibitor disappearing. Germination-inhibiting substances in great variety have been isolated from various seeds and fruits. These substances are usually found in the seed coat or in the tissues of the fruit; tomato juice, for instance, contains a powerful germination inhibitor. Presumably these inhibitors act by interfering in some enzyme reaction necessary for growth. Some of them are essential oils and are volatile, while others, such as coumarin, the substance responsible for the smell of new-mown hay, are gradually destroyed by enzyme action, so that the seeds are eventually able to germinate.

Dormancy in seeds is of obvious biological advantage. Premature germination before dispersal has occurred is usually a serious disadvantage to a plant and rarely occurs except in certain rather extreme habitats such as mangrove swamps and mountain tops. An after-ripening process that lasts through the winter enables a seed to germinate under favourable conditions in the spring and gives the young plant a better chance of survival than it would have had if it had germinated immediately on ripening. Dormancy is likewise of advantage in desert plants, but here the situation is more difficult to meet, since favourable conditions occur at rare intervals when there has been enough rain. The heavy showers which occur in places such as Death Valley, California, once every five to twenty years, are followed by a luxuriant development of plants, whereas the lighter showers that occur more frequently produce scarcely any growth. Seeds of many Californian desert plants, in fact, are able to distinguish between different amounts of rain, remaining dormant after a light shower whereas they germinate after heavy rain, even though in both cases they are equally damp for a similar period. Went (1957) found the same thing under laboratory conditions and showed that it happened because the seeds contain substances inhibiting germination. These substances are water soluble, and germination can take place when there has been sufficient rain to wash the seeds free of them. However, if this were all, one would expect that a succession of light showers would have the same effect as one bout of heavy rain, which is not so. It therefore seems that after light rains the supply of inhibitors in the seed must be replenished.

Seeds owe their survival through unfavourable periods to their quiescence, but cannot survive for ever. It is unlikely that all chemical change ceases in a resting seed; protein denaturation must go on slowly, and this or other changes sooner or later result in death. The life span of a seed may be from a few weeks to many years according to the species and the conditions under which it is kept. The seeds of some species of *Oxalis* will germinate when freshly released from the fruit, but drying kills them. The seeds of many trees, such as birch, beech, and elm, remain viable only until the spring following their production. Crop plants, too, have seeds which are relatively short-lived, lasting only one to three years. Stories of the germination of wheat grains taken from the tombs of Egyptian kings and four thousand years old are untrue. Microscopical examination of wheat grains which really are of this age shows that their living tissues have completely disintegrated and that it is inconceivable that they should germinate. Seeds of most weeds remain viable longer than those of cereals. Those of charlock (*Sinapis arvensis*) have been germinated after storage in an air-dry condition for eleven years, and seeds of dock (*Rumex crispus*) and of some other weeds have been found to be viable after having been buried in soil for eighty years (Darlington and Steinbauer, 1961). The record for longevity is held by the Indian lotus (*Nelumbo nucifera*). A seed of this, at least 237 years old, from a herbarium sheet in the British Museum (Natural History), was found to have germinated after being soaked after the bombing of the Museum in 1940, and others, found buried in peat in Manchuria and at least 120 and perhaps as much as 400 years old, have also been successfully germinated.

Besides showing the correlative dormancy which was discussed on p. 200, buds show a kind of dormancy which, like that of seeds, has the biological advantage of assisting the plant to survive unfavourable conditions. It is shown particularly by woody and bulbous species in temperate climates. Cold actually seems necessary for the proper development of such species, and if they are transplanted to the tropics they rarely survive even at high altitudes where the average temperature over the year is similar to that in their native habitat. In contrast, most annual plants have no such cold requirement.

A variety of treatments are known to be effective in breaking bud dormancy. These include exposure to an atmosphere containing ether vapour, hydrocyanic acid, or ethylene chlorhydrin; or injection of alcohol; or treatment with mineral acid or gibberellin. One of the simplest and most effective methods consists in immersing the twigs in a bath of lukewarm water (30–35° C.) for about 9 hours and afterwards keeping them in a warm greenhouse with their ends in water. The effectiveness of all these treatments varies according to the species of plant and the season; a treatment is more likely to be successful towards the end of the dormant period.

Many artificial means of breaking dormancy had been described before Coville in 1920 pointed out that under natural conditions it is the prolonged exposure to cold during winter that is effective in making dormant buds resume growth. The effective temperatures are usually below 9° C. for the trees and shrubs commonly cultivated in Britain, and the period of exposure necessary may be as little as 200 hours or as long as 3,500 hours, according to species.

The internal factors responsible for dormancy are not yet completely identified. It is generally found that dormancy is induced by short days. If plants are given extra illumination as the days begin to draw in at the end of summer the onset of dormancy is delayed, sometimes considerably. The tulip tree (*Lyriodendron tulipifera*) has been maintained in a state of continuous growth for as long as eighteen months by keeping it at a favourable temperature with a long daily period of illumination. This is not just a matter of more photosynthesis, for the extra illumination need only be weak. It is also evident that the onset of dormancy is not necessarily connected with leaf-fall. The dormancy-inducing factor, whatever it may be, is rather localized in its effects because Denny and Stanton (1928) found it possible to induce one of a pair of buds of lilac (*Syringa vulgaris*) to sprout by treatment with ethylene chlorhydrin, leaving the other still dormant.

Auxin, which, it will be remembered, is implicated in correlative inhibition of buds, does not seem to be involved directly in this kind of bud dormancy. Hemberg (1947, 1949) found evidence for dormancy in potatoes and in buds of ash being caused by growth inhibitors, and several subsequent investigations have supported this idea. Phillips and Wareing (1958, 1959) extracted buds and leaves of sycamore (*Acer pseudoplatanus*) with alcohol and were able to obtain from this extract a substance which had inhibitory effects on the growth of wheat coleoptiles, cress (*Lepidium sativum*) roots, and sycamore leaf discs, and on the germination of lettuce seeds. This substance was present in the greatest amounts in the buds in early winter and in least amount when active growth was taking place, although it was never absent altogether. Higher amounts of inhibitor were found in leaves and terminal parts of shoots given short days than in those given longer periods of illumination. The inhibitor appeared to be formed in the leaves and translocated from them into the terminal part of the shoot. It thus seems that dormancy in sycamore may be due to an inhibiting substance produced in response to the stimulus of shorter days at the end of the summer and that this gradually disappears, perhaps as a result of exposure to low temperatures, until in spring a low enough level is reached for bud break to occur. It remains to be seen if this picture is applicable to other species and what the chemical nature of the inhibitor is. Whatever the nature of the naturally occurring substances inducing dormancy, synthetic auxins are certainly effective in prolonging it. The use of these substances for this purpose has already been mentioned (p. 201).

We must now return to the subject of active growth. Even when kept under constant environmental conditions, some plant organs still show a daily rhythm in growth. This has been shown particularly clearly for *Avena* seedlings by Ball and Dyke (1954). They germinated the seedlings in continuous red light, then transferred them to continuous dark. This change was sufficient to set off a rhythmic variation in rate of elongation of the coleoptiles which lasted for two to three days. The first peak in growth rate happened 16 hours after the change-over, and the following peaks occurred at 24-hour intervals after this (Fig. 51). The seedlings had never been exposed to a 24-hour cycle of light and dark, and the rhythm showed no correlation with actual time of day, so it cannot be ascribed to some external condition showing diurnal rhythm which the experimenters had overlooked and not controlled. Furthermore, the 24-hour periodicity remained constant over quite a wide temperature range, 16–28° C. All this is very odd; one might expect that a push might start the metabolic balance of the seedlings oscillating, but that it should do so with this particular period seems more than a coincidence, and one seems forced to conclude that the seedlings inherited a rhythm of this period from the parent plants, which grew with the normal cycle of conditions. The independence of temperature is also strange, since the chemical reactions upon which the rhythm in growth surely depends must certainly be temperature sensitive.

Similar rhythms with periods of 24 hours or thereabouts have been found in all sorts of organisms. Man himself is reported as having some forty different diurnal rhythms. At the other end of the evolutionary scale even the simplest unicellular plants may show them; *Euglena*, for example, shows one in the rate at which it swims towards a light source. It has already been mentioned (p. 240) that tomato plants grow best when given a 24-hour cycle of light and dark. In plants, however, rhythms are most easily observed in leaf movements. These were studied as long ago as 1729 by the astronomer De Mairan, and detailed studies have

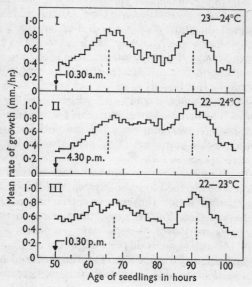

Fig. 51. Graphs showing mean rates of growth of *Avena* coleoptiles in three experiments started at different times of the day. The seedlings were grown in red light until 50 hours old, then transferred to darkness. The vertical dotted lines are exactly twenty-four hours apart. (After Ball and Dyke, 1954.)

been made recently by Bünning (1956), among others. All these rhythms have it in common that their period is almost independent of temperature, a low temperature stalling them altogether rather than slowing them down. By giving various light/dark cycles the maxima in the rhythmic variation can be shifted to any time of day, but the length of the periods can be altered only to a limited extent, and as soon as the abnormal light/dark cycles are replaced by continuous darkness the 24-hour rhythm reasserts itself. Red light of wavelength about 650 mμ has the most marked lengthening effect on the period of the rhythmic movements of runner-bean leaflets, causing it to be 3–5 hours longer than in continuous darkness. In far-red light the periods become shorter and the rhythm fades away (Fig. 52) – yet another manifestation of the red/far-red effect.

So far, only the hands, as it were, of these biological clocks have been studied, and the nature of the clockwork itself is unknown. The oscillations can be quite independent of the rate of metabolic processes such as respiration, and the temperature independence is most unusual for a function controlled by chemical reactions, which usually double in rate for every 10° C. rise in temperature.

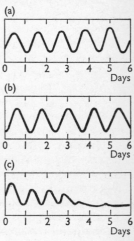

Fig. 52. The diurnal leaf movements of *Phaseolus*: (a) in darkness; (b) in continuous red light; (c) in continuous far-red light. In red light the oscillation shows longer periods, in far-red it shows shorter periods and dies away. (After Bünning, 1960.)

The behaviour of some sea-weeds shows a rhythm correlated with tides, and possibly lunar periodicities may occur in flowering plants too, but in these it is the seasonal periodicity which is most prominent. Especially in woody species, growth tends to occur at a particular time of the year, regardless of actual weather conditions. The bursting of buds in the spring is largely independent of weather, and growth is mainly confined to the spring and early summer, even though conditions apparently favourable for it may also occur later in the season. This is particularly noticeable in the beech, in which nearly all growth in shoot length is confined to two or three weeks during spring. A few 'Lammas shoots' may be produced later. Perhaps this is dependent on the shoot/root ratio, since it happens under conditions favourable to the growth of roots, which do not seem to show any period of dormancy and which grow whenever conditions are suitable. Otherwise, it is only in exceptional circumstances that shoot growth is resumed; loss of leaves as a result of a late frost or the ravages of caterpillars may cause this to happen. It is possible that much of the seasonal variation in growth of woody species may be explicable in terms of the balance between auxins and growth inhibitors, but as yet there is little definite information about this. On the other hand, a great deal of work has been done on the seasonal periodicity in formation of reproductive organs, and this we must now discuss.

The production of flowers and fruit in due season is evidently something which is to a considerable extent determined genetically, because the time of the year at which it happens depends so much on the species and variety of plant. As we saw in Chapter 8, not a great deal has yet come of the investigation of the internal factors requisite for flowering, and no specific substances responsible for the initiation of flowers have been isolated. However, it is clear that these internal conditions can be influenced to some extent by environmental conditions, since these, if unfavourable, can prevent it happening altogether. It has been established that of the various external conditions, light and temperature are often the decisive factors controlling flowering, and by manipulating them it is possible to prevent or induce flowering at will in many plants, even though we do not know what the mechanism is by which this is brought about.

The crucial importance which the period of illumination may have on the change from vegetative to reproductive growth seems to have been first noticed by the French botanist Tournois (1911), who found that hemp, a plant which remains vegetative when given long daily periods of illumination, could be brought into the flowering condition simply by artificial shortening of the day. Klebs (1913, 1918), who devoted many years to a search for the factors controlling development, also noticed that length of day had important effects. He found that the succulent, *Sempervivum funkii*, could be induced to flower in any month of the winter by giving it continuous illumination with low-power electric lamps. However, the best known of the early work on this subject is that of Garner and Allard (1920). In trying to carry out breeding experiments with tobacco they found that a new variety, Maryland Mammoth, would not flower when grown in the open near Washington, D.C., although it would do so in the greenhouse in autumn or winter in the same locality. Because of this, crosses could not be made between this variety and others which flowered in the usual way in the summer. After trying in vain every other treatment that they could think of to induce Maryland Mammoth to flower in the open, the effect of reducing the day-length, to correspond with that which the plants got when they flowered in the greenhouse later in the year, was tried. This was evidently done with little expectation of success, but it worked; by artificially shortening the day-length, by moving the plants into a dark cabinet after exposure to the desired number of hours of daylight, prolific flowering could be obtained at will. After this, Garner and Allard found that the ornamental plant, *Cosmos bipinnatus*, and some varieties of soybean (*Glycine soja*) were also prevented from flowering if given long days.

Sempervivum funkii and tobacco variety Maryland Mammoth thus seem to represent two contrasting types of *photoperiodic* behaviour. As instances multiplied it was found that plants could be classified into three groups:

   short-day plants, flowering best if subjected to light periods of 12 hours or less and including, besides hemp and Maryland Mammoth tobacco, *Chrysanthemum* spp. (Plate 22), *Xanthium* spp., some varieties of strawberry and rice, and most of the spring- and autumn-flowering species of temperate regions;

   long-day plants, flowering best if subject to light periods of 12 hours or more and including, besides *Sempervivum funkii*,

Hyoscyamus niger, Hieracium aurantiacum (Plate 23), beet, lettuce, wheat, potato, and all summer-flowering plants of temperate regions;

indifferent or day-neutral plants, the flowering of which is independent of day-length and controlled by other climatic factors and which include tomato, maize, dandelion, and the considerable number of tropical plants which have no flowering rhythm but which produce flowers, as well as leaves, all the year round.

This classification in no way corresponds with the natural classification of plants into genera and families. Indeed, as with tobacco, even varieties of the same species may belong to different photoperiodic groups. The geographical distribution of plants, of course, is very much dependent on photoperiodic response. In the tropics, where day-length is always about 12 hours, only short-day or day-neutral plants will be able to perpetuate themselves by sexual reproduction. Long-day plants, on the other hand, are restricted to high latitudes, where long days enable them to flower. Such plants remain flowerless indefinitely if grown in tropical regions.

As more exact experiments were carried out it became obvious that the classification of plants into short-day, long-day, and day-neutral types provides only a rough guide to their behaviour. The range of photoperiods under which flowering takes place is quite sharply delimited. For short-day plants there is a *critical photoperiod*, exposures longer than which are ineffective in inducing flowering. The critical photoperiod for Maryland Mammoth tobacco is between 13 and 14 hours and for *Xanthium* about 15·5 hours. Long-day plants flower only if illuminated daily for a period longer than the critical photoperiod. *Hyoscyamus*, for example, does not flower if the photoperiod is shorter than 10–11 hours. There is thus some overlap in photoperiod length, so that one of, say, 13 hours will induce flowering in both short-day and long-day plants. A rather arbitrarily distinguished class of 'indeterminate' plants, like long-day plants, flower only when the photoperiod is above a certain minimum, but this is shorter than the critical photoperiod for long-day plants. Then there are 'intermediate' species, which have two critical photoperiods and flower only when the photoperiod given lies between these two limits. It is also clear that different phases of development in the same plant may have different photoperiodic requirements. In Biloxi soybean, formation of flower initials at the growing points takes place in photoperiods between 2 and 13·5 hours in length, development of flowers from the initials takes place most quickly in 8- to 13-hour photoperiods and more slowly in photoperiods of up to 16 hours, but fruit growth does not take place when the photoperiods are longer than 13 hours.

The light treatment necessary to initiate flowering does not have to be continued until the flower buds are actually visible. If a short-day plant growing under long days is transferred to a short-day regimen for a little while then back again to long days, flowering may still occur. Soybeans require only two to four short days for flower formation, and *Xanthium* is even more sensitive, for only one cycle of a short day followed by a long night is sufficient to induce it to flower when it is otherwise kept under photoperiods unsuitable for flowering. A similar situation exists with long-day plants. However, although short photoperiodic induction is sufficient for flowering to be induced, longer treatment accelerates maturation of the flowers. Naylor (1941) found that *Xanthium* flowers took sixty-four days to mature when only one short-day treatment had been given, as against thirteen days when the plants were kept continuously under short days. Sensitivity varies with age, for old plants respond more copiously than young ones to brief photoperiodic induction. Most plants, in fact, have to reach a certain size, we might almost say that they have to attain puberty, before flower initiation is possible at all. The peanut (*Arachis hypogaea*) forms flower initials immediately after germination, but this is exceptional, and usually a minimum number of foliage leaves have to be formed first.

The photoperiodic effect depends more on the duration of illumination than on its intensity. With long-day plants, for example, it is sufficient to supplement a short day of natural daylight with artificial light of quite low intensity in order to obtain flowers. For most plants an intensity of 100 foot-candles – such as is obtained at about 18 inches from a 100-watt incandescent lamp – suffices, but some species are much more sensitive. Flowering in *Xanthium*, for example, can be suppressed by light of only 0·3-foot-candle intensity given for 8 hours to supplement 8 hours of sunlight. The sometimes eccentric behaviour of plants growing near a street lamp may be due to this sort of effect, although, if the lamp is a gas lamp, ethylene may be playing a part too (see p. 205). Of course, illumination at high intensity for some part of the photoperiod is necessary to allow sufficient photosynthesis to provide for growth, and the *number* of flowers formed generally increases with the light intensity given, but the low intensity required for initiation of flower initials suggests that this effect is not simply a matter of photosynthesis of food materials. Another thing pointing to the same conclusion is that the action spectrum for the photoperiodic effect is different from that for photosynthesis. Red light of wavelength 580–680 mμ is most effective, and blue light, 470–500 mμ, least effective in inducing flowering, whereas the efficiency of these two wavelength bands in photosynthesis is about the same.

Exposure to light is not effective in inducing flowering unless carbon dioxide is available at the same time. Parker and Borthwick (1940) grew soybeans in long days then gave them 6 short days (8-hour photoperiod) to induce flowering, afterwards transferring them back to long days. Plants given this treatment in normal air flowered, but similar plants in carbon-dioxide-free air during the short-day treatment completely failed to flower. This effect can hardly be due to starvation resulting from the prevention of photosynthesis, because it occurs even though the plants contain ample amounts of starch. As we saw in Chapter 7, the carbon dioxide uptake of succulents may be greater at night than during the day. In *Kalanchoë blossfeldiana*, an ornamental succulent, this pattern is dependent on the photoperiod, but it is not known whether the induction of flowering has any direct connexion with this.

In general, long-day plants will flower if given continuous illumination and do not require any dark intervals whatsoever for flower initiation. For flowering of short-day plants, however, a dark period is essential, and its length is just as important as the length of the light period. This is shown by the results of experiments in which the length of the dark period is varied while that of the photoperiod is kept constant. Biloxi soybean, for example, requires a minimum dark period of 10 hours for flowering, irrespective of the length of the light period (Fig. 53). This is why, when

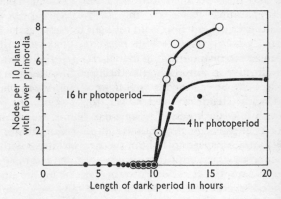

Fig. 53. Relation between length of the dark period and formation of flower initials in Biloxi soybean. (After Hamner, 1940.)

24-hour cycles of light and dark are given, the critical photoperiod for this plant is about 14 hours. Provided that 10 hours of darkness are given, the photoperiod can be longer, e.g. 16 hours, and flowering will still be initiated, indeed more vigorously than with a shorter photoperiod (Fig. 53). The flowering of short-day plants in short days thus happens because the dark periods are long, not because the light periods are short.

The importance of the dark period is also shown by the results of interrupting it with a brief light exposure. Hamner and Bonner (1938) found that if plants of *Xanthium* were exposed for 5 minutes to light of 150-foot-candles intensity in the middle of a 15-hour dark period, the initiation of flowering was completely prevented. The effectiveness of such a light break is greatest when it is given in the middle of the dark period. Harder and Bode (1943) found that whereas brief exposures of *Kalanchoë blossfeldiana* to light in the middle of a 14-hour dark period completely suppressed flowering, similar exposures towards the beginning and end of the dark period had much less effect. This suggests that some factor necessary for flowering is manufactured in the dark and that, although the final product is light-stable, the preparatory stages are completely reversed by light so that after a light break the whole business has to start afresh.

A most interesting finding is that it is red light which is most effective in suppressing flowering in this way and that its effect can be reversed by red light of longer wavelength (Borthwick, Hendricks, and Parker, 1952). Red light given during a long dark period to long-day plants, on the other hand, is effective in promoting flowering and, again, this effect can be reversed by light in the far-red. Just as with the lettuce seeds which require treatment with red light in order to germinate, the effect on flowering can be produced and annulled several times in succession. It looks very much as if the same reaction is involved in the two cases. A pigment which seems to be concerned in all the red/far-red reversible reactions has recently been prepared in a partly purified state and given the name 'phytochrome' (Butler, Norris, Siegelman, and Hendricks, 1959). Its nature has yet to be established, but it may turn out to be an enzyme which is converted from an active to an inactive state by absorption of radiation.

Photoperiodic responses are complicated by the effects of temperature. Maryland Mammoth tobacco, for example, blooms under a short photoperiod of 9–10 hours but not under a long photoperiod of 16–18 hours if the night temperature is 18° C., but blooms under both these photoperiods if the night temperature is 13° C. Thus, whether a plant is classified as a short-day plant or a day-neutral may be dependent on the temperature conditions. In general, the temperature during the dark period (that is, in normal circumstances, the night temperature) seems to be of more importance than the day temperature, and if it is low flowering may be inhibited altogether. Apart from modification of the photoperiodic reactions, temperature has its own effects on flowering, a matter which will be discussed shortly.

For both short-day and long-day plants it has been shown that it is the leaves, and not the growing points where the flower initials are actually formed, which perceive the photoperiodic stimulus. For example, spinach (*Spinacia oleracea*), which is a long-day plant, flowers only if the leaves are given long photoperiods. If the growing points are given long photoperiods and the leaves short photoperiods the plant remains in the vegetative condition. Grafting experiments point to the same conclusion: a leaf which has been given the appropriate photoperiodic treatment will induce flowering in a plant kept under conditions unsuitable for flower initiation if it is grafted on to it. A leaf of the garden plant *Perilla crispa* induced flowering in this way in seven plants on to which it was grafted successively before it finally died (Zeevaart, 1957). This capacity to bring about flowering can be induced even in detached leaves. The distance over which the stimulus can be transmitted depends on the kind of plant and on the conditions under which it is kept. Sometimes it is only the growing points near the leaf given the treatment which respond. In *Xanthium*, on the other hand, exposure of one leaf to short days causes initiation of flowers at growing points all over the plant. The general impression given is that the flowering factor moves in the phloem along with the main flow of sugars from the leaves.

It is not easy to account for all the variety of flowering phenomena with a single general theory. It does seem, though, that the mechanism of flower initiation is basically the same in short- and long-day plants. One fact that speaks for this is that varieties of a single species may belong to different photoperiodic classes, and one would hardly expect closely related plants to have widely different flowering mechanisms. Also the action spectrum for flowering is generally similar for long- and short-day plants. Another compelling piece of evidence is that a leaf of a long-day plant which has been exposed to long photoperiods to induce flower initiation will bring about flowering in a short-day plant if it is grafted on to it, and vice versa (Lang, 1952, 1954). The flowering of parasitic plants such as dodder (*Cuscuta* spp.) and broomrape (*Orobanche* spp.) seems to be determined by that of their hosts, presumably because the flowering factor is absorbed by them along with food materials. This suggests that the chemical factor bringing about flowering is of the same nature in all plants. On the other hand, our knowledge of the factors inducing flowering in day-neutral plants is scanty, and with some plants belonging to this class attempts have failed to demonstrate a flowering factor which can be transmitted by grafts. For the moment it is simpler to assume that in all plants a specific substance is manufactured in the leaves, from whence it is translocated to the growing points, in which it induces the formation of flower initials, but this idea may well have to be revised.

The best-known scheme to explain how this hypothetical flowering substance, which has been given the name 'florigen' but which we will denote simply by C, is formed in short- and long-day plants is one due to Gregory (1943). This is not necessarily incompatible with other suggestions that have been made, as, for example, that of Bünning (1948–58), who finds that there is a close correlation between rhythmic leaf movements and the effect of light on flowering, and who believes that flowering is dependent on diurnal rhythms in metabolism differing in sensitivity to light. In Gregory's scheme it is supposed that C is formed from carbon dioxide in a series of stages. The first stage, for which light is necessary, produces a substance A, which in short-day plants becomes transformed into an inactive substance X if the plant is given too long a photoperiod:

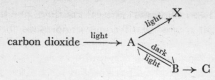

In the dark, however, A is transformed into B, and B, in turn, into C, the active flower-initiating factor. The transformation of A to B is reversed by light, but that from B to C is not. This explains why exposure to light has a maximum inhibitory effect on flowering if given in the middle of the dark period when the concentration of B is greatest. It may be that B is translocated from the leaf before being converted to C. One reason for thinking this is that if the tip of a *Perilla* leaf is given a short-day treatment and its base long-day treatment it does not induce flowering, although the reverse treatment, tip in long days and base in short days, is effective (Cajlachjan, 1945). Evidently B is decomposed on passing through the long-day barrier. In long-day plants conversion of the intermediate substance A′ into inactive X′ is supposed to take place in the dark:

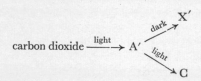

so that formation of the flower-initiating substance C is favoured by continuous light. On the evidence available C is identical in both long- and short-day plants, but A and A′ and X and X′ are not necessarily identical. Proof of these ideas requires that these various substances, A, B, C, etc., should be extracted from plants and identified chemically, but, as already mentioned, this has not yet been accomplished. Examination of 2,000 different extracts from flowering plants of *Xanthium* showed that none of them would induce flowering when applied to vegetative plants (Bonner and Liverman, 1949).

Apart from photoperiodic effects there are temperature effects which may be of equal importance for flowering. The most pronounced of these effects are exerted when plants are seedlings, long before they are in a condition to form flower initials. Certain plants, winter varieties of cereals being the best-known examples, flower sooner if they are exposed to temperatures round about freezing point while in the seedling stage. They get this treatment naturally if sown in autumn, and then they flower the following summer, whereas if they are sown in spring flowering does not usually take place in the same year, although it does in spring varieties of cereals sown at the same time. It was Gassner (1918) who discovered the importance of temperature for the flowering of winter cereals. He found that by germinating grain of winter rye (*Secale cereale*) at 1–2° C. before planting out in spring, flowering could be brought forward by as much as six weeks compared with that of plants grown from grain germinated at 24° C. Temperature had no such effect on the flowering date of spring rye. This treatment, because it enables the often heavier-yielding winter varieties of cereals to be used like the spring varieties, is of some practical value. It is now generally known as *vernalization*, literally, bringing to the spring condition, a name bestowed by Lysenko, who was responsible for its large-scale use in Russia.

The classical researches on vernalization were carried out with the Petkus variety of rye by Gregory and Purvis (1936–48). There are spring and winter races of Petkus. The spring one, when sown in spring under long days, produces 7 leaf initials on its main axis, then forms the ear. In short days it produces about 25 leaves before earing. The winter race when sown in spring produces 25 leaves before earing under short-day conditions or 16 under long days. If the grain of the winter variety is chilled for a sufficiently long period, however, it behaves exactly like the spring variety under long days, i.e. produces only 7 leaves before forming the ear. Incompletely vernalized seed gives plants which ear after producing some intermediate number of leaves. Vernalization thus only accelerates the onset of flowering. After the 25th leaf has been produced the growing point of an unvernalized plant of the winter race switches to the production of flower initials, and all attempts to change this by manipulation of the environment have so far been unsuccessful. Vernalization does not alter the rate of vegetative growth, it only results in this switch taking place earlier.

The seed need not be visibly germinating, but a minimum amount of water must be supplied, and the seed must have begun respiring at an appreciable rate in order for chilling to be effective. Inhibition of respiration by poisons or by deprivation of oxygen prevents vernalization, and its rate is reduced if the embryo is deprived of its supply of food materials by removal of the endosperm. The effective temperature is between 0° C. and 6–7° C., and exposure to this degree of cold for forty to forty-five days is necessary for complete vernalization. Interruption of vernalization by exposure to mild temperatures does not affect the degree of vernalization already achieved, but temperatures of 35° C. do cause a reversal, devernalization. This is not because of any general injurious effect of this high-temperature treatment, since spring rye treated in the same way shows no retardation of flowering.

Biennial plants, such as *Hyoscyamus* (Plate 15), celery, and the various kinds of beet, normally produce only a rosette of leaves in their first year, flowering in their second year after having been vernalized by chilling during the winter. This again is a matter of economic importance, especially with sugar beet, the sowing of which is a tricky business, as this must be done late enough to avoid vernalization, with the consequent production of flowering plants, useless for sugar production, in the first year, yet early enough for the plants to have the longest possible time for vegetative growth and sugar accumulation. A difference from the cereals, in which vernalization can take place in seeds still on the parent plant, is that these biennial plants are not readily vernalized in the seed, but only in the rosette stage. It is the growing point, not the leaves or root, which is sensitive to the cold treatment. Whereas grafting is not usually successful in cereals, *Hyoscyamus* can be grafted readily, and by this means Melchers and Lang (1937–48) have shown that the flowering factor can be transmitted from a vernalized plant to a non-vernalized one and cause it to flower. An unvernalized plant of *Hyoscyamus* can also be brought into flower by grafting on to it a scion of the annual race of *Hyoscyamus* which does not require vernalization. By grafting it has also been possible to show that the vernalization factor, 'vernalin', is distinct from the photoperiodic flowering factor, florigen. *Hyoscyamus* and beet are both long-day plants. It should be noted, however, that unvernalized plants are indifferent to day-length and that it is only after vernalization that the photoperiodic induction of flowering can take place. Development thus passes through phases, first temperature and then day-length being the controlling factors. The vernalization of *Hyoscyamus* is stable under short days, but beet is devernalized by short days and, even if it has begun to shoot, will then revert to the vegetative condition and form a 'perched' rosette.

Just as with photoperiodism, there is no connexion between the vernalization behaviour of a plant and its family relationships. Within the genus *Dianthus* (carnation), for example, there are to be found species with every possible degree of vernalization requirement. There is also no connexion of requirement for vernalization with any particular photoperiodic requirements. Plants requiring vernalization are, of course, confined to temperate and polar regions. On the other hand, some tropical plants, such as rice, appear to have a requirement for high temperature which may be related in nature to vernalization.

In summary it may be said that the factor necessary for producing the condition of readiness to flower, vernalin, is synthesized in embryos and growing points supplied with sugar and oxygen, some intermediate in the process being rendered inactive by moderately high temperatures in plants that require vernalization, so that its synthesis goes to completion only if the plant is exposed to low temperatures for some time. In spite of much chemical investigation, the mechanism of vernalization remains unknown. The grafting experiments indicate that the substances involved are similar in different species. For some plants a treatment with gibberellin will replace chilling in inducing flowering, but this substance does not have this effect on cereals, so that it is unlikely that it can be the only factor involved. It is probable that vernalization consists of several stages, only one of which is affected by gibberellin, and that different stages assume importance in different species.

CONCLUSION

*. . . the notion of individual parts is a practical makeshift
without final validity in the nature of things.*

J. C. SMUTS
(Presidential Address to the British Association, 1931)

CHAPTER 13

The Outlook of the Plant Physiologist

SCIENTISTS can consider plants from various points of view
– the statistical study of plant populations which a geneticist
may carry out, for example, involves a different kind of
approach from that of an anatomist investigating the development of a tissue by examination of sections under the
microscope. These different viewpoints are equally valid
scientifically, and if we are to obtain a reasonably complete
idea of the living organism they must be combined, as indeed they are increasingly tending to be. After all, our nice
distinctions between the various branches of botanical
knowledge are made purely for our own convenience, and
there is no corresponding antithesis of structure or functions
in a plant. However, in the study of plant growth it is undoubtedly the application of the concepts and techniques of
physics and chemistry which have been most productive
of results.

Whatever else it may be, a plant is a system in which
matter and energy undergo changes according to the laws
of physical science. In no case which has been carefully investigated has anything contrary to these laws been shown
to be going on in a plant. The plant physiologist must therefore be something of a physical scientist himself and must
also lean heavily on his colleagues in physics and chemistry
for help. In fact, men who are usually thought of as chemists

have been responsible for some of the most important advances in plant physiology. Thus, van Helmont in the early seventeenth century and Priestley in the eighteenth century laid the foundations for the scientific study of plant growth, while Calvin in the mid twentieth century has made contributions of great importance towards our understanding of photosynthesis. It may be remarked in parenthesis that the traffic has not been all one way, and that plant physiologists have been pioneers in several fields of physical science, e.g. Pfeffer in the study of osmosis and Tswett in the invention of chromatography.

From the physico-chemical point of view perhaps the most basic difference between non-living and living things is that whereas the former tend naturally to become increasingly disorderly, obviously obeying the second law of thermodynamics, the latter maintain a high degree of order within themselves so long as they are alive. This defiance of a physical law is more apparent than real, for, taken together with its environment, a living organism obeys the laws of thermodynamics as rigorously as anything else. What the organism does is to extract from its surroundings the means to maintain order in itself, so that order in one part is increased at the expense of the rest of the system. In plants the characteristic way of doing this is by photosynthesis, and an understanding of the nature of this process provides the key to the understanding of much of plant form and function. We have seen how the form and behaviour of a plant are largely determined by its need to absorb light and carbon dioxide from its surroundings and to maintain its water content in the face of the high rate of evaporation which is the almost inevitable corollary of photosynthesis if it is a land plant. Equally, on the chemical level photosynthesis occupies a central position in the life of a green plant. It is not a process apart, as was once thought, connected with the rest of plant metabolism only through carbohydrate as its sole product and the sole fuel for synthesis, but it intermeshes with many other processes and provides a flexible source of assimilatory power which can be used directly for a variety of different purposes. Of course, these academic considerations apart, the study of photosynthesis deserves special consideration from the physiologist as the *fons et origo* of the economic value of plants.

Investigation of photosynthesis and other metabolic processes of plants by physical and chemical methods has yielded a wealth of information, and our knowledge of a few processes, such as fermentation and the carbon fixation cycle in photosynthesis, may already be described as reasonably full and complete. We may confidently expect that rapid advance along these lines will continue and that in the near future we will have equally full information about many other processes. Yet the profusion and beauty of the biochemical findings should not mislead us into thinking that their mere accumulation will give a complete understanding of plant growth or that plant physiology is purely a matter of physics and chemistry, with no distinct features to make it a science in its own right. It is abundantly clear that the secret of life does not reside in any one substance or process but in the interrelation and organization of processes. It is this coordination, rather than the individual components, which is the proper study of the physiologist.

There are two contrasting experimental approaches to the understanding of the organization of a growing plant. One, the approach of the biochemist or biophysicist, begins with the isolation of individual components – they may be enzymes or whole organs – and the study of their behaviour under carefully controlled conditions. A disadvantage of this is that the experimental conditions are necessarily very different from those in the intact organism, and great caution is necessary in using the results to explain what is going on in the plant. The case of phosphorylase provides a warning example here. Starch-like substances can readily be synthesized by means of this enzyme in the test-tube, and it was thought for a long time that this was the means by which starch is made in plants too. Nevertheless, it appears that conditions in the cell do not favour the synthetic activities of phosphorylase and that quite a different enzyme system is actually responsible for the synthesis in the plant. Such difficulties are not necessarily avoided by using isolated tissues or organs, for even these may behave quite otherwise than they did when interacting with others in the whole plant. Another danger is that concentration of research on a particular component may lead to underestimation of the importance of the rest. Thus, it is tempting to regard desoxyribose-nucleic acid as the material which is ultimately responsible for all the phenomena of life. As we have seen, this class of substance undoubtedly has properties which are of profound significance for the maintenance of life, but it must always be remembered that these properties are only exhibited in the environment provided by the living cell and without this desoxyribose-nucleic acid is as lifeless as the bottle which contains it.

The other approach, that of studying the functioning of the intact plant, is equally fraught with difficulty. So complex are the interrelations of processes within the plant and between plant and environment that a particular treatment almost always affects more than one process, and the ambiguity of the results obtained contrasts sadly with the precision of those obtained by the biochemist working with simpler systems. Sometimes a situation may be found in which a particular process is controlled by a single limiting factor, as when gibberellins control extension growth in a dwarf variety of bean, and results may then be clear cut. But with another species of plant, or even with the same species at a different stage of development or grown under different conditions, some other factor may be the controlling one, and apparently conflicting results will be obtained. The processes of growth seem to depend on a delicate balance between many reactions, with sometimes one, sometimes another, factor assuming control. Only by patient experimentation, taking as many factors as possible into account, can a picture of what is happening in these situations be built up.

These two approaches are complementary and supplementary. The biochemical approach was first most successful in elucidating the mechanisms of breakdown. Now the mechanisms of synthesis are being unravelled; increasingly, mixtures of enzymes and isolated cell components are being used, and more account is being taken of the organization of living systems. As a result, we are beginning to have an idea of how the substance of plants is built up. Attempts to solve in biochemical terms the problems of how this material is organized in cell and tissue differentiation to form the elaborate structure of a flowering plant have so far had little success. Working downwards, the 'whole-plant physiologist', using ever more refined methods in his experiments, is playing an indispensable part by identifying the factors which are important, and so indicating the most profitable lines of attack to the biochemist. The two lines are converging and must ultimately fuse completely, but one may suspect that a full understanding of the complexities of plant growth will task the human mind to its limits.

FURTHER READING

GENERAL

THE works listed below are arranged in increasing order of difficulty. Anyone who has found this book too heavy going is implored to try again with Professor James's delightful *Background to Gardening*. The *Encyclopedia of Plant Physiology* will occupy over a yard of shelf space when complete, and more than half of the articles are in German, but it is an invaluable reference work.

JAMES, W. O., 1957, *Background to Gardening*. Allen and Unwin, London.

MEYER, B. S., ANDERSON, D. B., and BÖHNING, R. H., 1960, *Introduction to Plant Physiology*. Van Nostrand, Princeton and London.

THOMAS, M., RANSON, S. L., and RICHARDSON, J. A., 1956, *Plant Physiology*. J. and A. Churchill, London, fourth edition.

STEWARD, F. C. (Editor), 1959–, *Plant Physiology, a Treatise*. Academic Press, New York and London. (6 vols.)

1950–, *Annual Review of Plant Physiology*. Annual Reviews, Palo Alto, California.

RUHLAND, W. (Editor), 1955–, *Encyclopedia of Plant Physiology*. Springer-Verlag, Berlin. (18 vols.)

SPECIAL

STILES, W., 1961, *Trace Elements in Plants*. Cambridge University Press.

CRAFTS, A. S., CURRIER, H. B., and STOCKING, C. R., 1949, *Water in the Physiology of Plants*. Chronica Botanica Co., Waltham, Mass.

KRAMER, P. J., 1949, *Plant and Soil Water Relationships*. McGraw-Hill, New York and London.

DAVIES, D. D., 1961, *Intermediary Metabolism in Plants*. Cambridge University Press.

JAMES, W. O., 1953, *Plant Respiration*. Oxford University Press.

HILL, R., and WHITTINGHAM, C. P., 1957, *Photosynthesis*. Methuen, London, second edition.

BASSHAM J. A., and CALVIN, M., 1957, *The Path of Carbon in Photosynthesis*. Prentice-Hall, Englewood Cliffs, N. J.

RABINOWITCH, E. I., 1945, 1951, 1956, *Photosynthesis and Related Processes*. Interscience Publishers, New York and London. (2 vols.)

WEBSTER, G. C., 1959, *Nitrogen Metabolism in Plants*. Row, Peterson, Evanston, Illinois.

BONNER, J., 1950, *Plant Biochemistry*. Academic Press, New York.

JOHNSON, M. L., ABERCROMBIE, M., and FOGG, G. E. (Editors), *New Biology*, vol. 31, 'Biological Replication'. Penguin Books, Harmondsworth, Middlesex.

BRACHET, J., 1960, *The Biological Role of Ribonucleic Acids*. Elsevier, Amsterdam and London.

FREY-WYSSLING, A., and MÜHLETHALER, K., 1965, *Ultrastructural Plant Cytology*. Elsevier, Amsterdam and London.

AUDUS, L. J., 1959, *Plant Growth Substances*. Leonard Hill, London, second edition.

CLOWES, F. A. L., 1961, *Apical Meristems*. Blackwell Scientific Publications, Oxford.

WENT, F. W., 1957, *The Experimental Control of Plant Growth*. Chronica Botanica Co., Waltham, Mass.

SALISBURY, F. B., 1963, *The Flowering Process*. Pergamon Press, Oxford.

VAN DER VEEN, R., and MEIJER, G., 1959, *Light and Plant Growth*. Philips Technical Library, Eindhoven.

RUSSELL, E. J., and RUSSELL, E. W., 1961, *Soil Conditions and Plant Growth*. Longmans, Green, London, ninth edition.

The authors' names and dates for some of the more important research papers are given in the text. Full references for these may be traced through the *Annual Review of Plant Physiology*, *Biological Abstracts*, or *International Abstracts of Biological Science*.

INDEX